The Use of Models in the Social Sciences

The Use of Models in the Social Sciences

Edited by

LYNDHURST COLLINS

WESTVIEW PRESS

ISBN 0–89158–507–9

First published in 1976 in London England
by Tavistock Publications Ltd.

*Published in 1976 in the United States of America
by Westview Press, Inc.
1898 Flatiron Court
Boulder, Colorado 80301
Frederick A. Praeger, Publisher and Editorial Director*

Printed in Great Britain
by Cox & Wyman Ltd., London

LIBRARY OF CONGRESS CATALOGING IN PUBLICATION DATA

Main entry under title:

The Use of models in the social sciences.

Papers presented at a seminar held in July 1972 at the tenth annual meeting of the Seminars Committee of the Faculty of Social Sciences in the University of Edinburgh.
Bibliography: p.
1. Social sciences – Methodology – Congresses.
2. Social sciences – Simulation methods – Congresses.
3. Social sciences – Mathematical models – Congresses.
I. Collins, Lyndhurst. II. Edinburgh. University. Faculty of Social Sciences. Seminars Committee.
H61.U64 1975 300'.1'84 75–22018
ISBN 0–89158–507–9

Contributors

PETER ABELL Reader in Industrial Sociology, Imperial College, University of London

K. C. BOWEN Head of Research, Defence Operational Analysis Establishment, Ministry of Defence

LYNDHURST COLLINS Lecturer in Industrial Geography, University of Edinburgh

ROM HARRÉ Fellow of Linacre College, Oxford and University Lecturer in the Philosophy of Science

MARY HESSE Reader in Philosophy of Science, University of Cambridge

DAVID HOLLOWAY Lecturer in Politics, University of Edinburgh

C. A. ISNARD Professor of Mathematics, IMPA, Rio de Janeiro

JOHN LYONS Professor of General Linguistics, University of Edinburgh

DONALD MICHIE Professor of Machine Intelligence, University of Edinburgh

DAVID G. SMITH Defence Operational Analysis Establishment, Ministry of Defence

E. C. ZEEMAN Professor and Director of Mathematics Research Centre, University of Warwick

Contents

Editor's Preface

The most notable feature of the social sciences during the last two decades has been the dramatic increase in the use of models. The injection of complex philosophies, sophisticated mathematical formulations, and elaborate computer technology into the study of human behaviour has meant the transcending of traditionally narrow disciplinary boundaries of individual social sciences. Against this background of change, the Seminars Committee of the Faculty of Social Sciences in the University of Edinburgh was encouraged for its tenth annual meeting to sponsor a seminar which called upon the expertise of scholars in the related disciplines of Mathematics, Philosophy, Computer Studies, Engineering, and Linguistics as well as those within the social sciences to discuss *The Use of Models in the Social Sciences*. This volume contains the papers presented to the July 1972 Seminar.

The first two papers by Mary Hesse and Rom Harré concern the philosophy of model use. Hesse's paper focuses on the role of models in the natural sciences but holds and elaborates the view that an understanding of the place of models in natural science may illuminate theory construction in social science. Harré's paper extends the discussion of model use in the natural sciences to suggest an approach to model use in social psychology. The most unusual paper in the volume is perhaps that by Isnard and Zeeman, who introduce a new paradigm to the social sciences. Their elaboration of the catastrophe model, which in the seminar was illustrated by a mechanical analogue, is set within the framework of public opinion and government policy. The use of models with reference to government and political issues is a theme developed in two other papers. The first, by Bowen and Smith of the Ministry of Defence, employs notions drawn from systems theory to outline the role of models concerned with conflict problems, particularly problems of military strategy. In the second paper, Holloway examines the adoption of a cybernetics model by Soviet social science in its attempts to achieve optimal planning proposals. The remaining four papers are of a more diverse nature. Michie outlines the possibilities and implications of developing intelligent machines which will undoubtedly influence the model formulations of social scientists in the future, Abell explores the use of balance theory as a model of group decision-making processes, and Lyons illustrates the techniques of analysing language in a model framework. In the last paper, Collins demonstrates how a specific type of stochastic process model, calibrated from a large data source, can be employed to describe and predict spatial and structural changes in the industrial landscape.

The editor wishes to thank the Seminars Committee and the authors for their contributions to this volume.

L. C.

Models versus paradigms in the natural sciences

MARY HESSE

The question of differences in method between the natural and the social sciences has come to the fore again recently with the revival of concern within English language philosophy with continental characterizations of the so-called 'hermeneutic' sciences of man. The hermeneutic account of science takes its models from problems of interpretation of biblical and other esoteric texts, from problems of understanding alien cultures, both in the *Wissenschaften* of history and of anthropology and from the ideological challenge of Marxist and other potentially revolutionary interpretations of our own society and culture.[1] Some philosophers have gone on to argue from these models that the empiricist account of science as objective, cumulative, success-oriented, and value-free, is no longer adequate either as an ideal or as a methodological model for the social sciences. The challenge has even been carried into the domain of the natural sciences themselves in Kuhnian interpretations of the history of science (Kuhn 1962) in terms of successive paradigms and revolutions between which there are few or no rational links or accumulations of truth, and which are irreducibly dependent on their own social culture or on the sub-culture of their own scientific elites.

The programme of this conference indicates that there is one aspect of the methodological analogy between the natural and the social sciences that is still thought worthy of exploration, namely the role of models in the development of theory. It may seem that such a limited and workmanlike interest is a far cry from the global, not to say apocalyptic, concerns I have just adumbrated. However, for the following reasons, I think the two sorts of issues are not unrelated. First, the recognition and analysis of the role of models in the natural sciences arose as a conscious attempt to expose and remedy the shortcomings of earlier empiricist models of science, from logical positivism to the more sophisticated hypothetico-deductive account. In consequence, some of the wedges, which have been driven between the natural and the social sciences in the past, have been knocked away by a more liberal understanding of what it is to be a theory or explanation in natural science itself, and this liberalization makes empiricism a more flexible tool for analysing the social sciences. Second, however, from the point of view of the new hermeneutics, this new empiricism is as much under attack as the old, and therefore, is its applicability to the social sciences, and in particular the view that the role of models in natural science may illuminate theory construction in social science.

Any confrontation between the new empiricism, which derives from a natural modification and development of old empiricism, and paradigm-centred analyses, which derive from the hermeneutic interpretation of the social sciences, will have one out of four logically possible outcomes:

1 A take-over of social science. This is the behaviourist, reductionist programme on which Western science has been postulated for a century or more, and which looks increasingly problematic as the social sciences develop their own concepts and methods.
2 A take-over of natural science. This is the historicist, relativist, and ultimately irrational philosophy that now threatens from more extreme hermeneutics.
3 A stalemate, in which rigorous distinctions are maintained between the sciences of nature and of man, which looks increasingly unlikely to be viable in practice, and is in any case intellectually undesirable in theory.
4 A fruitful interchange of concepts, methods, and even tensions, in which careful comparisons and distinctions are made between specific sorts of examples, resisting the ever-present temptation of global denunciation from the standpoint of different ideologies.

It is the last of these possible outcomes to which I shall try to contribute. I shall do so by a particular consideration of the use of models in the natural sciences, for I am not competent from first-hand knowledge to discuss details of the social sciences. I shall rather outline a model of natural science itself, at which I have myself arrived in the course of a critique of traditional empiricism, and which will, I think, help to define the elements of natural science that are not transferable to the sciences of man.

The reader may already have noticed that an ambiguity has crept into my use of the term 'model'. Let me hasten to explain that this ambiguity is deliberate. There are models *in* science (models of crystal structure, cosmological models, models of conflict etc.), and there are also models *of* science (the positivist, the hypothetico-deductivist etc.). I have sometimes thought of distinguishing the second kind from the first by talking about *images of* science rather than models. But I think this admission of equivocation is undesirable for two related reasons. First, a model *of* science in history, philosophy, or sociology of science is a model *in* the sciences (*Geisteswissenschaften*) of history, philosophy, or sociology of science, since it is a model of a human and social enterprise, namely science, natural or social. Therefore, the use of models *in* and models *of* may help to illuminate each other. Second, the paradigm-critique itself compels us to consider self-reflexive situations in which the critique is turned on itself. That Kuhn gives an interpretation of science in terms of paradigms, itself both creates, and is a partial consequence of, a paradigm-change in the understanding of the history of science. However vertigo-inducing this insight may be, it implies that we cannot prematurely seek to escape the potential logical circle by trying to make distinctions which may only be appropriate to a pre-paradigm empiricism.

OBJECTIONS TO THE DEDUCTIVE MODEL OF SCIENCE

A convenient point to break into the potential logical circle is by means of characterizations of natural science which take account of the historical and philosophical studies that have explicitly devoted themselves to science as a rationally developing corpus of objective knowledge, yielding successful applications and predictions. Let us begin by contrasting the new empiricist model of natural science with the old.

An influential view of science in the old empiricism was the so-called *deductive* model[2] which was characterized by a number of radical dichotomies which were supposed to analyse and clarify its structure: theory versus observation, explanation versus description, discovery versus justification, induction versus deduction, and realism versus instrumentalism. In this account, science is supposed to be firmly based on empirical and experimental data expressed in observation statements whose meaning and truth-value are functions of ordinary descriptive language and independent of changing theories. It is supposed that pure description can be distinguished from any theoretical bias introduced by hypothetical explanations of the observations. Theoretical explanation cannot be arrived at by any logical method (where 'logic' is understood to be exhausted by 'deductive logic'), but theories must be guessed or conjectured, and then tested by deducing their consequences and comparing these with observation statements. If there is disagreement, the theory is falsified; if agreement, the theory may at best be said to be confirmed though of course not proved to be true, or sometimes, as in the Popperian account, the theory is said only to have survived to fight another day (Popper 1959; 1963). The process of conjecturing theories is one of creative discovery, the process of deducing consequences and testing them is that of justification. There is usually no room in this account for *inductive* justification of theories by means of an inductive logic, enabling us to pass from observations to theory. Moreover, there is no account of the way in which theories succeed one another in the historical development of science, other than their successive replacement by the next theory conjectured and tested in its turn. The successor theory does not necessarily have any rational connection with its predecessor except that they both explain the same accepted corpus of observations, and that it is often required to be a more general and powerful theory. In extreme versions of deductivism, the theory-observation dichotomy is taken to imply in addition that truth and falsity are properties only of observation statements, while theories are not propositional and do not purport to describe the real, but are only *instruments* for correlation and prediction of observations.

There are many objections to this logical empiricist model of science. The first objections arose out of two features that already appeared as anomalies in the model itself: the question of the nature of theoretical or 'unobservable' concepts, and the relation of the explanatory framework to the predictivity of theories. It is clear that many theories employ novel concepts which are not *prima facie* in the observation language: electron, meson, quasar, valency bond, gene, and so on. How are we to understand these theoretical terms? In purely formal or instrumental interpretations of theories, they are held to be mere signs, part of the deductive apparatus or black box into which observations are plugged, and out of which come further deductive predictions of observables. But this view does not seem to do justice to the almost universal sense of natural scientists that they are making discoveries rather than constructing black boxes; that in other words they are describing real, though unobservable, processes that provide causal explanations of observables. Reinforcing this objection is the need to understand how theories can be predictive. If theories are seen as being constructed out of a deductive system of uninterpreted signs, or if, less radically, they are seen as creative patterns of imagined strange entities and processes not derived in any way from observation, what justification does this give for us to apply the theory and make confident predictions in new domains where some identification of the concepts of theory with those of observation is required? To put this another way, for a deductive system in a theoretical language to entail observation statements in an observation language, some interpretive or correspondence rules are required from one language into the other. Where do these rules come from, if the theory is as little determined by observation as deductivists assert?

A further objection to deductivism arises from the *paradigm* model of science, which itself originated from a direct attack upon the notions of the invariance of the observation language with respect to changing theories, and the deductive relationship which is claimed to subsist between theory and observation (see Kuhn 1962 and Feyerabend 1962). It is pointed out that observation statements apparently derived from the empirical data may be corrected as to truth value by subsequent theory, and may even be changed in meaning in the same way. Examples are: the correction of Galileo's law that bodies fall to the earth with constant acceleration by Newton's theory according to which this acceleration increases on approaching the earth; and the change in meaning of such apparently basic predicates as 'light' and 'heavy' when Aristotelian mechanics give way to Newtonian – 'air is light' (i.e., it goes up) becomes false, and 'air is heavy' (i.e., it is composed of gravitating particles) becomes true. Extreme versions of the paradigm view become so impressed with the pervasive influence of theory on observation (the so-called 'theory-ladenness' of observation), that they are in danger of losing all sense of the continuity and objectivity even of natural science. It is held that the theoretical framework within which observations are interpreted so determines 'what we see' that there is ultimately no exit from the circle of theoretical ideas, no constraint from or access to 'what is' independently of our paradigm imposed upon it. Natural science itself becomes modelled on ideology. The vertigo which afflicts us when we contemplate the kaleidoscopic context of personal relations, or a skilful advocate in the courtroom, infects also our understanding of Greek science, the alchemists, the mechanists, and even our own science. There is no external point of reference from which we can meaningfully ask 'what is really the case here?'.

The paradigm model in its extreme form as just outlined is *prima facie* highly implausible when applied to the natural sciences. However, it does point to a process of mutual modification of theory and observation which undoubtedly does occur, and which is neglected in the logical structure of deductivism, with its requirement of stability of truth value and meaning of the observation statements. Moreover, even if circular self-reinforcement and self-correction between theory and observation were negligible in the natural sciences, it has been one of the generally accepted characterizations of the social sciences that even experimental description of social phenomena involves such a high degree of selection, classification, and appraisal, that this alone would cast doubt on their empirical nature. Recent examples given by Charles Taylor include the assumption that data for 'hard' social science must be gleaned by means of *verbal* answers by *individuals* to *questionnaires* – all potentially question-begging assessments of what are the essential ingredients of social life and behaviour – and the concepts of 'negotiation' and 'voting', which are used to express basic data, but whose social meanings pre-suppose a vast network of psychological and social interrelations (Taylor 1971:3). Where social data are thus theory-laden, changes of theory will bring changes of data, and it becomes difficult to see how observation can be sufficiently independent of theory to function as a deductive test of theory without circularity.

There are, therefore, three main objections to the deductive model of science: the need for non-formal interpretations or *understanding* of theoretical concepts, the need to give some justification of *inductive predictions* from theories, and the need to show that *self-reinforcement* or *self-correction* of observation statements by theory does not produce circularities of justification and the severance of science from empirical constraints.

THE FUNCTION OF MODELS IN SCIENCE

I believe that replies to all these objections can be given in terms of the use of material models in theories, at the cost of some modification of the original deductive account, but without falling into the extreme of paradigm-relativism.[3] (I use the term 'material model' to distinguish physical systems which constitute *analogues* for the systems to be explained by the theory, from purely mathematical or formal models, which are generally idealized *descriptions* of the data having no reference to any other physical analogue.) First, theoretical concepts are to be *understood* as derived by analogy from situations familiar in observation and describable in observational terms. For example, elementary particles and their properties are ultimately modelled on macroscopic particles. Second, such an analogy may give a basis for *inductive analogical argument* from systems that are known to exist and whose behaviour is known, so that by general induction, or what Newton called 'the analogy of nature', the behaviour of their less familiar analogues may be reasonably predicted.

The appeal to material models is in a sense a return to the original naïve realism in which atomic models, aether models, and the like, were seen as literal descriptions of mechanical particles and media similar to, but on a smaller scale than, the particles and fluids of ordinary observation. It is indeed a return to a kind of realism, but not a naïve realism. It no longer requires us to assume that the meaning of terms like 'particle' survives unchanged through analogical transfer into an atomic theory, for the properties and laws of behaviour of particles are found to be very different on the micro- and macro-scales, and to that extent the definitions and implications of 'particle' have changed. However, the analogical connection is sufficient to enable us to understand the theoretical concepts in a more than formal or mathematical sense of understanding, and also to draw further conclusions from the theories, yielding predictions in new observational domains.

This analysis of models has more than merely parochial interest within the structure of physical theories. It can be generalized by further scrutiny of the observation language itself, and indeed of all descriptive language, revealing that the commonly accepted distinction between literal and metaphorical or analogical meanings is as baseless there as is the distinction between theoretical and observation languages in science. *All* descriptive terminology is learned and subsequently used by a process of extension of application and meaning from similars to similars. I never re-apply the commonest term, such as 'green', in *exactly* the same circumstances in which I learned it, but always by making a (perhaps unconscious) judgment that this new situation is sufficiently similar to the old to merit application of the same universal term. My judgment is not arbitrary, since it is based on objective similarities which I am able to recognize, and is attested by the intersubjective understanding and general agreement of my language community.

The view of theoretical concepts in science as analogical extensions of observational terminology implies a continuous spectrum from elementary examples such as colour predicates, through less trivial metaphorical extensions of ordinary language, to the coining of new but immediately understandable theoretical terms such as electric *charge* (on analogy with a charge of gunpowder), electric *current* (which flows), *displacement current* in aether (on analogy with electric current in conductors), *curvature* of space (on analogy with curvature of a sphere), and so on, by continuous steps to the most esoteric terminology of modern physics. To recover, as against deductivism, the essential unity of the observation and theoretical languages in this way has its effect also on our understanding of the observation language itself. Metaphoric and poetic uses of ordinary language react back on the so-called literal uses from which they were drawn: for example, neither 'man' nor 'monkey' are understood in quite the same way after a man has been called an 'ape'; no 'democracy' after the peoples' republics have been called 'democratic'; and in the same way no 'brain' or 'machine' is quite the same after the brain has been compared to a machine, no 'billiard ball' after the laws of atoms have been derived and modified from those of billiard balls, and so on.

The upshot for the understanding of theory in the natural sciences is a much more flexible, and therefore less easily formalized, model of the interactions of the observable and that which explains it, with arguments going both ways, via inductive and analogical connections, as well as merely deductive, and a *network* of meanings which do not remain static as in a logical system, but are continually modified by new discovery and conceptual innovation. In particular, the model of science as consisting of such a network provides an analysis which is not subject to the three objections brought against deductivism. First, models render theoretical concepts and laws intelligible in terms of what is familiar, and hence help to clarify ambiguities and suggest possibilities of development; second, they sometimes give a basis for analogical argument and prediction from actual physical systems of similar kinds; and third, when understood as metaphoric extensions of the meanings of observational concepts, they help to explain how it is that some observation statements can be corrected in truth value and modified in meaning by continual interaction of theory and observation, but without losing contact with the empirical basis of science. A fourth role played by models in theories should also be mentioned here. This is the provision of *possibility* proofs by demonstrating in familiar terms that the entities and processes described by the theory can logically and perhaps also physically exist, that is, are not involved in hidden self-inconsistencies or conflicts with known physical laws. In the use of material models, the first, third and fourth of these features are always present; the second, inductive function, is sometimes present when the model is based on a real and not an imagined analogue, and when the analogue is close enough in enough respects to make analogical argument cogent.

This model of science is one of continuous evolution, proceeding by rational, though not necessarily deductive, steps from theory to theory, rather than one of revolutionary leaps between paradigms. How this rational evolution is to be worked out in detail is a largely unsolved problem, though some steps have been taken towards its further explication in studies of specific cases. Let us consider now whether we can specify the model more closely, and in doing so take advantage of some of the roles played by models *in* theories, to elucidate the character of natural science itself in terms of a model *of* science. Parallel with the roles just distinguished for models in science, such a model of science may, first, help to explicate and systematize the new empiricism; second, it may enable us to predict under what conditions the model will break down, for example when applied to the social rather than the natural sciences; third, it may cause us to modify some of our commonly accepted truisms about science; and fourth, it may show that science based on the principles of the new empiricism can actually exist. I shall now try to construct such a model by regarding natural science as essentially a *learning process*, and exhibit by means of it the infinite variety of ways in which science can retain its empirical and objective character without falling into either extremes of deductivism or paradigm-relativism.

SCIENCE AS A LEARNING PROCESS

With the exception only of the extreme paradigm model, all accounts of the structure of natural science have presupposed that the aim of science is to learn about the empirical world by means of interaction with the world, which provides data, tests, and reinforcements, and which is the subject of prediction and control. Consider a very simple learning machine which realizes these aims by going through the following stages of operation. Empirical *input* from the environment physically modifies part of the machine, which we will call its *receptor*. The empirical information thus conveyed is coded into machine language according to a programme present in the receptor, and produces the *initial data*, or initial set of observation statements of the system. This programme derives from the process of learning by means of which each language-using observer is provided with his stock of descriptive predicates. The initial data are now processed by some rules present in the machine which we will call *coherence conditions*. These tidy up the data according to whatever theoretical requirements are currently accepted: they may range from elementary curve-fitting and theory of errors, to more elaborate considerations regarding the economy, simplicity, and symmetry of theories, or their conformity with certain fundamental models or *a priori* conditions built into a theoretical framework, or even with very general metaphysical postulates of conservation or causality. The coherence conditions may be more or less restrictive in regard to the structure of theories. They may impose no more conditions than the deductive model does, that is to say, they may require only logical self-consistency and conformity to deductive rules, or, along the lines of the new empiricist model just described, they may contain rules for deriving theories inductively and analogically from the data, making use of familiar systems as models, and constraining the ways in which new concepts are introduced so that they remain intelligible in the enriched observation language.

We may now imagine the coherence conditions operating on the initial data so as to produce a best-fitting theory or theories, which can then be used to yield predictions and hence applications and tests in the external world. The external feedback loop, via test and consequent addition to the empirical input, may correct, modify, and extend the 'best theory' in the usual way. In addition, there is the possibility of building internal feedback into the machine in the following sense. The 'best theory', at any given stage of operation, need not be uniformly consistent with the initial data. Even without further external tests, it may modify that data by smoothing out curves, discarding minor anomalies, modifying part of the receptor programme, and reclassifying part of the data in the light of categories suggested as best-fitting for the rest of the data plus theory. This is only to make explicit practices which are commonplace in science, and involves no vicious circularity of theory and data so long as the bulk of the initial data remains unchanged at any given stage. In more familiar terms, *most* of the truth values and meanings of the observation statements will be stable with respect to local theory changes, but some small proportion may be modified by continuous interaction of input, data, and theory.

The learning machine can be developed in detail to constitute a model of an indefinitely flexible, hierarchical, self-organizing process which represents the interaction of the corpus of scientific knowledge and the world. There is no need to claim that a machine as crude as that described here could be built as a real 'discovery machine' which would dispense either with the language-using observer or with the creative scientist. So far, it is intended only to indicate what relations must subsist between scientific learning and the external world if the empirical character and objectivity of science is to be maintained. Anything said about the receptor programme or the coherence conditions could be conceived to be programmed directly into the machine by an observer or scientist-programmer in whatever way it is that observers do learn their descriptive language, or theoretical scientists do in fact brood on their data to produce explanatory theories. To complete the 'mechanization' of *these* processes would of course itself be a major undertaking in the psychology and physiology of learning, and in the psychology, sociology, and logic of discovery, and is perhaps ultimately unformulatable.

However, the machine does provide a model consistent with all views of science which have two features in common: namely, that the test of scientific knowledge is, first, over-all agreement with facts as represented at any given time in a descriptive language, and, second, success in making predictions to test correct learning of the structure of the environment. The machine is in fact the model of empiricist objectivity which lies behind the search for natural knowledge from Greek astronomy to modern physics. Like all models it shows that such objectivity is *logically* possible, given the notion of an external world satisfying certain conditions that I shall outline below. It also explicates the notion of objectivity and suggests extensions of it. In terms of this model, the extreme paradigm model of science is the limiting case in which all feedback is internal, that is, no external constraint causes modification of theory, because the receptor is programmed to produce data which are wholly determined by the coherence conditions and not at all by the world. In such a paradigm model there is a multiplicity of sets of coherence conditions and hence 'best theories', and no empirical method of choosing between them.

In terms of the natural sciences, the paradigm view is unproven and unnecessary, for all the objections to classic empiricism which led to its development are accommodated in less extreme form in the general learning model. Of course, this is not to say that the success-oriented science thus specified is indefinitely possible in practice, or is a necessary condition of civilized life, or is even socially or morally desirable. But that it has existed in the past three centuries or so of natural science seems an inescapable interpretation of the history of that science, however culturally relative some of its 'paradigms' may be shown to be. However, the applicability of the learning model to the social sciences is far less evident. In conclusion I shall use the model to suggest some possible points of breakdown when the environment is the social and human world.

OBJECTIVITY IN SOCIAL SCIENCE

First, notice some points at which the natural-social analogy need *not* break down. It is not the case that use of theoretical terms is forbidden in the natural sciences, for they may be introduced by analogies and models. They may be introduced in the same way in the social sciences. It is not the case that natural science is dealing with unproblematic observation situations where what is perceived is independent of theory. Properly understood, interpretation of the sun as a distant fiery ball is dependent on *both* sensory input and accepted coherence conditions and theories, just as is interpretation of behaviour as 'angry', or a signature as a pledged word.

However, it is the characteristics of prediction, test, and subsequent modification of theory that may be missing in the social sciences. On the assumption that there is a 'social world' to act as environment of the learning machine in the way the 'natural world' does for the natural sciences, there are at least three ways in which the learning process may be conceived to break down.

1 The process of data collection may so interfere with the antecedent external state of the world that empirical input ceases to represent its state independently of that process. Input becomes an artefact of learning. Hermeneutic philosophers often compare this situation to the uncertainty principle in quantum physics where the attempt to measure the position of a fundamental particle is said to interfere irreducibly with its momentum, and vice versa. But it should be noticed that the analogy is not necessarily an apt one, for our information about this kind of interference comes not from direct observation, but from a complex theory of fundamental particles, other aspects of which *are* known by the usual objective learning process. In other words, we cannot argue to the non-objectivity of physics from the uncertainty principle, since that principle itself is only known by depending on some cases of relative objectivity in physics.

   Similarly, although the *logical possibility* of irreducible interference can be understood in terms of the learning model, this cannot be used to *prove* that particular parts of the social sciences are non-objective without depending on the relative objectivity of other parts. For example, if it is suspected that questioning members of a tribe about the significance of their ritual produces defensive and misleading responses, this suspicion must rest on *other* relatively objective information about the likely nature of such rituals, or on our own introspection that we are likely to be defensive and misleading in response to such questions. To decline to recognize possible *degrees* of independence and objectivity here is to abandon the practice of science in any recognizable sense.

2 The learning model also yields a logical possibility of internal breakdown of the learning process. Prediction may become impossible because manipulable amounts of data may not sufficiently represent the fine structure of the external world, so that errors and loss of information in receiving and coding data may cumulatively diverge, leading to extreme underdetermination or undue instability of 'best theories' with respect to changing

data. Where natural science has been successful, we must assume that the structure of the world is sufficiently simple relative to the structure of the learning process to permit learning. The social world may not, of course, be so simple as to be similarly learnable.

3 In the case of both natural and social science, the very operation of the learning process may change its own goals. For example, the level of predictive success of the natural sciences has already led to questioning of the concept of technological manipulation to which it has given rise, and has suggested changed criteria of success itself. Perhaps the goal of natural science should rather be abstractly mathematical, as in Plato, or purely aesthetic or 'hedonist', as recently in Feyerabend (1970: 209). In either case, it should be noticed, these suggestions lead not to *disproof* of the possibility of objectivity, but to its voluntary abandonment as a social *value*. In the case of the social sciences, it is likely to be the absence of predictive success rather than its presence that leads to comparable suggestions. But to draw the conclusion that the objective model should be abandoned in favour of some sort of total ideological interpretation is to be guilty of logical confusion. Ideological interpretations of society are themselves supposed to be persuasive and causative of action. In other words, they themselves presuppose that *there are* predictable regularities in the social world. However, these regularities are just the kind of whose nature we know little, and of whose effects practically nothing. Unless all attempt to understand the social world is to be abandoned, we had better continue patiently to try to isolate relatively independent areas of the social world, making explicit though critical use in our methodology of the objective model of scientific learning, for it is indispensable, and its possibility has not been disproved.

NOTES

1 For a cogent critique of positivist accounts of science from the viewpoint of hermeneutics, see especially Habermas (1972).

2 The *locus classicus* of deductivism is Nagel (1961).

3 I have developed at greater length some of the points of this and the next section in *Models and Analogies in Science* and in *The Structure of Scientific Inference*. What I call 'material' model is what R Harré calls 'iconic' model in the paper which follows in this volume.

REFERENCES

FEYERABEND, P. K. 1962. Explanation, Reduction, and Empiricism. In H. Feigl and G. Maxwell (eds.), *Minnesota Studies in the Philosophy of Science*. Minneapolis: University of Minnesota Press.

——1970. Consolations for the Specialist. In I. Lakatos and A. Musgrave (eds.), *Criticism and the Growth of Knowledge*. Cambridge: Cambridge University Press.

HABERMAS, J. 1972. *Knowledge and Human Interests*. Trans. J. J. Schapiro. London: Heinemann.

HESSE, M. 1966. *Models and Analogies in Science*. New York: University of Notre Dame Press.

——1974. *The Structure of Scientific Inference*. London: Macmillan.

KUHN, T. S. 1962. *The Structure of Scientific Revolutions*. Chicago: Chicago University Press.

NAGEL, E. 1961. *The Structure of Science*. London: Routledge.

POPPER, K. R. 1959. *The Logic of Scientific Discovery*. London: Hutchinson.

——1963. *Conjectures and Refutations*. London: Routledge.

TAYLOR, C. 1971. Interpretation and the Sciences of Man. *Review of Metaphysics* (25): 3.

The constructive role of models

ROM HARRÉ

PART I MODELS IN THE NATURAL SCIENCES

The general notion of a model

A model is a representative device. But it is unlike either of the two main traditional classes of sign. It is unlike a natural sign in that there is no causal relation between a model and its subject, while a natural sign like smoke is related causally to the fire that it signifies. It is unlike a conventional sign, since the choice of a particular model as a representation is not wholly arbitrary. The selection of a model is based upon real resemblances and differences between the model and what it represents, and decisions as to what are the proper degrees of likeness and unlikeness can be the subject of argument. The term 'model' captures the main features of this mode of representation better than the somewhat similar notion of 'picture'. Its range of significance is more suited to the role of this kind of representative device in science than that of the latter term. For example, a model may be a concrete object capable of comparable performances to the thing modelled. The behaviour itself may be the model, in which case we would quite properly want to call that behaviour a process that is a model of another process. We may want to speak of something imaginary that is not yet realized or may not be capable of concrete realization, as a model. The mode of representation in pictures, at least traditionally, is more thoroughly projective than that by which certain important categories of models are related to their subject matter. The likeness between a model and its subject matter may be no more than a formal homology. I shall use the word 'model' as the most general term of this kind, reserving 'picture' for a certain class of models. Diagrams, using highly schematized representative devices, but following certain projective conventions between themselves and their subject matter, form the borderline case of that sub-class of models, properly called pictures.

Why the study of models has come to the fore in philosophy of science

The notion of a model has appeared in recent philosophy of science in response to the failure of the 'logicist' programme. This was the attempt to express all that was characteristic of natural science in terms of concepts drawn exclusively from formal logic (see Hempel 1965: Chapters III, IV). The paradoxes and problems thrown up by that programme have led many philosophers of science to turn away from the apparatus of formal logic in their search for analytical concepts, and instead to look for them in the realities of scientific practice. In so doing, they have identified some intellectual processes that seem quite crucial to scientific thinking and which lie outside the possibility of formal analysis (Harré 1970). These processes involve the disciplined scientific imagination, in its task of constructing conceptions of processes and structures that are immune from empirical investigation, and yet, they must be assumed to underlie and be productive of those patterns which can be studied empirically. In the attempt to understand the imaginative processes that are involved in creative scientific thinking the notion of a model has turned out to be particularly illuminating. Not only has the new turn in the philosophy of science extended the domain of discussion in that field, but because it has involved a close scrutiny of actual scientific thinking, it can be of considerable use to scientists in drawing their attention to the sources and status of many of their most fruitful conceptions. In this task, neo-realism is in striking contrast to the logicist (or positivist) programme, which because of its fear of anything that smacked of psychology falsified the intellectual processes of science. The effect of copying the prescriptions of logical positivist theory of science has been disastrous for the social sciences, because only a very small and rather trivial part of scientific method was capable of being identified through the use of the concepts embedded in the positivist programme.

Examples of the restrictive effects of taking the formalist programme too seriously

The bad effects of positivism derive from two sources. One is the over-restrictive conceptual system associated with this point of view, which eliminates by default most of the realities of scientific thinking. The other is the positivist choice of favoured paradigms. The theories that come closest to meeting the positivist criteria are the very bare, very general theories of mechanics, which, since they are concerned with the processes underlying all others, are atypically irrational in their foundations, depending upon relations of bare concomitance between the states they ascribe to physical systems. To apply the form of such a paradigm to other areas of science would lead to the advocacy of a chemistry without atoms, a genetics without genes, a psychology without thoughts and so on. Don't think these haven't been tried! The temptation to ease the burden of science by taking the positivist way out is perennial. More than a hundred years separate Brodie's Calculus of Chemical Operations and Skinner's *Beyond Freedom and Dignity*, but philosophically they are very close kin.

The decline of positivism has then had a somewhat unexpected bonus. It has initiated a train of thinking that has led to the identification of a whole range of concepts which may prove to be of very considerable help to scientists in those areas where there has been some uncertainty as to method, and some uneasiness as to the status and indeed legitimacy of certain techniques, both empirical and theoretical. With the help of new insights into the structure and method of established natural sciences, partly deriving from taking sciences such as chemistry rather than mechanics as models, it has been possible, for instance, to show not only the legitimacy of the new movements in social science, comprised under the ethogenic banner, such as ethnomethodology, but to see them as meeting the requirements of the established sciences a great deal better than the apparently 'scientific' psychology of the laboratory tradition (Harré and Secord 1972).

Varieties of models

Philosophers have not always clearly distinguished sentential from iconic models. A sentential model is a set of sentences in some kind of correspondence with another set of sentences. An iconic model is a thing, structure, or process in some kind of correspondence with another thing, structure, or process. In this sense, a model is something real or imaginary which sentences can be *about*. Diagrammatically the actual situation in a science may sometimes be something like this:

Sentences of Set I correspond to sentences of Set II
are about are about
Subject Matter I which corresponds to Subject Matter II

If Subject Matter II is some kind of iconic model of Subject Matter I, that is, is like it in some ways, then some of the sentences in Set II which describe it, will correspond to sentences in Set I, which describe Subject Matter I.

There is a theorem in formal logic, the Skolem–Lowenheim Theorem, which can be interpreted to say that for a system of concepts of the kind of complexity that would be needed in a science, there are infinitely many sentential models of a given set of sentences. So for instance, if the Set I of sentences states the gas laws, there will be infinitely many sets of sentences which match those sentences. But if one set of sentences is to explain the facts described by another set, there must be some constraint on the multiplication of sentential models. The fact that there is only one acceptable theory of gases, namely the kinetic, illustrates the crucial role played in science by the subject matter of the second set of sentences. It is only because we are prepared to accept the picture of moving molecules as the most plausible icon of the empirically unknown structure of a gas that we are able to settle upon the sentences describing such movements as the best candidate for a theory of gases. Thus, in actual science we have two modelling relations of wholly different kinds. There is a correspondence between sentences, linking the sentences in a model with the original set of sentences, and there is the relation which obtains between the subject matters of each which includes such matters as real likeness and difference. These can be represented symbolically so that we have the following structure:

Sentential Set I
is about
Subject Matter I

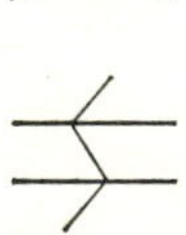

Sentential Set II
is about
Subject Matter II

This is the basic schema and I shall show how it can be put to work to bring some sort of order into the immensely complex intellectual processes involved in creative theory construction, as well as simpler representative tasks.

There is one remaining ambiguity in the notion of model which must be dealt with before one can begin. So far I have been using 'model' solely in the sense of 'analogue' i.e. model of something. But it is also used in the sense of 'ideal'. One example of this use, is the way we speak of a model as something to be copied. The model *for* a theory, in this usage, is the source or basis of the concepts in the theory. It is in this sense that we speak of mechanics as a model for molecular kinetics. To cut through these ambiguities a terminology has been growing up. That upon which something is modelled, the model *for* something has come to be called the model-*source*, or just 'source'. Analogues of various sorts have been distinguished as various kinds of *-morphs*, or forms. Those *-morphs* whose role is representational have been called 'iconic -morphs'. I shall elaborate some of the important categories of '-morphs' in later sections.

The role of models in creative theory construction

Natural scientists have traditionally undertaken two distinct tasks. They have tried to sort out the non-random patterns in nature from the enormous multiplicity of happenings and phenonema, and they have tried to explain these patterns. The task of explanation requires answers both to the question of the conditions under which the patterns are created, and the question as to the mechanisms which generate them, under these conditions. This is not just an epistemological distinction, but involves metaphysics. The conditions which bring a pattern into being are of the character of events, temporally patterned changes, while the mechanisms which produce the patterns are of the character of things, permanent occupants of space with all sorts of latent powers and capacities and usually internally complex.

Things and substances are logically complex, that is they require to be specified both in terms of their behaviour and in terms of their nature. This duality is forced on us by the persistence in existence of things and substances at times when they are not manifesting their potential behaviour. Events are logically simple since, because they do not persist, they have no potentials and thus require no inner nature. They are nothing but what they seem. The pattern of scientific explanation reflects this metaphysical distinction. Behaviour is explained by reference to the natures of things. For example in chemistry the behaviour of a material is explained by reference to its chemical composition and stereostructure, where at least in principle both the behaviour and the chemical structure or nature of the material can be investigated empirically. At the other end of this spectrum are cases like Freudian psychology, where the nature of a person is specified in terms of a system of concepts that seem to imply the impossibility of the independent empirical investigation of the nature they ascribe (MacIntyre 1967).

But both cases have in common the fact that the process by which the nature is first ascribed in developing an explanation is psychologically an exercise of the imagination and philosophically an analogy. The process can be given some kind of form and thus becomes subject to a rational critique by a double application of the model schema I developed in the first section. When a non-random pattern is identified, the first step is to undertake a series of experiments to determine the range of conditions under which it appears. Then the processes which generate the pattern are to be looked for in the natures of the things and materials involved. It is the fact that these are usually not known that brings into action the model building process. The creative task is to invent a plausible analogue of the mechanism which is really producing the phenomenon. Mendel did not know what mechanism produced the Mendelian pattern of characters, generation by generation, so he proposed the genetic factor ('gene') as the basis of such a mechanism. Philosophically speaking what he proposed was an analogue of the then unknown mechanism of inheritance. It was *adequate* as an explanation since analogues of the observed patterns could be deduced from it, and it was *plausible* as a mechanism since it fitted in with the predominantly atomist conceptions of low-level, Victorian science, and did no violence to established, biological ideas. But it took a hundred years to *establish* the hypothesis as an independent fact about organisms. In the end it was established that genes *existed* and that they were *causally productive* of the observed patterns. The conceptual complexity of the process is illustrated, I hope, by the italicized terms. Three concepts are from epistemology, 'adequacy', 'plausibility', and 'establishment', and none of these is capable of reductive analysis in terms of 'truth'; while two are from metaphysics, 'existence' and 'causal production'. To work out the full consequences that derive from looking at science in this way is an enormous task (Harré 1970). I want here only to draw your attention as it were to 'the facts of the case', since I can then proceed to examine the forms these processes of thought take in the social sciences.

The account just given can be expressed as a schema:

FIGURE 1

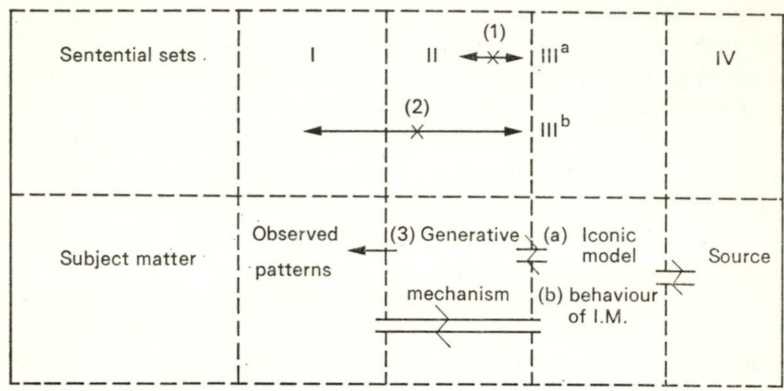

(1) Concerns structure etc.

(2) Concerns behaviour

(3) Causality

Usually Sentential set II is empty. That is, the nature of the actual mechanism producing a pattern is often quite unknown, and the gap is filled by imagining a mechanism and the processes in it which would produce patterns like those actually observed. And we can say that our iconic model is an analogue of whatever is actually producing the patterns. In order to achieve plausibility the iconic model must be modelled on a suitable source, and the sentences descriptive of it will be in some kind of correspondence with the sentences describing the source. One should notice just how complex this structure is. The iconic model is in a relation of analogy in three ways: it is analogous to its source (gas molecules are only analogues of little things); it is analogous to the real structure in which the generative processes occur (a swarm of molecules is, at least in the first instance, only an analogue of the real nature of a gas); and it must behave analogously to the way gases really behave (so that the laws which we derive for the imagined swarm of molecules must be analogous to the laws which we observe to obtain for gases). I am afraid it cannot be made any simpler than this. But however complex it is, I hope that the structure is now clear. This structure represents the process of creative model building, since the work of imagining an iconic model leads to the postulation of novel processes, hitherto unobserved structures and even novel kinds of things, perhaps with novel properties. The maintenance of a relation with a source constrains the imagination so that whatever is imagined retains a measure of intelligibility, while the maintenance of a relation with the real processes and patterns of nature constrains the model builder to make his models adequate as the basis of explanation.

One must insist over and over again that there is nothing in this schema that demands that the iconic models be simply pictorial. Sometimes quite new and wholly unpicturable models may be developed by using the schema. The concept of the 'field of potential' is such a concept. Maxwell used mechanical, picturable sources for developing the concept, but these are detachable once they have given an intuitive grasp of the notion.

Finally, I should like to emphasize that the logical structure of the schema above is resistant to expression wholly in terms of deductive connection. Of course, each of the three sentential sets, I, III, and IV can be organized in a deductive manner, but since the relations between the subject matter of the three sets is only one of analogy it is impossible to complete, *a priori*, a set of transformation rules which would enable deductive connections to be established horizontally in the schema.

But what about sentential set II? This can grow by two processes. As the iconic model comes to seem more and more plausible, sentences from set III can be the sources of sentences in set II. But the model may also serve as the basis for existential hypotheses. On the basis of Mendel's model, one may generate existential hypotheses, of the form 'Do genes exist?'. The model, if sufficiently articulated, can lead to quite precise specifications of the search area and the mode of its investigation. In the gene example it suggests that the nuclei of cells be searched, and that the mode of investigation be first the microscope, and then the techniques of molecular biology. Should such a search prove successful, then the Sentential set II may grow by direct investigation of the generative mechanism itself. At this stage, the analogue structure ceases to be a part of the theory, and can be filed away as a part of the history of science. The schema, it should now be evident, is a dynamic structure, representing an intellectual *process*. The neo-realist philosophy of science conceives of the role of models in just this dynamic way, since it aims to give an account of the process of theory construction, as well as a static analysis of the structure of theories at various stages of development.

The representative and analytical role of models

In this account, the role of the model is creative. Formally speaking, this creative role is possible because the model is located in a structure in which its source is necessarily different from its subject. Thus, an analogue of the subject (the unknown generative mechanism) is built up by drawing on a source (the known nature and behaviour of some class of things or some well understood process). Models are also used for tasks more representative than creative. In such cases the model's subject is also its source. If a biologist sets about making a model of the blood vascular system of an organism he draws upon that very system for the knowledge that he expresses in the model which he constructs. Such a model is both a model *of* the vascular system and modelled *on* it. Its role is primarily representative. It may have certain desirable features built in such as simplicity, abstractness, idealization and so on. Such models may, in certain circumstances, have a residual creative role in that, when the structure of the original is expressed in the special way of the model, new relations may be capable of being observed, which had been obscured by contingent features of the original.

Models whose subject and source differ have come to be called 'paramorphs' and those whose subject and source are the same 'homoeomorphs'.

Just as paramorphs may be the subject matter of sentential models, so too may homoeomorphs. The description of a homoeomorph may be treated as a sentential model of the description of its source-subject. I am inclined to think that this is the kind of modelling that is found in mathematical models in economics. The sentences in the mathematical model can be treated as descriptive of a homoeomorph of the real economic system. On the whole, economists are not to be thought of as offering descriptions of icons of the generative mechanisms that produce economic patterns.

I am firmly convinced that anthropology and related social studies, like social psychology, should take chemistry as a methodological model rather than, say, Newtonian mechanics. This is as much as to say that they are perfectly entitled to use their own versions of the model building processes described above in developing their knowledge, without being thereby 'non-scientific'. The idea that Newton's *Principia* is the sole paradigm for acceptable science has had a disastrous effect in social psychology, perhaps more than in any other area of social studies, and it has brought with it the largely empty rhetoric of statistics and 'measures'. I need not go into all that here (Cicourel 1967).

PART II APPLICATIONS OF THESE NOTIONS IN SOCIAL SCIENCE

The ethogenic point of view in social science

The ethogenic point of view in the social sciences conceives of human beings, not just as passive responders to the contingencies of their social world, but as agents deploying in their social lives a theory about people and their situation, and a related social technology. Ethogenists believe that this point of view has been kept alive in anthropology, and the symbolic interactionist tradition in sociology, while it was denigrated or denied in those branches of social science that were nearer psychology. Nevertheless, one is not merely preaching to the converted in laying out the principles involved in this theory, since I think it survived as a largely unexamined assumption and is still in need of explicit formulation.

Any individual person's theory about himself and others, and their social world, is like the kind of theory we have identified in sciences like chemistry, in which the pattern of events and the mechanism productive of the pattern are capable of separate description, and frequently of separate empirical investigation. Theories of social action, whether they are those held by an ordinary social actor in terms of which he develops his own action and construes the actions of others, or whether they are those special versions of that kind of theory developed by social scientists, have a similar structure. On the ethogenic view, a person's social capacities are held to be related to the relevant cognitive equipment he possesses, and this equipment includes items most naturally treated as models. These may range from very specific representations of the natures of his near and dear, to a typography of schemata for managing the identities of those who are more remote. And any given person's social theory will also contain representations or models of the social order, one or more of which may be models of that order which have diffused through from social science. 'The class system' is a case in point.

All this cognitive equipment is remote from inspection even perhaps from the actor himself[1] and any other person, be he social scientist or layman, must perforce conceive a model of relevant fragments of the cognitive structure of the person he interacts with. In this way, he forms a model of cognitive elements which are themselves models of varying degrees of abstractness.

The fact that some kind of social order exists shows that our models of each others' models and of the social order have some degree of homology, i.e. formal correspondence. This seems to be ensured amongst humans by the existence of common languages and other forms of symbolic interaction by which a psychic community of shared meanings is created, ensuring a sharing of symbolic forms. This is one of the points at which structuralist ideas assume great importance. In *The Savage Mind*, and in other places, Lévi-Strauss (1966) can be understood to be offering hypotheses about the shared sources of models for representing certain abstract structures, an understanding of which plays an essential part in the management of social life, and representations of which must be supposed to be present among the cognitive resources of each member of the community. This is the sense I give to his famous concept of *bricolage*, i.e. it is the common source of each individual's models, that ensures that they will be sufficiently homologous to create a common social world.

Not only are representative models shared, but so too are models in the sense of ideal types. The stylistic features of performance by which a person projects a chosen image of himself in public, suitable for what he takes that interaction to be, must be adjusted to the range of types recognized as authentic by his audience (Goffman 1969). Otherwise he will fail to be understood and his efforts at self-presentation are liable to be written off as weird and idiosyncratic aberrations. The aetiology of such models as these is extremely complex, but it is clear that they may involve both imitative or iconic modelling as well as elements which could more properly be taken to be arbitrary. Contrast the loose, hip-swinging walk of the young men entering Harold's Club in Reno, Nevada, by which a culturally standardized image of 'big spender' is projected, derived from well-known human exemplars, and the head-toss of a young woman, an equine metaphor by which 'unbridled autonomy' is indicated, with the open and shut palm with which an Italian waves goodbye. The young man may surround his walk with further iconic accoutrements, such as a string tie, big hat, and so on, derived from his exemplar, though for the young woman to elaborate her point with a whinny would be regarded in most circles as extravagant.

Occasions for model use in the social sciences

An ethogenist sees a social world existing primarily in the episodes of individual encounter, and the constraints exercised on previous and subsequent conduct by the possibility and realization of culturally sanctioned forms of microsocial interaction. In a sense, we know such episodes well and our techniques for their successful management are really remarkably good. But as social scientists, we must join with Machiavellians, con-men, and theatrical producers in both occupying roles and taking distance from our social performance. By this means, we become conscious of a complex reality, in need of analysis. Following Burke (1969) and Goffman (1968; 1969), I will assume that we must take a generally dramaturgical perspective, and look for the broad principles of construction of homoeomorphs of the episodes of microsocial life in such concepts as Burke's dichotomy between scene and action. By seeing the social world as a self-directed production on the stages available in home and factory, in office and airliner, one possible, skeletal structure emerges from the complexity of the action, a skeleton capable of enormously fruitful development.

What must people be like for them to be capable both of the action as conceived in the dramaturgical perspective and of the distancing by which controlled social action, and social science (one of many possible forms of commentary upon the action) become possible?

The natures, psychological 'mechanisms', and cognitive resources of the actors are by and large unknowns, and for these an interrelated system of paramorphs will be outlined, using as a common source the resources and intellectual skills of the most self-aware Machiavellian. Finally, the macrostructures of the social world, existing themselves only as iconic models within people's minds, as part of their cognitive resources for interaction management, will be looked at very briefly. The fact that social scientists describe such structures as if they had an independent reality serves merely to illustrate their instrumental role as images, since in the minds of both social scientists and ordinary men such images have the very same function. To take this view of the representation of the social macrostructure is already to adopt a radical stance to the problem of the form of its reality (Berger and Luckmann 1967). Indeed, in each problematic area the model bears a different relation to reality. Homoeomorphs of microsocial episodes are abstractions from an independent reality; paramorphs of the natures of people are representative anticipations of a possible reality, while the totality of individuals' models of the larger social order exhaust the reality of that order itself.

Models of microsocial episodes

Whether we are looking at the matter from the point of view of a layman or social scientist, it makes sense to begin the task of social analysis with an analytic of social episodes. With that begun, we can then turn to the prerequisites required of people that they have the necessary powers to operate in the way we find them operating. In this way, the model of the social order and a close analysis of the forms of microsocial interaction logically precedes the development of a model of man, though as a good ethogenist I take it for granted that if there is any priority in causality between the two essential elements it is human powers that are ontologically basic and the social order is one of their epiphenomena.

Social action can be examined from a great many points of view, but I shall begin, somewhat arbitrarily it may seem at first sight, from the aspect of the performance of those overt and conscious social acts by which the social order is created and maintained. I do not wish to imply by this choice of priority that I am not aware of a vast covert (i.e. non self-conscious) stream of interaction which is also functional in this way. I mean the stream of paralinguistic interaction, and other mutual influences of a non-verbal kind by which a kind of atmosphere, social aura or tone is created and maintained (see Argyle 1972).

I begin then with such overt social acts as the interaction among a group of people by which a certain status hierarchy is maintained and reaffirmed. Such interaction episodes can be arranged along a spectrum by means of which we insert a source for fine-structure models within the general model of the staged performance. At one pole are the wholly formal, in which every move is laid down in advance and the actors do what they do by explicit reference to the rules. In a state banquet, status is affirmed and confirmed by explicit acts according to a strict protocol. We commonly identify formal episodes in which formal social acts are achieved as rituals. At the other pole are wholly informal interactions where a pattern of action directed to the performance of the social act is manifested but where there is little or no explicit attention to an antecedent specification of a procedure, and where the actors may not be conscious of the ceremonial character of the episode in which they are engaged. The ceremonial character may be capable of being seen only from the standpoint of a detached observer of the scene, though of course it will affect the perceptions and expectations of the actors who have taken part in it (Goffman 1972: 114–16). As an example of an episode at this end of the spectrum I have in mind a family quarrel, which seems to the participants to be open, that is, various outcomes seem to be possible. But if an outsider could observe it, the various phases of a sequence, sufficiently strongly patterned as to lead to the humiliation of one of the participants and the triumph of the other, would seem inevitable to him. One might, from the point of view of that perception, follow Lévi-Strauss in glossing the quarrel as a ceremonial reaffirmation of a status differential which was once the result of a genuinely problematic quarrel (Lévi-Strauss 1966: 30) At the formal end, both actors and outsiders, privy to the forms of the society, agree on the social act brought about by the action, while at the informal end though social acts *are* brought about, the lack of antecedent specification of the form of the action may lead to disagreement between social commentator, be he scientist or family friend, and the actors. It is the possibility of such disagreement that allows a social therapist room to manage the perceptions of the actors in such a way that they come to see the episode as falling within a class of episodes having a formal structure which, though they acted it through, they were too involved to perceive. As I see it, this is the use of a process of modelling.

Let me make this somewhat clearer with the help of a schema. For any given social act we can order the episodes by which the act is performed along a continuum, from the formal, to what I shall now more properly describe as the enigmatic, that is those for whom the underlying productive processes are unknown and for which there are, *a fortiori*, no explicit rules. People who think they are quarrelling nevertheless follow, day by day and quarrel by quarrel, a highly stylized and very stable form. But they are not aware of the sources of this ritualistic feature of their quarrels nor even perhaps that their quarrels have taken on a ceremonial character. To describe the quarrel as an 'informal ritual' as I have done in introducing the case is to subsume it under a model, that is to conceive of it as produced according to some analogue of the process by which the structure and actions of the formal episode is produced and to have an analogous structure and social meaning to an explicit ritual directed at achieving the same or a similar end. This is to model the enigmatic on the formal in two different dimensions. It is to offer an analytic for the *episode*, under which the various things that happen will have a different construal from that given to them by the actors, and to offer a model of the generative process which would produce an episode like that which actually occurs, were the episode formal. And this last step may lead to empirical hypotheses about the cognitive equipment of the actors, about the development of their social skills and even, by a further process of modelling, about the structure of their nervous system, as I shall explain in the next section. Thus, the structure of an enigmatic episode is conceived of on the model of a formal episode comparable as to social act achieved, while the mechanism by which the episode is produced is conceived of on the

FIGURE 2 Structure of analytical modelling for episode analysis

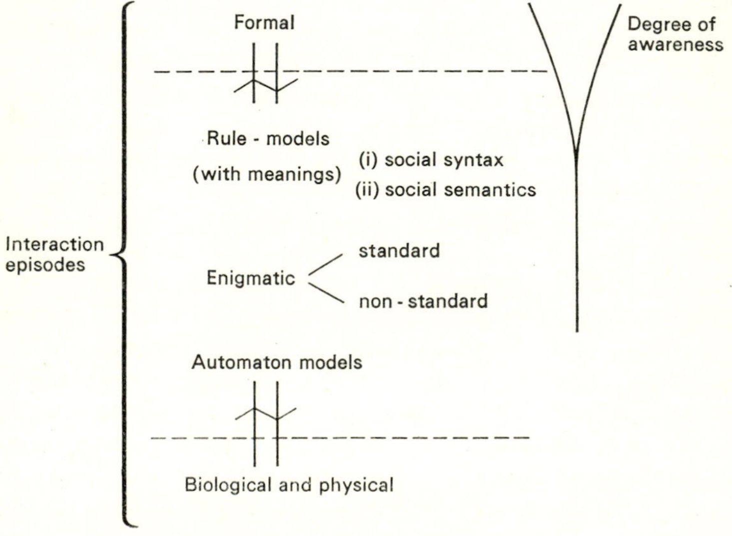

model of the mechanism by which the formal episode is produced, namely explicit rule-following. In this way we generate both a homoeomorph of the episode, and a paramorph of the processes of its production.

This kind of double use of the formal model is part of the methodology of Goffman (Harré and Secord 1972: 205–26) in his studies of the forms of everyday life, and it is clearly an important part of the technique of field anthropology. But the anthropologist's use of the technique is problematic in a way which Goffman's is not. There are etiquette books and manuals of instructions about in our culture, so that Goffman knows which part of his subject matter is genuinely enigmatic and which part is the formal product of explicit rule-following, or of residual habits having their source in formal prescriptions. In many cases, an anthropologist's notes provided the very first etiquette book that a society may have known. Of course, the fact that he is *told* that there is an oral tradition specifying the forms of tribal ritual may mean no more than that the oral traditions start from here. It must be immensely difficult for an anthropologist to distinguish the formal from the enigmatic, and once having distinguished it, prevent his perception feeding back into the society converting the enigmatic to the formal.

Ritual (or the liturgical model) is not the only source of, i.e. model *for* analytical concepts and paramorphic models of the generating processes of the action. Of equal importance is the game or agonistic model (Scott and Lyman 1970). Both fit within the generalized dramaturgical perspective.

But the idea of using the formal as source for concepts for analysing and explaining the origin of the enigmatic has recently led ethogenists towards a complementary perspective. The game-ritual source of concepts provides a device for analysing the content of the elements, moves, actions, and sayings of social interactions. One might naturally be inclined to say that the application of this conceptual scheme enabled one to understand the social meaning of gestures, expressions, sayings (and non-sayings), and so on. It would be natural to call the products of this analysis a social *semantics*. From this point, it is a simple step to the *linguistic analogy*. Perhaps there is a social *syntax* that determines the structure of interaction rituals and games. Perhaps the order of kinds of actions in an interaction (say a greeting 'ceremonial') is as rule-governed and fraught with significant propriety as the order of the component elements in a saying. The pursuit of the study of social syntax is at a very rudimentary level (Lehner 1969). It has been suggested (Tiger and Fox 1971: 12–13) that the linguistic analogy might be taken so seriously as to encourage the pursuit of structural universals on the lines proposed by Chomsky for language (see Katz 1966). At this stage, one can only say that the linguistic analogy opens up the possibility of intriguing lines of research.

Having found out what people are doing, and this, as I have argued involves identifying the social meaning of what is done, i.e. what social *act* has been performed, and may involve the discovery of the rules governing the structuring of the component actions by which the act is performed, the next phase of modelling is to conceive of a model of man such that people are capable of doing what we know quite well they do in fact do. I believe that in our everyday interactions with people we are pretty thoroughly behaviourist, identifying people by their appearance, and thinking about them only in so far as we form opinions as to what they will be likely to say and do. The best we usually hope for is some kind of untroubled passage through an encounter. But social *scientists* must do better, they must do at least as well as moderately sympathetic and intelligent laymen do from time to time. They must try to get at what it is to be that very person. They must explore the phenomenology of the social world.[2]

Models of people

When we turn our attention to the problem of modelling people we find a situation fraught with complexity and heavy with the debris of history, exploded myth, and of sustained prejudice. It can hardly be disputed that human beings are physico-chemical mechanisms *and* conscious, self-monitoring, rule-following, intention-pursuing, meaning-endowing agents. I propose to turn my back on the siren simplicities of reductionism, and offer a set of model schemata, complex enough to capture our presently perceived reality, but open enough to be capable of absorbing a certain range of future discoveries, conceptual or biochemical.

To do justice to what we know about people, *four* kinds of person model are required, each individual being capable of being minimally represented in his social capacity by a set containing one of each. They are the ethogenic, the cybernetic, the system theoretic, and the physiological. What is required is in fact something more than just a set of models. I shall be outlining something more in the nature of a set of skeletal theories, each with an embedded model. In short, an adequate account of human social functioning requires, even at our present elementary state of knowledge, a fourfold application of the theory schema sketched in Part I. The ethogenic theory, with its embedded models, is required to do justice to the intentional agency of human action, exemplified in such activities as conceiving, critically reviewing, and realizing a plan. The physiological theory is required, not only because one can hardly deny that people are ultimately physiological mechanisms, but also because some straightforward physiological responses, such as the trembling hands of the nervous, are an intimate part of social life, in that they are both indications of a state, and are absorbed into the ethogenic model as the bearers of meaning.

The ethogenic model An ethogenic theory takes as the source of its models of the generative mechanisms of enigmatic human action the known modes of acting of human beings when they follow a rule, or conceive and realize a plan, in full awareness of what they are doing. In the course of such action the fully self-aware man monitors those actions, and monitors the monitorings, making himself thereby capable both of stylistic control and commentary upon (or accounts of) what he is doing, thus justifying his actions and explaining them at the same time (Harré and Secord 1972: 84–100). One kind of such account is social science.

How does the most self-aware person plan his social actions? He imagines a situation and his own and others' actions therein, adjudicating the propriety of what he does by reference to the imagined judgment of a few significant others; the provincial try-out before the opening night, one might say. He may run over several possible scenarios in the theatre of his imagination. I claim that this is what happens, as a matter of fact, in the most self-conscious form of social planning. I acknowledge that most social action is habitual action, and there is little self-consciousness about the actions and mind of the confident and experienced social actor. But I am advocating the adoption of the state of mind of the adolescent and the consciousness of self-management of a Machiavellian, as sources of models for the cognitive processes of the mature social actor whose self is lost in the interest of the action. This closely corresponds to the phenomenologist move from the 'natural attitude' to retrospective and reflective attention.

I am inclined to think that the analysis of the inner lives of adolescents and Machiavellians yields four main components relevant to the genesis of appropriate social action. They are 'situations', 'selves', 'arbiters', and 'rules for the development of the action'. There is a certain number of standard social situations which we must be able to recognize. In each situation, there are appropriate social selves to be presented in a recognizable way (see Goffman 1972: 47–95). There are usually a few people whose opinion of our social skills and performance we would be shamed to forfeit. Finally, each situation and its proper self constitute a scene in which action may develop in a limited number of permissible ways. One can imagine a set of rules, like the rules of a ceremony, which prescribe the proper course of the action.

This complex of definitions and rules, images and imagined actions, constitutes not only a resource for an individual, but knowledge of it is the central stuff of social science. Knowing the cognitive resources of the people of a society we know its possible social forms, and thus, the only ways action can develop which can be recognized as such. These resources could be laid out diagrammatically as a matrix, each element of which is a conceptual complex, to the unravelling of which the methods of Kelly might be appropriate (see Bannister and Mair 1968). Social action is intelligent action utilizing these resources, or it is the habitual residue of what was once intelligent action of that sort. The ethogenic point of view repudiates the idea that the human social world comes into being as a kind of automatic, multiple reproduced response to the signals of one's conspecifics.

FIGURE 3 Ethogenic model-schema for cognitive structures for social problem-solving

$$\begin{array}{ccccccc} S_1 & - & p_1 & - & j_1 & - & (r_1) \\ - & - & - & - & - & - & - \\ - & - & - & - & - & - & - \\ - & - & - & - & - & - & - \\ S_n & - & p_n & - & j_n & - & (r_n) \end{array}$$

S_1 ... situation-type
p_1 ... persona-type
j_1 ... arbiter of propriety
(r_1) ... rules

The cybernetic model In the cybernetic model the rules and plans which are perceived or imagined as guiding the conduct of the self-managing man of the ethogenic image are expressed formally, and 'following as a conscious act' is replaced by the formal 'following' of the operation of an algorithm. The cybernetic model must be functionally equivalent to the ethogenic, for any given person in any given culture, i.e. the algorithms must generate prescriptions of patterns of action etc. which are sufficiently similar to those generated by the workings of the ethogenic model, which are themselves sufficiently similar to what people actually do. This model is a formal expression of the ethogenic, and could be treated as not independent at all, but as a homoeomorph, ideal and abstract, of the ethogenic. Its formal instructions would be related to the naturalistic rules of the ethogenic model as their direct formalization.

The system-theoretic model There is no place in the cybernetic model as such for a representation of the hardware capable of functioning in the way the formal algorithms of the model do. This deficiency is made up by the conception of an abstract structure capable of performances formally described in the cybernetic model. The systems so conceived must be functionally equivalent to the algorithms of the cybernetic model. The system-theoretic model can be conceived of as an abstract homoeomorph of the real physiological system, and as a paramorph of the mechanism responsible for the abstract operations of the cybernetic model; and through the functional equivalence of that model to the ethogenic, as a paramorph of the mechanisms responsible for the actual, concrete operations of conscious, human agents.

The physiological model The abstract structure of the system-theoretic models can take concrete form in iconic models of putative, real structures in the nervous system, thus generating physiological hypotheses. This form of model closes the circle, since physiological models are models of the nature of man, that man who in real life, with his real resources and real cognitive and imaginative powers, can think and act in the manner represented in the ethogenic models. Physiological models will then be homologous to certain favoured system-theoretic models, the homology being a reflection of the fact that we can conceive of the system-theoretic model as an abstract and idealized form (a homoeomorph) of the concretely realized physiological model.

Models of the social order

I have claimed that the social order is nothing but a series of homologies between models of an imaginary structure each of which are part of the cognitive resources of people involved in the management of social interaction. It is just because we can form models of reality that we have the power to create a reality by conceiving of a structure which has the status of a model but whose subject we create on the basis of the model. As natural scientists and protoscientists we create a model of an existing world: as social actors we create a world for an existing model. For example, social power is an endowment to an individual from us, as we give him deference. It derives from the place in our image of social reality reserved for somebody of his kind. Of course, he and his kind may be part authors of our image, but his social power lasts no longer than the image with our place for him persists.

Perhaps the most accurate placement of our images of a social world can be obtained by comparing them to the metaphysical component of the full theory-schema set out in Part I. In the metaphysics of a science, we set up a kind of general vision of reality in which the kind of things that can exist and the kinds of events that can occur are represented. Of course, it is an empirical question as to which possibilities are realized, and as to what exact form that realization takes. In an analysis of the theories about people and their social actions that we deploy in the management of our self and our interaction with others, images of society have the place that metaphysical visions of the world have in natural science. The image of society gives us our ideas of what roles there can be, and then we discover empirically if they are filled, how and by whom – the only difference from natural science being the crucial fact that we can and do construct worlds to fulfil images. Finally, it is important to notice that in social theories a viable set of interactions may exist between people whose images of society are very widely different, provided only that some minimal homologies exist in terms of which some structure of meaning can be given to an interaction. An important area of empirical study here awaits a bold and unprejudiced observer. The cognitive structures which we ascribe to other people are given form and content by an imaginative process similar to that by which develop our own cognitive resources. They are invented but not wholly freely. People have ways of representing abstract social realities in which they employ analogues having similar formal relations to the structure they wish to represent, but which may reflect only the logical or formal relations of that structure. This, as I have suggested, is how we should interpret the homologies of Lévi-Strauss.

Each person has a mode of representing to himself the structure of the social world, and he manages his social action, when rules and habits run out, by reference to that representation. One device by which the social order might be stabilized and the necessary homologies between each actor's societal image be guaranteed would be a ritual reaffirmation of the legitimacy of the local mode of representation. It is very important to remember that the modes of representation may be realistic, and have an immediate relation to real differences in the world, such as a world conceived of as male and female; or the mode of representation may be wholly fictitious in form, such as a social world pictured as hierarchically structured by class, or ordered as in the feudal pyramid.

The world of male and female is a really real world, while the world of man and wife, though superficially resembling the world of male and female, gains its reality through the relative and potential universality of the homologies that exist between conceptualizations of an image of order. A marriage ceremony creates a set of homologous images, it does not manufacture bonds. The ceremonial element in social life, whether formal or informal, is the one ineliminable and universal prerequisite for a social world since it is the means by which homologies are continuously created, and the social world brought into being and sustained.

The only place I know where the physical layout of the people is an exact homologue of their status hierarchy is at the wives' end of the room during an American middle-western faculty party. The florid extravagance of this form of analogue can be grasped if we reflect that even at the court of the Sun King the metaphor would have been deemed too banal. Despite the fictitious form of the *representation* the method of concretely visualizable metaphor may serve as a useful model for preparing solutions to the microsocial problems with which one is likely to be beset, and those images are an important part of the cognitive resources of competent social actors. *We* play with Durkheimian ideas of social facts at our peril. But no doubt the great man was aware in his heart of the metaphysical points just made.

PART III CHECKING THE AUTHENTICITY OF A MODEL

Testing models by simple prediction

All this talk of the role of the imagination in science must not be allowed to obscure the necessity for bringing its products into some kind of contact with reality. Models must be checked for authenticity. Once again, we find ourselves faced with a very complex situation, by contrast with the elegant economy of the older view of science. The older view saw a theory as a logically organized structure of hypotheses, from which predictions were made by deducing the consequences of supposing that certain boundary conditions held. If the prediction turned out to be correct when those boundary conditions were realized, inductivists held that this added a modicum of weight to the theory, while if it turned out to be mistaken, fallibilists held that this showed that the theory was worthy to be rejected. Something of this structure survives into the era of models. If the adoption of an iconic model leads to the incorporation of statements in a theory from which testable predictions can be drawn, then the outcome of those tests will bear upon the acceptability of that model. But the source of a model of the unknown inner structure of some entity is usually sufficiently rich to allow ameliorating additions to be made to the original model should it fail hypothetico-deductively, additions whose pedigree ensures they escape the stricture of being merely *ad hoc*. The most striking case of this is the continuous modification of the gas molecule, as it becomes more and more like its source, namely a solid thing, under the pressure of the discovery of the breakdown of the original forms of the gas laws in extreme conditions.

But iconic paramorphs can be the source of other kinds of hypotheses, particularly existential. I have already pointed out that an iconic model is often a model of the unknown inner structure of a thing or material, and often has the form of a system of elements, organized in some way. The commonest form of such organization in the natural sciences is spatial. For instance, the von Laue explanation of X-ray diffraction describes a model of the inner structure of crystals in which the crystal is envisaged as a lattice, at the vertices of which are ions. From this, an existential hypothesis can be derived, since the lattice vertices specify places at which a definitive search can be made for specified kinds of things. Should ions be found at the specified places the model has been authenticated. Its status changes from a simulation of the unknown inner nature of crystals to that of a realistic picture.

But there are very obvious limits to the existential checking of iconic models. These are the limits of observation. From an existential point of view, it seems proper to draw the line at the limit of what might be called the 'extended senses'. Just where this line is to be drawn is a nice point, and could be the subject of argument. But it is also obvious that much of science transcends the most permissive drawing of such a line. How then do we judge the authenticity of the imaginative simulation of reality? Jacques Monod (1972) argues, in his recent book, that science is made possible only by the acceptance of the possibility of such simulation. Our trust in it, he argues, can be rationally grounded in the fact that our powers of imaginative simulation are the product of an evolutionary process. But their adaptiveness might as much derive from systematic self-deception as from genuine authenticity, it seems to me. I am inclined to think that we must seek yet another method for checking the authenticity of our creations.

The final criterion is that of plausibility according to the prevailing metaphysics of the period. This criterion, while being perhaps the most powerful of all checks upon scientific theorizing, is both vague and evanescent. It is vague because the metaphysics of an era determines only in very broad outline what is assumed to be obviously real. Consider the variety of forms the material atom took, each of which was acceptable at some time and to some members of the scientific community. It is evanescent since powerful new models of reality may lead to shifts in the metaphysics of a cultural community, while changes in the groundwork of metaphysics have often enlarged imaginative possibilities in one direction while closing them in others. Both directions of influence can be discerned in the history of the field as a model of the fundamental physical reality. *Naturphilosophie* and the Romantic movement prepared the metaphysical ground, while the scientific development of the concept by Faraday and Maxwell has encouraged the growth of a metaphysics of potentiality.

Science is pursued under the intellectual discipline of plausibility, and the empirical discipline of fact.

The replication of reality

I have already argued that the humdrum methodology of chemistry provides a better scientific exemplar for social studies to follow than does the heady but atypical methodology of fundamental physics. In addition to the processes of testing I have outlined above, chemists use a technique of checking their models of reality, the development of the analogue of which by Mixon (1972: 145–77) for the social sciences must be regarded as a methodological breakthrough of considerable importance.

Organic- and biochemists not only try to discover the structure of the compounds that come their way, and to check their hypotheses as to that structure by seeing that the predicted products of decomposition actually appear, but they regard the ultimate triumph of their science as consisting in the synthesis of the very compounds they have analysed. The crowning achievement of chemistry is the replication of reality.

The analysis of accounts both from actors and the ethogenically-aware participating spectators of social action yields three main kinds of interlocking material: images of the self and others; definitions of situations; and rules for the proper development of the action. Mixon has shown how, by ferreting out this material and constructing a sufficiently detailed scenario, a particular range of social realities can be replicated by amateur actors, complete with appropriate feelings! The method is in its beginnings, but I believe that in its further development lies much the most promising line for future empirical research in social science. On the analytical side the phenomenological tradition has much to contribute, while the pursuit of the linguistic analogy, and the further identification of non-verbal components can complement and complete the dramaturgical perspective. By the exploitation of homoeomorphic models of episodes, paramorphic models of the human resources necessary for action in those episodes, we can create model social worlds, complete, as they say in the model railway catalogues, 'in every detail'. Our capacity to do this is the measure of our achievement as social scientists.

Testing people models

Criteria of authenticity, including the replication of reality, provide the most pertinent method for the checking of those models in use in the social sciences which simulate cognitive features of individual people. I have argued that the development of such models is essential to the ethogenic approach in social science, which emphasizes the construction and management of the social world by individuals. Such models represent the cognitive equipment with which one tackles the problematic character of the social world, and is, of course, one of the items put to the test in a Mixonian replication of reality.

But developing a model of the unknown, cognitive structure of a human being not only passes limits analogous to those of the extended senses, in that it may involve elements and structures of which we are unaware (and perhaps never could become aware), but it may also involve modes of organization that are not found in ordinary experience. It will certainly involve modes of organization that are not found in the structures that the traditional natural sciences study. For instance, it may be necessary to explain the succession of one thought by another by the principle that the latter is a reason, in a context of justification for the other; rather than that the former is the cause of the latter. How can we check the authenticity of such models?

Corresponding to the use of the microscope is the reportage of participants in a social encounter. But it is clear that cognitive modelling in the service of explanation goes far beyond what can be identified in accounts. To provide a justification of modelling in such terms I shall elaborate the concept of functional equivalence already introduced in Parts I and II. In discussing the necessity for introducing models of unknown mechanisms I argued that the model would have to behave in such a way that it could be thought to produce patterns of phenomena analogous to those patterns produced by whatever was the real mechanism. If the model produces a pretty good simulation of the known patterns it could be said to be functionally equivalent to whatever was really producing the patterns. In the case of natural science the check on functional equivalence is confined to the effectiveness of simulation of the observed patterns.

But in the human sciences the situation is more complex and for once the complexity is to be welcomed. In the very long run, one wants to say that the mechanisms producing the patterns of human action are physiological. A cognitive model capable of simulating known patterns of social behaviour (or of language-using for that matter) must, in the last analysis, be functionally equivalent to some physiological mechanism. Suppose, for instance, that the cognitive models required to explain the genesis of human social action are all of at least the degree of complexity of a system that can not only monitor its behaviour but monitor that monitoring, and in the light of what it learns, controls not only what it is doing but the manner or style of that doing, then the physiological mechanism by which our sort of organism brings this off must be at least of that degree of complexity and have at least that measure of structure as a system. Thus, functional equivalence between cognitive model and physiological structure requires that certain homologies hold between them, mediated by the intermediate levels of modelling that I have christened the cybernetic and the system-theoretic.

Thus, we have a third check upon our modelling, though in the present state of the art the realization of this check may be very distant. Only if there are identifiable physiological mechanisms capable of performing the control and monitoring functions of the cognitive models are those cognitive models authentic. These checks operate with no regard whatever to the deliverances of introspective awareness.

NOTES

1 This fact raises a further series of difficult questions as to the status of these alleged cognitive elements. I do not propose to deal with them here.

2 The close parallel between ethogenic social psychology and phenomenological sociology can be seen in Schutz (1972).

REFERENCES

ARGYLE, M. 1972 Non-Verbal Communication in Human Social Interaction. In R. A. Hinde (ed.), *Non-Verbal Communication.* Cambridge: Cambridge University Press.

BANNISTER, D. and MAIR, J. M. M. 1968. *The Evaluation of Personal Constructs.* London: Academic Press.

BERGER, P. L. and LUCKMANN, T. 1967. *The Social Construction of Reality.* New York: Doubleday.

BRODIE, B. 1866. A Calculus of Chemical Operations. *Philosophical Transactions* **156**: 781–859.

——1877. A Calculus of Chemical Operations. *Philosophical Transactions* **167**: 35–116.

BURKE, K. 1969. *A Grammar of Motives*. Berkeley and Los Angeles: University of California Press.

CICOUREL, A. 1967. *Method and Measurement in Sociology*. New York: The Free Press.

GOFFMAN, E. 1968. *Stigma*. Harmondsworth: Penguin.

——1969. *The Presentation of Self in Everyday Life*. London: Allen Lane, The Penguin Press.

HARRÉ, R. 1970. (reprinted 1972). *The Principles of Scientific Thinking*. London: Macmillan; Chicago: Chicago University Press.

HARRÉ, R. and SECORD, P. F. 1972. *The Explanation of Social Behaviour*. Oxford: Blackwell.

HEMPEL, C. G. 1965. *Aspects of Scientific Explanation*. New York: The Free Press; London: Collier-Macmillan.

KATZ, J. J. 1966. *The Philosophy of Language*. New York and London: Harper and Row.

LEHNER, A. 1969. Semantic Cuisine. *Journal of Linguistics* **5**: 39–55.

LÉVI-STRAUSS, C. 1966. *The Savage Mind*. London: Weidenfeld and Nicolson.

MACINTYRE, A. C. 1967. *The Unconscious*. London: Routledge and Kegan Paul.

MIXON, D. 1972. Instead of Deception. *Journal for the Theory of Social Behaviour* **2** (2): 145–77.

MONOD, J. 1972. *Chance and Necessity*. London: Collins.

NEWTON, I. 1947. *Principia*. Trans. A. Motte, 1729. Edited by F. Cajori. Berkeley: California University Press.

SCHUTZ, A. 1972. *The Phenomenology of the Social World*. London: Heinemann. (1st edition: 1932 Vienna.)

SCOTT, M. B. and LYMAN, S. L. 1970. *A Sociology of the Absurd*. New York: Appleton-Century-Crofts.

SKINNER, B. F. 1972. *Beyond Freedom and Dignity*. London: Cape.

TIGER, L. and FOX, R. 1971. *The Imperial Animal*. London: Secker and Warburg.

Some models from catastrophe theory in the social sciences

C. A. ISNARD AND E. C. ZEEMAN*

INTRODUCTION

Phenomena involving sudden large variations traditionally have been assumed to be outside the reach of mathematical treatment, because they lacked what was considered to be an essential precondition, the continuity of the dependence relations between the variables. Recently, a branch of mathematics called catastrophe theory, one of the creations of the French mathematician René Thom (1972), has been applied to such discontinuous phenomena in biology (Thom 1969; 1971a; 1973a; Zeeman 1972a; 1974a) and physics (Fowler 1972; Shulman and Revzon 1972; Thom 1971b; 1973a; Zeeman 1972b; 1973; 1974c). The authors of the present article hope that their modest examples may suggest to specialists in the social sciences the possibility of applying catastrophe theory to similar discontinuous phenomena in their fields. (See also Harrison and Zeeman; Thom 1970; 1973b; Zeeman 1971; 1973; 1974c; 1974d; 1975.) The objective, in each of our examples, is the qualitative characterization of those points where small variations in some variable may cause large variations in a dependent variable, in other words those points where 'catastrophic change' may occur. This is the reason for the name catastrophe theory.

There is also a related phenomenon of 'divergence', where the

* Sections 1–11 are the joint work of both authors, and sections 12–16 are by E. C. Zeeman only.

discontinuity may occur with respect to a variable other than time. For example sharp divisions of opinion can emerge in a population, even though the opinion of each individual may have evolved gradually and smoothly. By contrast the exact sciences are convergent in the sense that small changes in initial data usually cause only small changes in the ensuing motion, and so those sciences displaying divergence have been labelled 'inexact', because again they were thought to be impossible to model.

However, the creation of catastrophe theory has now revealed that sudden change and divergence are not only natural, and interrelated, but also amenable to rigorous mathematical treatment. Our objective is to use the theory to give qualitative understanding and global insight. The next objective, which we do not attempt here, is to provide quantitative models for experimental testing. In this sense catastrophe theory, as Thom himself has pointed out, is not a theory but a method. It is a mathematical tool, like the theory of differential equations, that can be applied to scientific theories, in order to explain and confirm them, or disprove them. The paper is intended to be an introduction to this method.

Contents

1 THE INFLUENCE OF PUBLIC OPINION ON POLICY

In our first example, we consider the influence of public opinion upon an administration, or, more precisely, the effect that changes in the distribution of public opinion have upon the ensuing policy adopted by the administration. We are supposing that this policy is influenced by the opinions of a large group of people that we call the *population* – it may be the total population of a nation, or part of it, for instance the membership of a large party, class, or military group, etc.

In order to illustrate the model more precisely, we shall work with a specific example, although the whole theory that we develop can be applied to almost any situation where there is a continuous spectrum of policies (or several spectra). The specific example we choose to work with is the case of a nation deciding upon its level of action in some war, either a hot war or a cold war. Let the variable x represent the possible alternatives, so that the higher values of x represent stronger military action, and the lower values weaker action, with the lowest values representing withdrawal or surrender. At a given moment, let P(x) be the number of people in the population who would approve of policy x, in other words would approve of the adoption by the administration of the level x of military action. The number P(x) can be weighted, if one wishes, to take into account the relative influence that different segments of the population may have on the administration. Also, the function P can be normalized, if one wishes, in other words scaled down so that there is a unit area under the graph. Hence P can be regarded as the probability distribution of public opinion.

FIGURE 1 Public support for different policies

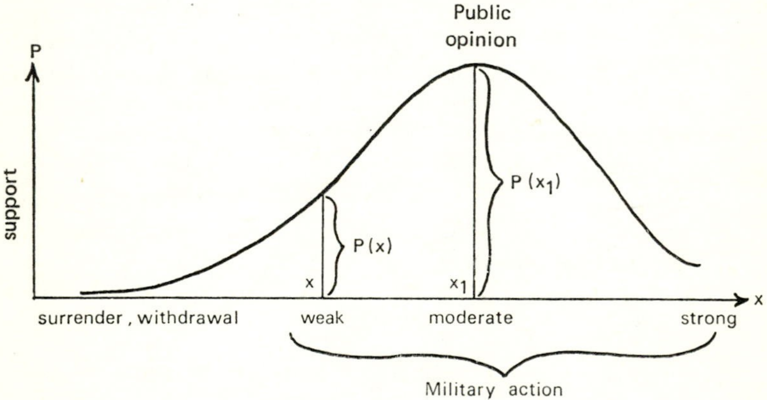

We suppose that *the aim of the administration is to maximize support*. This is, of course, an ideal assumption, made to isolate the particular cause-effect relationship that we want to study below. Also, it is not clear what the word 'maximize' should mean when we come to more complicated distributions, and so we shall need to introduce explicit rules in the next section. But at any rate, given the distribution of public opinion shown in *Figure 1*, then the policy adopted would be x_1. We say that the *behaviour*, at that moment, is x_1.

We choose to use the word 'administration' rather than 'government' in order to emphasize that we are modelling the spirit of the civil servant rather than the elected leader; the obligation of the administrator is to carry out the wishes of others rather than his own, to follow public opinion rather than to lead it.

Remark about maxima and minima This type of mathematics in which a function P is maximized, or minimized, appears in many different fields of application. For example, in economics P might represent profit, or cost, and an agent might choose his behaviour so as to maximize profit, or minimize cost. In psychology, P might represent anxiety level, and an individual might choose the behaviour that is anticipated with least anxiety. In sociology, P might represent the internal tension of a group, and the group might choose the behaviour to minimize this tension. In physics, P might represent the potential energy of some system, and the system would seek a stable equilibrium state, in other words a behaviour that minimized P (see Shulman and Revzon 1972; Zeeman 1972b). In fact, the considerations that follow can be applied to all these phenomena, and many more, and will show how catastrophic changes, and divergence, can occur mathematically in any deterministic model of this nature.

2 MAXWELL'S RULE AND THE DELAY RULE

We return to our original example. Suppose that with time public opinion becomes divided, so that there are now two local maxima at x_2 and x_3, as in *Figure 2*.

FIGURE 2 Split public support

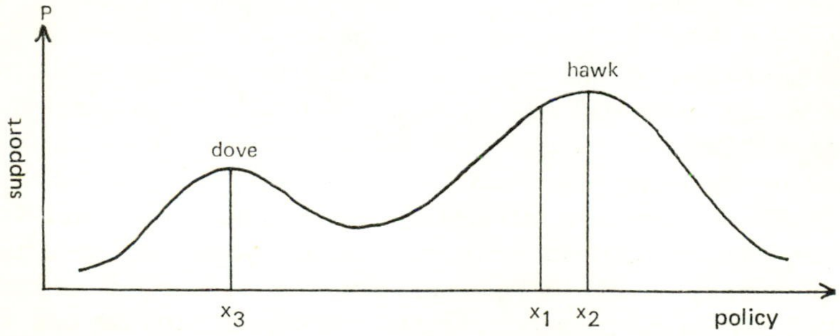

The majority has swung to the right in favour of stronger military action, and a minority has swung to the left in favour of less, or in favour of withdrawal. The contemporary fashion is to label these two groups, or their spokesmen, as *hawks* and *doves*. We suggest that an administration that had been engaged in policy x_1, if it was trying to 'maximize support', would immediately switch to policy x_2, in order to obtain larger support. In this way, as the distribution of public opinion changes with time, so does the adopted policy, or the behaviour. Moreover, if the distribution of *Figure 1* changes smoothly, meaning differentiably with respect to time, into that of *Figure 2*, then the behaviour will change smoothly from x_1 to x_2.

Suppose now that some time later the distribution of opinion changes a little more to *Figure 3*.

FIGURE 3 The Maxwell and Delay rules

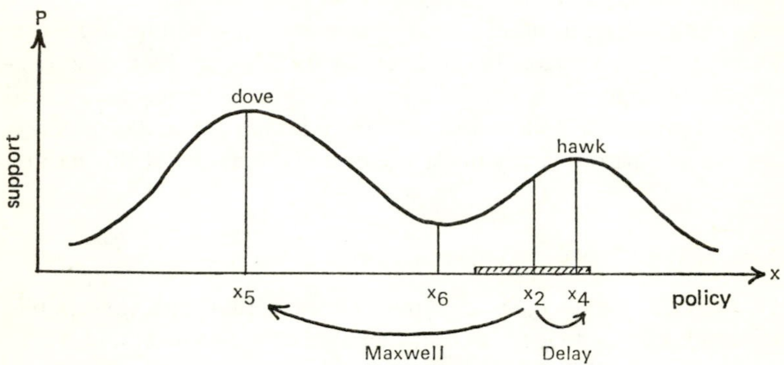

The majority opinion has now swung to the doves (and in so doing may have made both dove and hawk maxima slightly more hawkish). The administration, which had been engaged in policy x_2, now has a problem: should it adapt smoothly to the nearby local maximum x_4 of the hawks, or should it make a 'catastrophic' change of policy to the distant dove maximum x_5, where it would obtain maximum support? One thing is certain: the administration is least likely to try and average everyone's opinion and choose policy x_6, because this would have minimum support, and would incur the criticism of both doves and hawks. Therefore the problem is to choose between the two maxima. We can formalize the procedure by laying down two rules, as follows, and resolve the choice by agreeing to obey one or

other of the two rules. Rule (1) will imply choosing the dove maximum x_5, while rule (2) the hawk maximum x_4.
The rules are:

(1) *Maxwell's rule. Change policy to where support is maximum.*
(2) *Delay rule. Change policy in the direction that locally increases support.*

The directions of the arrows in *Figure 4* illustrate the directions of policy change under the Delay Rule, when this is applied to the distribution in *Figure 3.* At each point the direction of the arrow is determined by the slope of the graph, because this indicates which direction causes the support to increase. The arrows point towards

FIGURE 4 Policy movements under the Delay rule

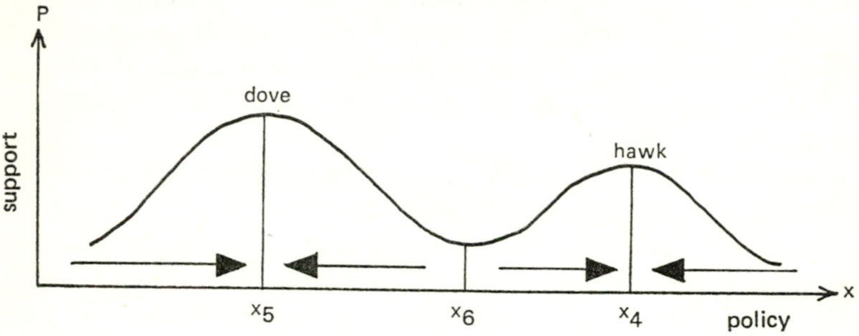

the two local maxima, and therefore under the Delay rule the policy changes until it is at one of the *local maxima*, whereas under the Maxwell rule it always changes to the *over-all maximum.*

Under both rules we assume the policy change happens *instantaneously*. The justification for this is that in practice any change of policy by an administration is usually so much swifter than the slow rate of change of distribution of public opinion, that compared with the latter the policy change can be regarded as instantaneous (see Zeeman 1972a). The reader may well ask the question: if under the Delay rule the policy change is instantaneous, why call it 'Delay'? The answer will become apparent in Sections 4 and 8 below, where we show that (instantaneous) adherence to the Delay rule can cause an administration to delay its response to swings of public opinion. Moreover, in the next section we give several reasons for suggesting that administrations do in general obey the Delay rule. This may help to explain why the delayed response is so common a phenomenon in practice.

Now let us return to *Figure 2*, and verify what happens under the two different rules as *Figure 2* evolves slowly into *Figure 3*. Maxwell's rule would imply a *catastrophic* jump from the old hawk policy x_2 to the new dove policy x_5, as soon as the dove maximum overtook the hawk maximum. Meanwhile, the Delay rule would imply a *smooth* policy change from the old hawk maximum x_2 to the new hawk maximum x_4. In this case, the emerging majority of doves would have been ignored because to change policy in that direction would initially have incurred a decrease of support, until the minimum x_6 had been passed.

Remark about minima There is a small mathematical point here: what if we found ourselves at the minimum x_6 and had to operate the Delay rule? The answer is that such a situation is unstable, and if it did occur, could only be a transient phenomenon, because P is always changing, and as soon as the minimum had moved, then x_6 would no longer be at the minimum, and so we could operate the Delay rule.

Remark about choice of rule At this stage, in any application of catastrophe theory, one must make a choice between rules (1) and (2), because they lead to slightly different models. One can devise other rules, for instance choosing the peak with the largest area beneath might be called the Voting rule. But in each case, the choice of rule must depend upon the particular application, and the one that seems to be best for most applications is the Delay rule. In fact, whenever the behaviour is determined by a differential equation (such as $dx/dt = \partial P/\partial x$) the Delay rule is a theorem, and so holds automatically (Zeeman 1973). For instance, in a biological example like the beating of the heart (Zeeman 1972a) the Delay rule is a consequence of using a differential equation to describe the underlying chemistry. In an economics example about the behaviour of stock exchanges (Zeeman 1974b) the Delay rule is a consequence of using a differential equation to describe the feedback of the market index upon investors. It is only when averaging devices are used that Maxwell's rule applies: in physics, for example, density measures the average packing of molecules in a volume, and consequently Maxwell's rule is used in Van der Waals's equation to describe the catastrophic jump in density as a liquid boils (Fowler 1972; Shulman and Revzon 1972; Thom 1971b; 1972). In fact, it is called

Maxwell's rule after the nineteenth-century Scottish physicist J. C. Maxwell, who formulated an equivalent rule for this particular phenomenon. In most applications to the social sciences, the Delay rule is more appropriate, but nevertheless in each case, at this stage of the argument, its use must be justified.

3 SOCIOLOGICAL JUSTIFICATION OF THE DELAY RULE

We return to our original example. Here we choose to use the Delay rule, and justify our choice as follows. There are broadly speaking five types of reason for preferring the Delay rule to Maxwell's rule: lack of information, intuition, sociological pressures, inertia, and past history.

First, the lack of information. In spite of prolific intelligence services, news media and opinion polls, administrations today are still often in serious doubt as to the weight of public opinion, and may not be able to gauge at all accurately at any given time whether the dove or hawk maximum is higher. Furthermore, it is also difficult to ascertain the precise distant policy that would receive the most support (in other words the position of the point x_5 in *Figure 3*). There is also a serious mathematical point here (which we return to at the end of Section 10 below) because it is possible to alter the relative heights of the two maxima by suitably manipulating the horizontal scale; for example, we could raise the hawk maximum by shrinking the hawk-end of the scale, and simultaneously lower the dove maximum by stretching the dove-end of the scale.

Usually, it is much easier for an administration to gauge the extent of support for nearby alternative policies than for a major shift of policy. It is generally simpler, and may seem relatively safer, to adapt policy smoothly so as to stay at the local maximum, rather than to make the sudden major shift of policy to another maximum which may or may not be higher.

Second, intuition. Compared with the difficulty of determining the global distribution function P, the local determination of which direction brings increased support is relatively easy, and can often be seen by intuition (the analysis required is local, and demands only the ordering by size of the support for nearby alternatives, rather than a full quantification). This becomes important when administrators have to make quick decisions off the cuff, in which intuition plays a greater role.

Third, the sociological pressures. Besides the natural face-saving reluctance to undertake reversals of policy there may be deeper sociological reasons against so doing. It may happen that an administration considers views too distant from its own to be hostile already on a personal level, and therefore the support of the holders of those views would be unconquerable, even by a radical reversal of policy. Such an administration tends to keep a close dialogue restricted to a smaller group of people, whose opinions are closer to its current policy, and amongst whom it tries to maximize support, while dismissing the excluded opinions as extremisms. In *Figure 3*, the shaded interval on either side of x_2 represents the opinions of this restricted group, and therefore the 'viable' near-by alternatives under this view. Within the viable alternatives x_4 commands the maximum support.

Fourth, inertia. It may take a great deal of time, effort, and money to reverse a policy, both in human persuasion and communication, and in the redeployment of resources. Meanwhile, public opinion may be volatile, and if a large proportion of the population is undecided, then the two maxima of doves and hawks may be oscillating slowly up and down like a seesaw – in which case it could be foolish, if not impossible, to indulge in the erratic behaviour of a reversal of policy at every oscillation of the seesaw.

Fifth, past history. The two rules display a significant difference in that Maxwell's rule takes no account of past history, whereas under the Delay rule the recent behaviour plays a crucial role in determining the current behaviour.

Summarizing: the above five reasons all argue in favour of the Delay rule and against Maxwell's rule. They all point towards the administration pursuing a policy that changes smoothly, through the continual successive comparison of the adopted policy with all near-by alternatives, and, at each stage, the adoption of a new policy if it brings larger support – in other words the Delay rule. Exceptions can happen during times of election. For if public opinion, during an election, is divided over some issue as in *Figure 4,* and if there happen to be two main parties that take the two peaks of opinion as their main election planks, then the election itself can perform a simple operation of the Voting rule. However, in our model we are more interested in the behaviour of a single administration during its tenure. Therefore, from now on we assume the Delay rule. In its behaviour the administration will cling to the protection of its local

FIGURE 5 Catastrophic jump in policy

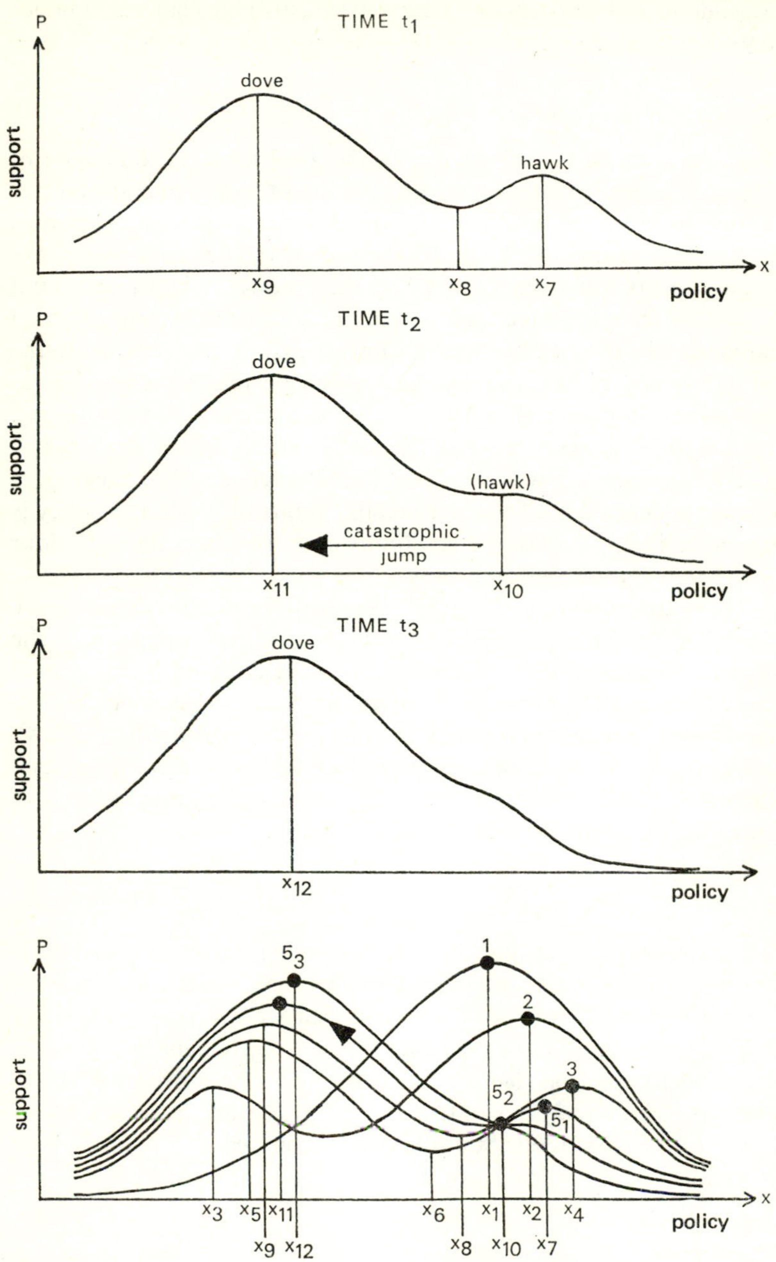

maximum, and will delay making any catastrophic changes in policy until forced to do so, which eventuality we now examine.

4 THE CATASTROPHIC CHANGE

Suppose that the behaviour was in the local hawk maximum x_4 of *Figure 3*. Suppose then that the distribution of public opinion evolves smoothly with time through the three successive distributions shown in *Figure 5*, at times t_1, t_2, t_3. By the time t_1 the behaviour will have changed smoothly from x_4 to x_7. By the time t_2 the hawk maximum x_7 and minimum x_8 have coalesced at x_{10}, and the behaviour is poised momentarily in unstable equilibrium at x_{10}. A moment later, the equilibrium vanishes, and by the Delay rule the behaviour has to make the instantaneous catastrophic jump to the dove maximum x_{11}. By the time t_3, the behaviour has settled stably in the dove policy x_{12}. We can now see why the Delay rule is so called: the catastrophic change is delayed until the last possible moment, when the policy is forced to jump because the local maximum in which the behaviour 'was caught' vanishes completely.

The bottom diagram of *Figure 5* shows all the distributions that we have had so far superimposed, with the numbers referring to the previous figures, and the blobs indicating the adopted policy in each case. Although the population is steadily becoming more dove-like, the track of the adopted policy is quite different. Initially the hawk policy escalates, and continues to escalate for most of the time; then there is a brief de-escalation before the catastrophic jump to the dove policy, after which the latter hardens slightly.

5 CONTROL FACTORS

What influences the changes in public opinion? We begin to elaborate the model by trying to pinpoint certain causes, which we shall call *control factors*. This is not to suggest that we necessarily have any control over them, but merely that this is a convenient terminology. It is actually the dependence of the behaviour x on the control factors that we wish to analyse. Control and behaviour are cause and effect.

We continue with our example of a nation deciding upon its level of action in some war. Consider the two control factors:

$a =$ threat
$b =$ cost.

In other words, *a* is some scale or index that measures how much the population feels their territory is threatened or their security is at stake. Meanwhile, *b* is some scale measuring the cost of the war, in casualties and money. (Possibly cost-per-achievement might be a more significant factor.) The effect of *a* and *b* on public opinion is qualitatively different, because a sense of common danger tends to unify opinion into a fighting mood, while a costly war tends to divide the population. We shall therefore call *a* a *normal factor* and *b* a *splitting factor*.

In order to make these concepts precise, we shall introduce sociological hypotheses, and translate them into mathematics. The deep theorems of catastrophe theory will enable us to synthesize the mathematics. We can then translate the synthesis back into sociological conclusions. It is not immediately apparent, without the use of the intervening mathematics, that the sociological hypotheses imply the sociological conclusions, and that is the purpose of using catastrophe theory. In this manner we shall see how the terms splitting factor and normal factor can be defined abstractly, and so acquire a new depth of significance, that can give insight into a wide variety of applications.

But first we explain how the dependence of the behaviour upon the control factors can be visualized as a graph.

6 THE CONTROL-BEHAVIOUR GRAPH

Let C be a horizontal plane with co-ordinates a,b. We call C the *control space* or *parameter space*. A point c = (a,b) in C is called a *control point*, and represents a particular threat + cost. The control space parametrizes the distribution of public opinion; in other words each control point c determines a particular distribution P_c of opinion x. We can incorporate the parametrized family of distributions into a single *support function* P, by defining

$$P : C \times X \longrightarrow R$$

by the formula $P(c,x) = P_c(x)$.

Let G_c denote the set of maxima of P_c. For example, if P_c is a distribution as in *Figure 1*, with a unique maximum at x_1, then G_c consists of the single point x_1. If, on the other hand, P_c is a distribution as in *Figure 2* with two maxima at x_2, x_3, the G_c consists of the pair of points $\{x_2, x_3\}$.

Now, let X be a vertical line with co-ordinate x. We call X the *behaviour space*, because it represents the possible levels of military action. Then G_c is a function from C to X, which is sometimes single-valued and sometimes double-valued. Our objective is to analyse this function. Now, the best way to visualize a function is to draw its graph. Therefore, let G denote the graph of the function G_c. To be precise, the graph G is contained in three-dimensional space, $C \times X = R^3$, and is defined to be the set of points

$$G = \text{closure}\,\{(c,x);\ c \in C,\ x \in G_c\}.$$

In fact, G will be a surface in R^3, and we claim that it will be equivalent to the folded surface pictured in *Figure 11* of Section 11 below. This is a strong and surprising claim, and to prove it we shall need to define equivalence and assume five hypotheses. Four of these are local sociological hypotheses, local in the sense that they are assumptions about the shape of P_c for particular cases of threat + cost. The other one is a mathematical hypothesis about P as follows.

Hypothesis 1. P is smooth and generic.[1]

This is a technical but harmless mathematical assumption, that enables us to use catastrophe theory in order to weld the four local sociological hypotheses into the single global picture of *Figure 11*, and hence determine G.

7 SOCIOLOGICAL HYPOTHESES

For convenience, let us use the language: *opinion is unified* if the distribution P_c of public opinion has a single maximum as in *Figure 1*, and *opinion is split* if it has two maxima as in *Figures 2–4*.

Hypothesis 2. If the cost of the war is low, then opinion will be unified, and the greater the threat, the greater will be the level of military action called for.

Therefore, keeping *b* fixed small and letting *a* vary, we shall have G_c as a single-valued increasing function of *a*. Moreover, G_c is smooth, since P is smooth by Hypothesis 1. Therefore, we obtain the graph shown in *Figure 6*. We label this G because it is a plane section, b = constant, of the three-dimensional control-behaviour graph G defined in the last section. This graph, and Hypothesis 2, is an initial formalization of what we mean by saying *a* is a normal factor.

FIGURE 6 Threat-action graph for low cost

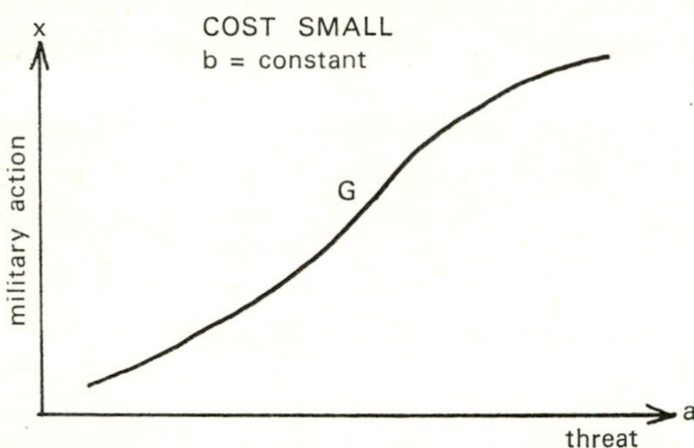

Hypothesis 3. If the cost is high, and the threat moderate, then opinion will be split between doves and hawks.

Therefore, keeping *b* fixed large, and letting *a* vary, the graph of G_c will have two branches called dove and hawk, as shown in *Figure 7* below. This is an initial formalization of what we mean by saying *b* is a splitting factor.

Hypothesis 4. If the cost is high, but the threat very great, then opinion will be unified in favour of strong military action.

Therefore, in the graph in *Figure 7*, only the hawk-branch extends over the right-hand end of the *a*-axis. Therefore, the dove branch must terminate at some point, B. Similarly we have the complementary hypothesis:

Hypothesis 5. If the cost is high, but the threat very small, then opinion will be unified in favour of withdrawal.

Therefore, only the dove-branch extends over the left-hand end of the *a*-axis. Therefore, the hawk-branch must terminate at some point, A. The precise fashion in which the hawk branch terminates is illustrated by the sequence of distributions in *Figure 5*. Here we are envisaging a situation in which the sense of threat is diminishing, taking decreasing values $a_1 > a_2 > a_3$ at times $t_1 < t_2 < t_3$, and therefore the hawk-branch will terminate at time t_2 at the point $A = (a_2, x_{10})$.

In *Figure 7* the unbroken line illustrates the graph G of maxima G_c, while the dotted line illustrates the analogous graph of minima. Although the dotted line has no sociological significance (as we pointed out in Section 2, above), nevertheless, it is mathematically interesting that the two graphs continue to give a smooth curve.[2] The two points A, B where the hawk and dove branches terminate are called *fold-points*, because these are the points where the combined graph folds over. In other words, the singularities of the projection $G \to C$.

FIGURE 7 Threat-action graph for high cost

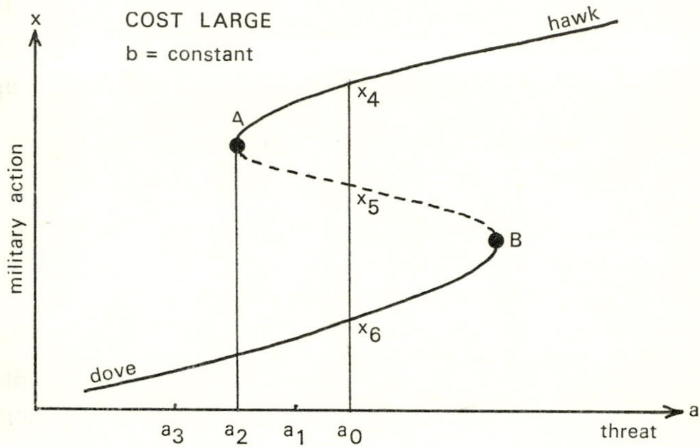

Let $b = b_0$ denote the fixed value of high cost for which *Figure 7* is drawn. Now, also fix $a = a_0$, and let $c = (a_0, b_0)$. Then suppose that the corresponding distribution P_c is illustrated in *Figure 4* with x_4 = hawk maximum, x_5 = dove maximum, x_6 = the minimum. This explains why the vertical line $a = a_0$ in *Figure 7* meets the combined graph in those three values of x.

Summarizing: we have translated the four sociological hypotheses into mathematics by drawing the graphs in *Figures 6* and *7*. These will be the plane sections, b = constant, of the three-dimensional graph G that we are seeking. The problem arises: how does the section shown in *Figure 6* evolve into that in *Figure 7*? The main theorem of catastrophe theory tells us that qualitatively there is only one way for this evolution to occur. It enables us to synthesize the mathematics into a single global picture, and then translate the mathematical properties of that picture back into sociological conclusions. A similar technique was used to study the unstable behaviour of stock exchanges (Zeeman 1974b).

But before we move on to the more complicated three-dimensional geometry in Section 11, let us first illustrate in the next section the type of qualitative conclusion than can already be drawn from *Figure 7*, and then digress in the following section to explain more precisely what the word 'qualitative' means.

8 THE DELAY BEFORE THE CATASTROPHIC CHANGE

We can now begin to put together the two main threads of our model so far:

(i) The variation of public opinion under different situations of cost +threat (described by Hypotheses 1–5 in Sections 7–9).
(ii) The resulting behaviour of an administration, that is seeking to maximize its support by operating the Delay rule (described in Sections 3–6 above).

Suppose we have a war-like situation with high cost (b = constant). The cost may not necessarily be due to military action, but could be due to a cold war, necessitating a high level of military preparedness, and a consequent crippling burden on the economy. Under varying

FIGURE 8 The delay before declaring war or making peace

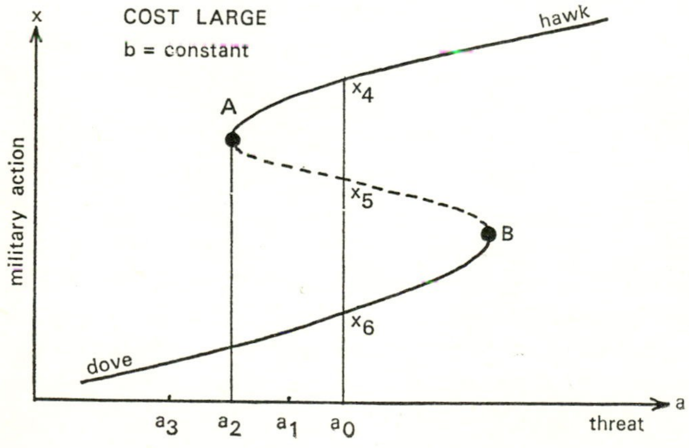

levels of threat, *a*, the maxima of public opinion will be represented by *Figure 7*, which we draw again in *Figure 8* below.

By the Delay rule the administration's policy behaviour will follow the graph G. Therefore, if the threat is small, the administration will pursue a dove policy. If the threat increases the administration will follow the dove graph, changing smoothly to a slightly tougher line, but essentially still pursuing a policy of appeasement. When the critical point B is reached, the administration will suddenly make a catastrophic change in policy to the point B′ on the hawk graph, by, for example, declaring war, or launching a military attack. Notice that the point B occurs some time after the majority of opinion has swung in favour of the military action, and so, fortunately for the human race, there is a built-in delay in the process of declaring war. Moreover, the higher the cost the greater the delay, because the S-shape of the graph in *Figure 7* becomes more accentuated as the constant b is increased.

Now, consider the reverse process of what happens if the threat subsequently diminishes. The administration having once adopted the hawk policy will remain on the hawk graph until the critical point A is reached, when it will suddenly make a catastrophic change in policy to the point A′ on the dove graph, by, for example, agreeing to a cease-fire, withdrawing, or surrendering. This time, the built-in delay is less fortunate, because the administration will remain entrenched in its war-like policy, possibly causing unnecessary loss of life, some time after the majority of opinion has swung in favour of abandoning that policy. The reason for this delay is illustrated in *Figure 5*. Again, paradoxically this time, the higher the cost the greater the delay. The explanation often given during the delay period for not withdrawing from a costly war is that such withdrawal would make a mockery of the sacrifices already made.

9 DIGRESSION ON THE MEANING OF 'QUALITATIVE'

There are fundamental reasons why the qualitative point of view is important in the social sciences, and therefore it is worthwhile digressing at some length in order to define 'qualitative' and explain the point of view. The reader is also recommended to read Thom's philosophy on the subject (Thom 1969; 1970; 1972; 1973b).

The whole of mathematics rests on three types of structure (i) order, (ii) topological, and (iii) algebraic. In a subject like physics all three types of structure can be given physical meaning, but in the social sciences only the first two types generally have any sociological[3] meaning.

(i) *Order structure* As soon as one uses comparisons such as 'higher' cost or 'greater' sense of threat, one is giving sociological meaning to concepts of order.

(ii) *Topological structure* As soon as one uses any kind of continuous scale to describe proximity one is giving sociological meaning to topological concepts. Furthermore, one can begin to use concepts of calculus, like smoothness. At this juncture, it might not be amiss to quote some observations of Tolstoy on calculus from *War and Peace*. Although he is writing in 1869, his words are strangely pertinent today:

> A modern branch of mathematics, having achieved the art of dealing with the infinitely small, can now yield solutions in other more complex problems of motion, which used to appear insoluble.
>
> This modern branch of mathematics, unknown to the ancients, when dealing with problems of motion, admits the conception of the infinitely small, and so conforms to the chief condition of motion (absolute continuity) and thereby corrects the inevitable error which the human mind cannot avoid when dealing with separate elements of motion instead of examining continuous motion.
>
> In seeking the laws of historical movement just the same thing happens. The movement of humanity, arising as it does from innumerable arbitrary human wills, is continuous. To understand the laws of this continuous movement is the aim of history . . . Only by taking an infinitesimally small unit for observation (the differential of history, that is, the individual tendencies of men) and attaining to the art of integrating them (that is, finding the sum of these infinitesimals) can we hope to arrive at the laws of history. (Tolstoy 1869, *War and Peace*, Book XI, ch. 1; see 1970, Vol. III, p. 3; also p. 225.)

Tolstoy puts his finger on exactly what catastrophe theory is trying to do.

(iii) *Algebraic structure* By contrast, algebraic concepts such as addition and multiplication seldom have any sociological meaning.

For example, one cannot 'add' two senses of threat to give a third, and even 'twice' the cost can become meaningless if one tries to include in the cost of a war the measure of human suffering.

Roughly speaking, in mathematics those properties that depend upon the order and the differential-topological structures are called qualitative, while those that depend upon the algebraic structure are called quantitative. More precisely, we begin by framing the first qualitative definition.

Definition: Let X, X′ be two scales describing the same data. We say the changes of scale from X to X′, and from X′ to X, are qualitative if they are both smooth and order-preserving.[4] *In this case the two scales are said to be qualitatively related.*

Notice the important feature of this definition is that the change of scale can be non-linear; therefore, although the order and topological structure of the scale are preserved under the change, the algebraic structure may not be.

In most mathematical models in the social sciences, if one uses a scale X for the convenience of making experimental measurements, or displaying data, then any qualitatively related scale X′ is as valid. Therefore, any conclusion based upon the use of the particular scale X is only valid provided the same conclusion also holds using X′. Such a conclusion is called *qualitatively invariant*, or, more briefly, a *qualitative conclusion.*

There are exceptions: if the scale happens to measure physical quantities like population or raw materials, then it is permissible to restrict attention to *linear* changes of scale, but even then, if other non-physical scales are also involved, it still may only be valid to draw qualitative conclusions. Of course, in the physical sciences one is justified in restricting attention to linear changes of scale, due to the translational symmetries of space and time, and therefore one can expect physical laws to be expressed in quantitative language or formulae, for example like Boyle's law, $PV = RT$. Rutherford's remark that 'qualitative is just poor quantitative' does indeed contain an element of truth in the physical sciences.

However, it would be a fundamental mistake to expect to be able to express the laws of the social sciences in such language, because the language itself is not qualitatively invariant. It is equally mistaken to expect that since we cannot use quantitative language there are no laws. To state the laws of the social sciences we must expect to have to use qualitative language, in other words, mathematical terms that are invariant under qualitative changes of scale.

Of course, to *scientifically prove* any scientific law, social or physical, it is necessary to adopt the classical scientific method of choosing a quantitative model, predicting, and verifying experimentally.[5] To perform an experiment the social scientist must *quantify* each variable, that is to say, select a particular scale, and a particular method of measurement. Two different experimenters may select different scales that are only qualitatively related,[6] and therefore may finish up with graphs that are only qualitatively equivalent. *Therefore, although each experiment may produce a quantitative graph, only the qualitative properties of those graphs can be admissible conclusions.*

Compare again with the situation in physics: two physicists independently checking Boyle's law, for instance, may choose to use different temperature scales, centigrade and Fahrenheit, which have different origins and different sized units, but the essential point is that these two scales are linearly related. Therefore, when one experimenter obtains a straight line graph relating temperature and pressure (under fixed volume), he knows that the other experimenter will also obtain a straight line, and he is therefore entitled to attach significance to the straightness of it, and to express this fact in a formula.

By contrast, consider two social scientists performing experiments to check *Figure 6*, the dependence of action upon threat (under low cost). If one experimenter happened to quantify so as to obtain a straight line graph, then he would *not* be entitled to attach significance to the straightness of it, because he knows that the other experimenter may have chosen only qualitatively related scales, and consequently obtained a curved graph. Now the only qualitative properties possessed by *Figure 6* are single-valuedness, smoothness, and increasingness. Therefore, the only type of law that he could extract from *Figure 6* is that 'action is an increasing function of threat'. In essence this is what we have taken as our Hypothesis 2.

The social scientist may complain, with some justification, that this is a pretty feeble kind of law – and ask if this is the best example that qualitative mathematics has to offer? If we are not allowed to use formulae, what else has qualitative mathematical language to offer? Until recently the mathematician would have had to admit that there were only a few words in this language, because only a few[7] qualitatively invariant terms were known, terms such as 'greater than, increasing, maximum, single-valued, double-valued', etc. It is hardly enough to constitute a language. Not only that, but the terms themselves, although containing hidden subtleties for the mathematician, must have seemed rather unsubtle to the non-mathematician; so translucent, in fact, to our visual intuition, that they had already long been perceived, and incorporated into everyday language, well before the advent of mathematics. As a result, the laws that could be written in qualitative mathematical language were regarded as non-mathematical, because they could be translated into everyday language. For example, in our statement of Hypothesis 2, instead of using the qualitative mathematical language 'action is an increasing function of threat' we found it preferable to use the more familiar translation 'the greater the threat the greater the action'. As a result, qualitative mathematical language was, until recently, too limited and too obvious to be useful in the social sciences, except perhaps for expressing proverbs.[8]

Scientific statements that are written in terms too obvious are generally criticized for being both trivially true and trivially false, in spite of the fact that these criticisms are contradictory. Perhaps this is because of the swiftness with which the mind can leap on to the truth of the statement, and then leap off again to consider all the exceptions. On the other hand, if the statement is more subtle, packs more punch, incorporates more special cases, or more varied phenomena, contains more insight, has the power to arrest the mind with more surprise, then the mind is more ready to dwell upon the statement, sufficiently long perhaps to admit that it might be called a law (or a proverb), and to forgive the exceptions by renaming them as modifications. For example, this is certainly the case with Boyle's law, which is patently false near the critical point of a gas, and therefore needs to be modified as Van der Waals's equation (Fowler 1972); but in spite of this we still call it a 'law' because it still packs the punch.

A scientific law is an intellectual resting point. It is a landing that needs being approached by a staircase, upon which the mind can pause, before climbing further to seek modifications.

Summarizing what we have said so far: the qualitative mathematical language is the natural language for expressing the laws of the social sciences, but until recently it was useless.

Now, with the advent of catastrophe theory, this language has suddenly been unexpectedly enriched in two vital ways. The language has been transformed from being useless to becoming potentially useful for expressing rigorously an unsuspected array of laws in all the social sciences (as well as the biological and physical). First, catastrophe theory has contributed several new qualitatively invariant terms, such as 'fold-point, catastrophic change, cusp catastrophe, divergence, normal factor, splitting factor, bias factor, butterfly catastrophe', etc. Second, these new terms are subtle, and have no familiar translation into everyday language. Therefore, the new scientific statements that can be made using them have new power to synthesize ideas, to lend new insight, and to arrest the mind, perhaps sufficiently to be called laws.

10 EQUIVALENT GRAPHS

So far, we have used two different types of diagrams, probability distributions as in *Figures 1–5*, and cause-effect or control–behaviour graphs as in *Figures 6–8*. In catastrophe theory we are particularly interested in multivalued control-behaviour graphs, as in *Figures 7, 8*, and wish to study their qualitative properties. Therefore, we introduce a definition of equivalence between two such graphs, that is slanted towards catastrophe theory in the sense that it will later enable us to state the theorems precisely.

Definition: Given two planar graphs G, G′ we say they are qualitatively equivalent if there is a diffeomorphism[9] *of the plane that maps vertical lines to vertical lines and maps G to G′.*

Example 1 *Figure 9* illustrates two graphs that are qualitatively (but not quantitatively) equivalent.

Example 2 Let C, C′ be the two horizontal scales measuring control, and let X, X′ be the two vertical scales measuring behaviour. Let ΨC: C→C′ and Ψ_X: X→X′ be two qualitative changes of scale. Let Ψ denote the product map $\Psi = \Psi C \times \Psi_X$. Let G′ = ΨG. Then G is qualitatively equivalent to G′ by the diffeomorphism Ψ. Notice that in this example not only are vertical lines mapped to vertical lines, but also horizontal lines to horizontal lines.

Remark 1 In general, the diffeomorphism Ψ in the definition can have an extra freedom over and above that given by a product of two

FIGURE 9 Qualitatively equivalent graphs

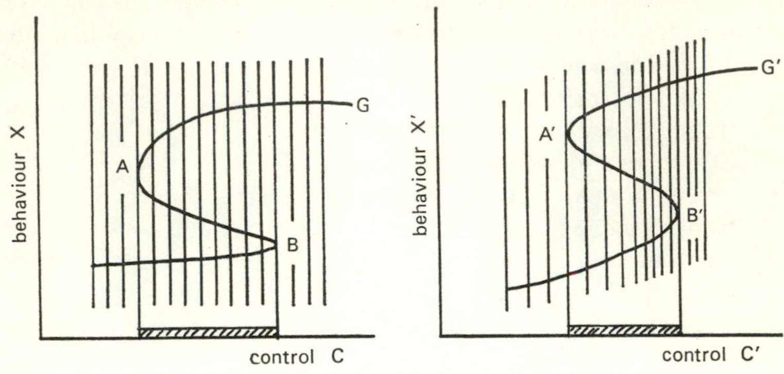

qualitative scale-changes, because the definition is biased in favour of verticals rather than horizontals. There are two reasons for this extra freedom, as we now explain. Since vertical lines are parametrized by the horizontal control axes C, C′, and since Ψ maps vertical lines to vertical lines, Ψ induces a unique map $\Psi C: C \to C'$. If, further, ΨC preserves orientation then ΨC is a qualitative scale-change. On the other hand, Ψ does not induce a unique scale-change on the vertical behaviour axis, but rather a smooth family of scale-changes, one for each vertical line. The main reason for allowing the extra freedom of varying vertical scale-changes is that it is mathematically necessary for the main classification theorem of catastrophe theory (see Mather 1969; Thom 1972; Trotman and Zeeman 1974; and Sections 11, 13 below). But also, the extra freedom can be given sociological meaning, because different experimenters may prefer to vary their behaviour scales differently under different conditions of control.

Remark 2 Since qualitative changes of scale are a special case of equivalence, properties that are invariant under equivalence are qualitative properties.[10] *Figure 9* above illustrates two such properties, *fold-points* and *multi-valuedness*. Fold-points of G are where the vertical lines are tangent to G, and are invariant because smooth maps preserve tangency. Therefore, the fold-points A, B of G are mapped to the fold-points A′, B′ of G′. Consequently, the shaded interval of C, over which G is three-valued, is mapped to the shaded interval of C′, over which G′ is three-valued; the complement where G is single-valued is mapped to the complement where G′ is single-valued. In Section 8 above we have already seen the importance of fold-points in applications, representing thresholds of catastrophic change, while the shaded interval represents the extent of delay.

Remark 3 Fold-points and multi-valuedness are the only qualitative properties of planar graphs that we shall use. We are now ready to pass on to higher dimensions, representing situations where there are two or more control factors influencing one or more modes of behaviour. The crucial question is: what are the higher-dimensional analogues of fold points? Thom (1972) calls these *elementary catastrophes.* His remarkable achievement was to recognize them and classify them for up to five control factors. Siersma (1973) has extended the classification to eight control factors, and higher dimensions are currently being studied.

Remark 4 One advantage of the qualitative point of view is mathematical simplicity. For, when studying qualitative properties of an application, instead of having to work with an analytically awkward graph (such as G in *Figure 9*), which may have been thrown up by the statistical data from experiment, we are at liberty to replace it by any equivalent graph (such as G′). Generally, the most convenient procedure is to choose a graph G′ that is algebraically the simplest, given by a polynomial equation: we call this graph a *canonical model.*

Remark 5 Canonical models are particularly useful in higher dimensions. From the quantitative point of view, although it is fairly easy to comprehend and visualize the infinite variety of two-dimensional graphs, in higher dimensions the complexity coupled with the difficulty of visualization might well cause the mathematician to despair. He finds it difficult to comprehend them, let alone clasisfy them. However, the qualitative point of view turns this despair into delight, because the problem is now largely solved. Locally, any graph is equivalent to one of the elementary catastrophes. Therefore, it suffices to look at canonical models of the elemetary catastrophes. There are only a few of these, and they provide the new qualitative language. This language enables us to describe how two or more control factors can interrelate and interfere with one another in influencing behaviour. If the social scientist wishes to acquire the language in order to frame rigorous laws, all he need do is to master the geometry of the elementary catastrophes (Poston and Woodcock;

Thom 1972), the two most important of which, the cusp and the butterfly, we describe in Sections 11 and 13 below.

We must now extend the definition of equivalence from two-dimensional graphs to higher dimensional graphs. First consider the extension to three dimensions. Here we envisage a situation where two control factors are influencing one behaviour mode, similar to the application in Section 6 above of cost + threat influencing action. For convenience we represent the two control factors as horizontal axes, and the behaviour mode as the vertical axis. The graph will be a surface in three-dimensional space, R^3. The definition follows almost word for word the two-dimensional case.

Definition: Given two graphs G, G′ in R^3 we say they are qualitatively equivalent if there is a diffeomorphism of R^3 that maps vertical lines to vertical lines, and maps G to G′.

Now, consider the general case, allowing for arbitrarily many controls and modes of behaviour. Suppose there are k scales or factors of control, so that the control spaces C, C′ are represented by k-dimensional Euclidean space $C = C' = R^k$. Suppose that $X = R^n$, representing n scales or modes of behaviour, and $X' = R^{n'}$, representing n′ modes of behaviour, where n, n′ may, or may not, be the same. The control–behaviour graphs G, G′ will be k-dimensional manifolds in $C \times X = R^{k+n}$, $C' \times X' = R^{k+n'}$. Call the n-planes, n′–planes parallel to X, X′ in $C \times X$, $C' \times X$, *vertical.*

Definition: Given two graphs G, G′ in $C \times X$, $C' \times X'$ we say they are qualitatively equivalent if there is a smooth map $C \times X \to C' \times X'$ that maps vertical n–planes to vertical n′–planes, and induces diffeomorphisms $C \to C'$ and $G \to G'$.

The reader may ask why in the general case do we allow n to be different from n′. There are two reasons. First, mathematically it enables the classification theorems below to be stated in a much more powerful form. Second, in applications we may have $n > 1$, with X representing several behaviour modes simultaneously, while $n' = 1$ and G′ is a canonical model. Therefore, the use of canonical models does not impose any restriction upon the description of behaviour. For an example of this in an application see Section 15 below.

Remark We emphasize that all we have said about equivalence refers only to control–behaviour (or cause-effect) graphs. Before concluding this section, a word of caution needs to be said about probability distributions, which are the other types of diagram that we have been using. The main point to be made is that a probability distribution is a quantitative tool, and part of the experimental procedure leading to the presentation of data in the form of a control-behaviour graph.

$$\text{Experiment} \xrightarrow{\text{quantitative}} \begin{array}{c}\text{Control}\\ \text{behaviour}\\ \text{graph}\end{array} \xrightarrow{\text{qualitative}} \text{Conclusion}$$

Therefore in general it is meaningless to apply qualitative arguments to raw probability distributions. We illustrate this point by stating a sociologically meaningless mathematical lemma:

Given any raw probability distribution P on a scale X, and given any interval I of X, then it is possible, by shrinking I to I′, to choose a qualitatively related scale X′, such that the new distribution P′ has a new maximum in I′, as high as we please.

Proof: $\int_I P = \int_{I'} P'$. See *Figure 10*

FIGURE 10 Probability distributions (as opposed to support functions)

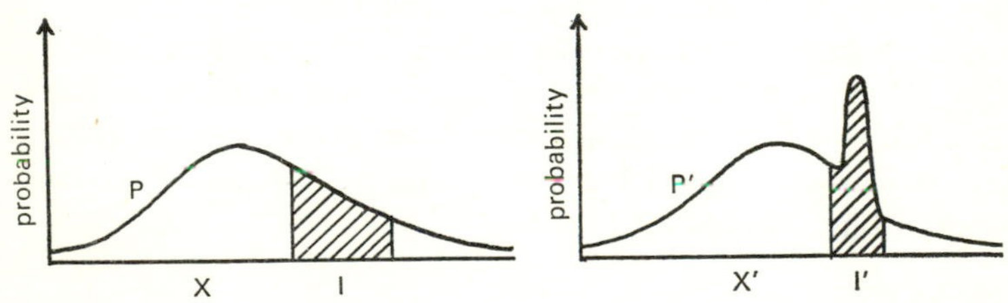

On the other hand, if two experimenters took a scientific hypothesis, tested it by experiment, chose qualitatively related scales, collected statistics giving raw probability distributions, chose methods of weighting and adjusting their data that seemed to them the most accurate way of transforming the raw material into qualitatively meaningful distributions of public support for the various policies, and finally produced the two distributions in *Figure 10*, then this would be another matter. This would be an experimental result that threw doubt upon the scientific hypothesis.

Here in this paper, we are not presenting experimental data, and therefore not giving the quantitative half of the process, but we are concerned with presenting the qualitative half. The ambiguity suggested by *Figure 10* does not enter into our discussion, because in the sociological hypotheses, in Section 7 above, we have assumed that opinion is either unified or split, that is to say, the distribution has one or two maxima, depending upon the control conditions. Therefore, we can proceed rigorously from these hypotheses to the conclusion in Section 12 below. To test the theory, the social scientist would have to test the hypotheses by experiment, or by interpretation of historical data.

11 THE CUSP CATASTROPHE

The simplest elementary catastrophe is the fold-point. The next simplest is the *cusp catastrophe*, and we now describe its canonical model (Thom 1969; 1972). For the benefit of those readers who have not met it before we describe it in some detail, and also pedagogically recommend reading (Zeeman 1971; 1972b).

Let M be the cubic surface in R^3, given by the equation:

$$x^3 = a + bx.$$

Here a,b are horizontal control axes, and x the vertical behaviour axis, as in Section 6 above. The surface is illustrated in *Figure 11*, where, for convenience the control space C is drawn as a horizontal plane below the origin (rather than through the origin). The *fold curve* F is where vertical lines are tangent to M, and is given by differentiating with respect to x:

$$3x^2 = b.$$

The projection of F down onto the control space is called the *bifurcation set* B. Although F is a smooth cubic curve, B has a cusp at the origin, and that is where the name[11] comes from. The equation of B is given by eliminating x from the two equations above:

$$27a^2 = 4b^3.$$

F separates M into two pieces, both of which have F as their common

FIGURE 11 The cusp catastrophe

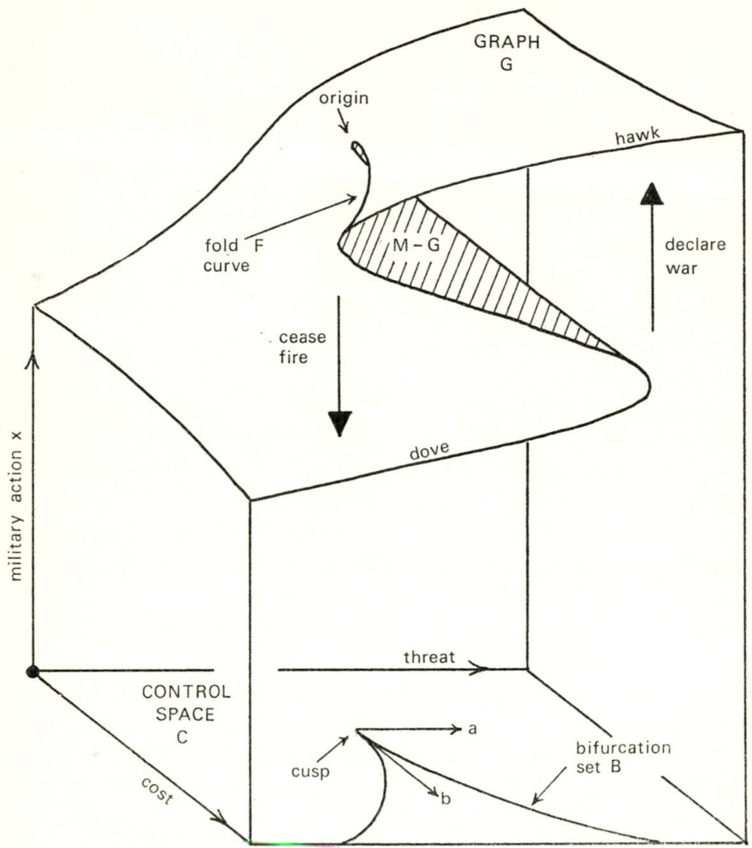

boundary. The larger piece, given by $3x^2 \geqslant b$, is the *graph* G that we want. G is single-sheeted outside the cusp, and double-sheeted inside the cusp, where the upper and lower sheets, marked hawk and dove, overlap. The smaller piece, M–G, given by $3x^2 < b$, and shown shaded, consists of a single sheet over the inside of the cusp, in between the hawk and dove sheets. The piece M–G is sociologically meaningless like the dotted part of *Figure 7*, and so, from now on, we concentrate on G rather than M.

There are many[12] probability functions P giving rise to this particular graph, for which G is the set of maxima, as defined in Section 7; M–G is the set of minima, and M is given by the equation

$\frac{\partial P}{\partial x} = O$. However, we are less interested in the probability function than the graph, because the probability function is a quantitative tool, part of the experiment, leading not to the canonical model, but only to an equivalent graph. We are more interested in the qualitative properties of the canonical model, because these properties are automatically shared by both graphs. We have already mentioned some qualitative properties, for example:

(i) The projection B of the boundary F of G has a cusp.
(ii) B is the set of control points over which the qualitative type of distribution changes, or bifurcates.
(iii) G is single-sheeted outside B, and double-sheeted inside.

Now, consider the plane sections of G given by $b = \text{constant}$. For $b < 0$ the sections are equivalent to *Figure 6*, and for $b > 0$ to *Figure 7*. Therefore, the cusp catastrophe answers the question how these plane sections can evolve into one another. The deep result is the uniqueness of that evolution, which follows from the main classification theorem below. But first we verify that the evolution can be written in invariant qualitative language.

In the control space define the *splitting factor* to be the direction of the axis of the cusp (at the cusp point). Define a *normal factor* to be any transverse direction, oriented towards $a > 0$. This gives invariant definitions of normal and splitting factors, that agree with the a,b–axes in the canonical model. In a neighbourhood of the origin any section of G transverse to the splitting factor, b, will be smooth increasing if $b < 0$, and split if $b > 0$. The splitting causes the fold curve to appear and hence the resulting catastrophic effects. We are now ready to state the main theorem.

Classification Theorem 1: Let $C = R^2$, $X = R$, P be any smooth generic probability function on $C \times X$, and G the resulting graph in R^3. Then the only singularities of G are fold-curves and cusp-points.

Remark 1. Here, by *singularity*, we mean a singularity of the projection of G onto the control space, C, in other words, a point where the projection is not locally a diffeomorphism. The theorem is so called because it classifies the only two elementary catastrophes that can occur with two control factors. The theorem remains true, word for word, if $X = R^n$, in other words, we allow simultaneously arbitrarily many modes or scales of behaviour. In Section 13 below we state the analogous result for four control factors.

Remark 2 The theorem and conception of proof are due to Thom (1969; 1972) and the details of proof to Mather (1969). See Trotman and Zeeman (1974). The proof is much more complicated than the statement, but the latter can be used without necessarily knowing the proof.

Remark 3 The graph G in the theorem may be many-sheeted, and may have several fold-curves and cusps. But all the fold-curves are alike, and each cusp-point is locally-equivalent[13] to the cusp catastrophe or its dual.[14] Hence, the cusp catastrophe is the most complicated situation that can happen locally. It is stable and persists under small perturbations of P. It is the unique way a sheet can split, and therefore the unique way that continuous sections can evolve into split sections.

FIGURE 12 Normal and splitting factors: conflicting factors

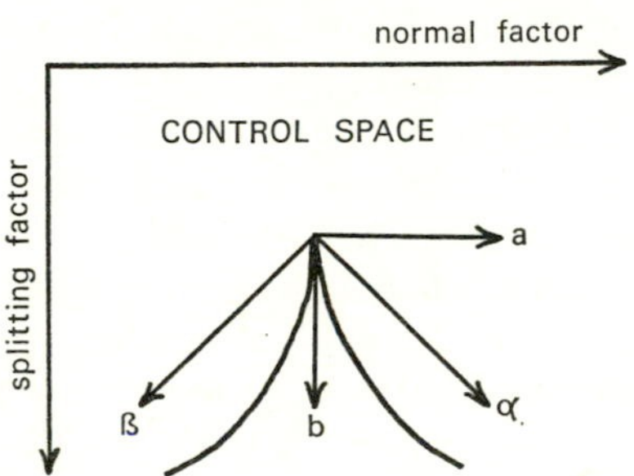

Notation If there is only one cusp, and no other fold curves other than those associated with the cusp, then the graph is equivalent to the canonical model, and we can choose suitable axes a, b in the control space. We abbreviate the statement of equivalence by saying:

a *is a normal factor and* b *a splitting factor influencing* x.

In some applications one does not use the splitting factor, but rather two normal factors either side of the cusp, such as $\alpha = b + a$, $\beta = b - a$.

In this case we say

α,β are conflicting factors influencing x.

The reason for this terminology is that the control α tries to push the behaviour on to the upper surface, while β tries to push it on to the lower, and inside the cusp the two controls conflict. Examples of this nature are 'rage and fear are conflicting factors influencing aggression' (Lorenz 1966: 81; see Zeeman 1971), or 'pressure and temperature are conflicting factors influencing density' (which is Van der Waals's equation (Fowler 1972; 1–7)).

We emphasize that both of the above notational statements are precise qualitative statements that the graph of x as a function of the controls is equivalent to the cusp catastrophe.

Each statement can play several roles: it can serve as:

(i) a *theorem*, provable from simpler hypotheses, as in the next section,
(ii) a *hypothesis* (or conjecture) providing the theoretical framework for design of experiment,
(iii) a *law*, summarizing experimental results.

The statement itself is a synthesis of many ideas, with the following aspects:

Profundity due to the mathematical uniqueness and stability, depending on deep theorems.

Universality In any aspect of nature, or any scientific experiment, where two factors influence behaviour, where splitting and discontinuous effects are observed, and where smooth genericity may be assumed, the graph must contain the cusp catastrophe.

Insight From the model one can explain, predict, and relate a variety of phenomena that previously may not have appeared to be related. As an example we return to the problem on hand.

12 APPLICATION OF THE CUSP CATASTROPHE

Theorem. Threat is a normal factor and cost a splitting factor influencing the level of military action

We are entitled to label this statement as a *theorem* because it is an immediate corollary of the classification theorem and the graphs in *Figures 6, 7* arising from the five hypotheses in Section 8. Alternatively, we could label it as a *hypothesis*, and then the four previous sociological hypotheses would be corollaries, testable by experiment. An 'experiment' in this case might take the form of analysing the behaviour of a particular nation over a period, and would involve quantifying, that is to say inventing methods of measurement from historical date of indices of cost, threat, and action. If sufficiently many experiments were successful, that is to say, the results of different methods of measuring different nations were qualitatively equivalent, and the exceptions were explicable by suitable modifications, then the statement would become a candidate for a *law*.

We now illustrate the use of the statement to explain what happens under varying conditions of cost and threat upon a population, and the resulting behaviour of its administration. Consider the various cost–threat paths in the control space, illustrated in *Figure 13*. As the pressures on the population follow the path in the control space, the administration dutifully follows the path on the graph G, vertically above, obeying the Delay rule.

Path 1 A nation with plenty of resources feels increasingly threatened and, unified, gradually moves into moderate action. The resulting

FIGURE 13 Paths in the control space

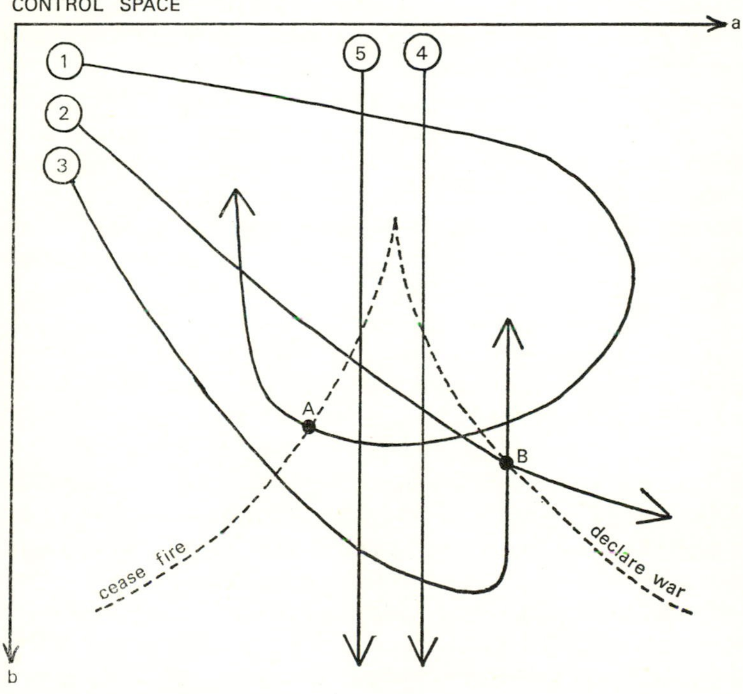

cost escalates, and as a consequence the action also gradually escalates. The threat subsides, and as a result opinion becomes divided between doves and hawks, but the administration's policy is caught entrenched in the hawk opinion, and delays until A before making the (catastrophic) decision to withdraw, after which the cost subsides. The catastrophic change of policy at A is precisely the catastrophe discussed in Sections 5, 9 above, and pictured in *Figures 5, 8*.

Path 2 A nation with more limited resources feels a similar increasing threat, but at the same time feels the escalating cost of military preparedness, and so delays any action until B, when it (catastrophically) declares war.

Path 3 A nation initially finds the cost of war prohibitive, but subsequently, due perhaps to the development or purchase of new defence weapons, may find that war becomes feasible. Therefore, to its enemy's surprise, it may suddenly declare war in the middle of a stable period of constant threat. This is called the *surprise reversal* phenomenon, and tends to appear in many applications, for example in committee behaviour (Zeeman 1973: Example 4).

Paths 4 and 5 Two nations confront each other, and, both feeling threatened, start a costly arms race. As a result, opinion in both nations becomes divided between hawks and doves. Although they may both start in moderately hostile moods that are very close, in one nation the hawks prevail, because path 4 passes just to the right of the cusp, and so this administration gradually adopts a more aggressive posture. Meanwhile, in the other nation the doves prevail, because path 5 passes just to the left of the cusp, and so that administration gradually adopts a posture of appeasement. Both changes are smooth, and this illustrates the phenomenon of divergence.

A similar phenomenon can occur when an international crisis blows up between two nations, or two groups of nations (or for that matter between any institutions where conflict can arise). During the short period of the crisis, lasting perhaps a month, or even as short as a week, the two administrations involved become increasingly aware of the cost of further escalation, and not infrequently the crisis is resolved by one administration standing firm, path 4, while the other backs down path 5. It is well known by diplomats that it is essential for the administration standing firm, path 4, to leave open for their opponents a clear avenue of retreat so that they can follow path 5, and not to succumb to the euphoric temptation to victoriously close all avenues, otherwise, by driving their opponents into a corner, they may marginally increase the feeling of threat experienced by the opposing population. This tiny margin may be sufficient to convert their opponents' path 5 disastrously into path 4. Then as both nations follow path 4, war will probably ensue.

Together, the five paths illustrate the close interrelation between discontinuous and divergent behaviour.

13 THE BUTTERFLY CATASTROPHE

The next sophistication in our model is to investigate the emergence of a compromise opinion, represented by the appearance of a new maximum in the probability distribution as in *Figure 14.*

FIGURE 14 Emergence of compromise opinion

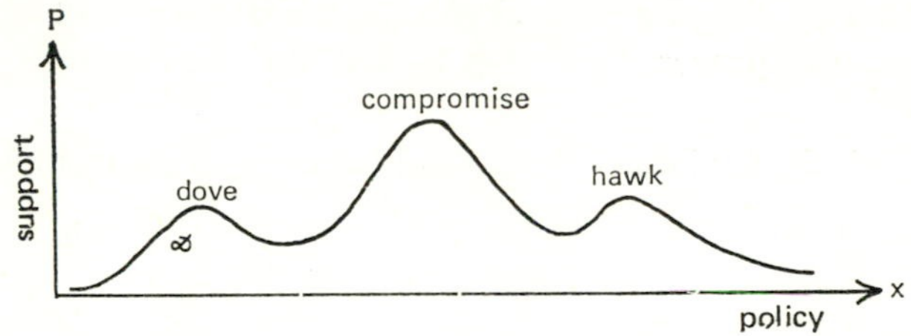

If opinion has become polarized between doves and hawks in a stalemate, then it is of importance to understand the mechanism underlying compromise. This same mechanism applies to nearly all social phenomena where compromise plays a part.

We have seen by Classification Theorem 1 above that mathematically the only way a two-peak distribution can evolve from a one-peak is by means of the cusp catastrophe, which required two control factors. The next theorem states that the only way a three-peak distribution can evolve is by means of the *butterfly catastrophe*, which requires four control factors. Indeed, in everyday experience, to hammer a compromise solution out of a polarized situation generally does need two more factors, some new ingredient plus time.

We now describe the canonical model (Thom 1972) of the butterfly catastrophe. We give it in a form that illustrates it as a generalization of the cusp catastrophe. The control space $C = R^4$ of the butterfly has 4 control factors:

a = normal factor
b = splitting factor
c = bias factor
d = butterfly factor.

The behaviour space X = R, with

x = behaviour mode.

Let M be the four-dimensional manifold in C $\times$ X = R^5 given by the equation

$$x^5 = a + bx + cx^2 + dx^3.$$

Let G be the four-dimensional submanifold of M given by

$$5x^4 \geqslant b + 2cx + 3dx^2.$$

Then G is the desired graph of the butterfly catastrophe. Since we cannot draw a five-dimensional picture, the best way to understand the qualitative properties of G is to first draw in *Figure 15* various

FIGURE 15 Sections of the butterfly catastrophe bifurcation set

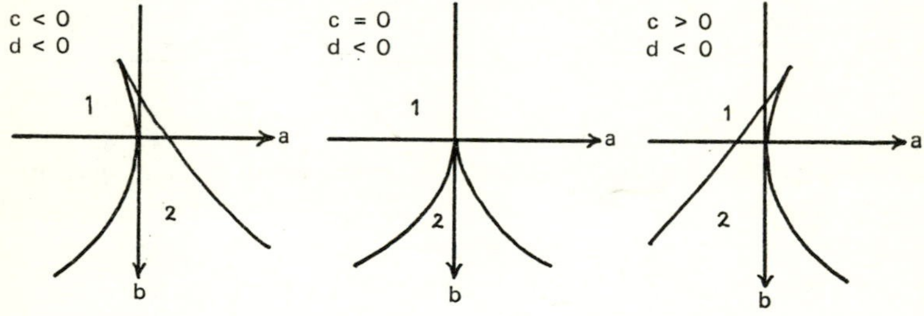

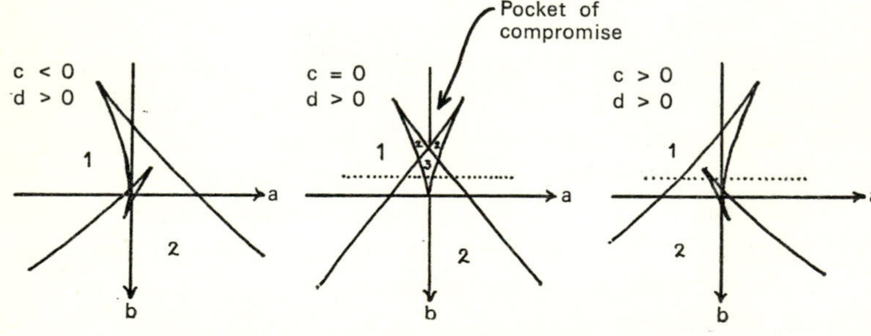

two-dimensional sections of the control space C. Each section is an (a,b)–plane drawn for (c,d) = constant, and illustrates what the bifurcation-set looks like in that section.

Notice the effect of the bias factor, c. When $d < 0$, the effect of the bias is to bias the position of the cusp, as shown in the top three pictures. When the bias is positive the cusp is biased in the positive direction of the normal factor, and vice versa.

Now, consider the effect of the butterfly factor, d. When this comes into play, $d > 0$, the effect is to bifurcate the cusp into three cusps, as

FIGURE 16 Section of the butterfly catastrophe

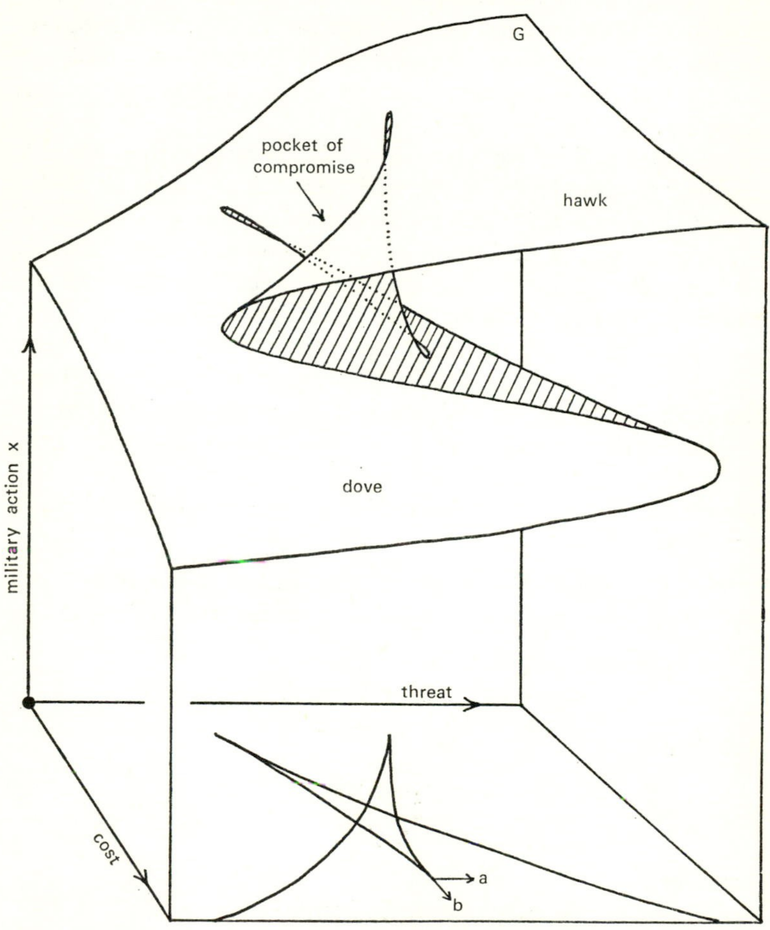

shown in the bottom three pictures. The number in each region indicates the number of peaks in the corresponding probability distribution, and hence the number of sheets of G over that region; as the control point crosses the bifurcation-set the number changes because the distribution bifurcates.

If one turns the central picture upside down it looks a bit like a butterfly, which explains the name. The V-shape in this picture represents the emerging pocket of compromise opinion. There are in fact two Vs, an outer-V with vertex at the cusp at the origin, and an inner-V with vertex at the intersection point above the origin. The compromise maximum exists at all points inside the outer-V, and is the unique maximum at all points inside the inner-V. In between the two Vs, the compromise is competing with the dove and hawk maxima, and inside the little diamond shape all three maxima are competing.

To illustrate this, we now draw the corresponding control–behaviour graph in *Figure 16*. We add the x–axis as a third dimension to the (a,b)–plane, and draw the section of the graph G above this particular section of C. Comparing *Figure 16* with *Figure 11* shows how the pocket of compromise is emerging in between the hawk and dove sheets. Notice that in *Figure 16* each of the two upper cusps is a cusp catastrophe, while the lower cusp is a dual-cusp catastrophe.

The effect of a positive bias, $c>0$, on *Figure 16* is to distort it and raise it all slightly in the x-direction. This effect is so important in applications that we state it as a lemma and prove it.

Lemma 1: The effect of more bias is to make behaviour more aggressive.

Proof Let $c_1 < c_2$ be two values of bias. Fix the values of b, d and consider the two graphs M_1, M_2 of a_1, a_2 as functions of x given by

$$a_1 = x^5 - bx - c_1 x^2 - dx^3$$
$$a_2 = x^5 - bx - c_2 x^2 - dx^3.$$

Therefore

$$a_1 - a_2 = (c_2 - c_1)x^2$$
$$> 0, \text{ for all } x \neq 0.$$

Therefore

$$a_1 > a_2, \text{ except when } x = 0.$$

Now, look at these same two curves M_1, M_2 the other way round as graphs of x_1, x_2 as functions of *a* given by

$$x_1^5 = a + bx_1 + c_1x_1^2 + dx_1^3$$
$$x_2^5 = a + bx_2 + c_2x_2^2 + dx_2^3.$$

Restrict attention to the subgraphs G_1, G_2 given by

$$5x_1^4 \geqslant b + 2c_1x_1 + 3dx_1^3$$
$$5x_2^4 \geqslant b + 2c_2x_2 + 3dx_2^3.$$

These are the two control–behaviour graphs corresponding to values of bias c_1, c_2. Since $a_1 > a_2$, we see that $G_1 < G_2$ in the sense that for each point (a,x_1) in G_1 there exists a point (a,x_2) in G_2 such that

FIGURE 17 Sections of the butterfly catastrophe

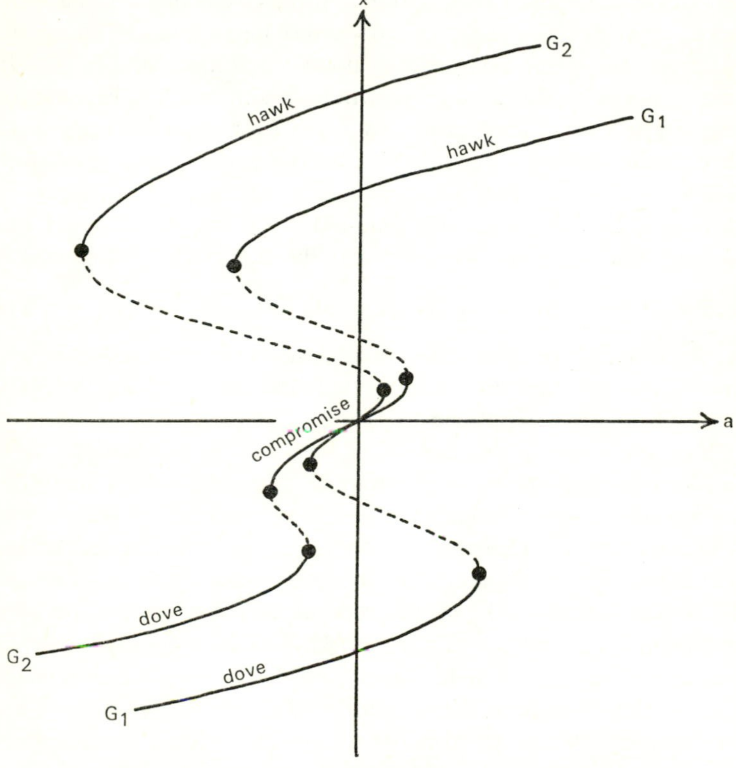

$x_1 < x_2$ (except possibly when $x_1 = x_2 = 0$). Therefore the higher bias c_2 causes behaviour G_2 that is more aggressive than G_1, as required.

Figure 17 illustrates the graphs $G_1 < G_2$ for particular values $b > 0$, $c_1 = 0 < c_2$, and $d > 0$, corresponding to the dotted horizontal lines in the two bottom right pictures of *Figure 15*. If the paper is turned round so that the a–axis if vertical, one can see how the result is caused by the formula

$$a_2 = a_1 - (c_2 - c_1)x^2.$$

Before concluding our description of the butterfly catastrophe we make a small qualitative point about the butterfly factor, d. In many applications d = time, and so at d = 0 the compromise begins, and as time progresses the pocket of compromise grows. In the lower central picture of *Figure 15* the lower cusp is fixed at the origin a = b = 0, and the pocket grows by the two upper cusps moving upwards and outwards. Qualitatively, we could just as well choose to have the pocket growing by the upper cusps moving outwards along the a–axis and the lower cusp moving downwards along the b–axis. In some applications this kind of growth makes more sense because the compromise pocket then gradually takes over the whole plane. In other applications, as in real life, the compromise can grow lopsidedly, or can wax and wane, and each of these growths can be achieved by choosing a suitable time–axis in the canonical model. For example, the downwards growth can be achieved by choosing a curvilinear time–axis along the parabola $(a,b,c,d) = (0, -\frac{9t^2}{20}, 0, t)$. Qualitatively, there is nothing to choose between a straight or a curved time–axis, and since this parabola has the d–axis as tangent at the origin we are still entitled to refer to d as time.

This completes the description of the butterfly catastrophe sufficient for our applications. More accurate, computer-drawn, quantitative pictures of the canonical model can be found in Poston and Woodcock (1974). The reader who is primarily interested in the applications may now proceed to the next Section; see also Zeeman (1973). But before we leave this section, in order to highlight the fundamental importance of the butterfly, and put it in its correct perspective, we would like to state a four-dimensional version of the Classification Theorem. Thom (1969; 1972) proved that there are seven elementary catastrophes for a four-dimensional control space (together with three duals). However, we maintain that only three of these apply to probability distributions, the fold, the cusp, and the butterfly, and hence these are the most important catastrophes for the social sciences. Therefore, we introduce a definition that singles out the cusp and the butterfly.

Definition: Let G be the graph of maxima of a probability function on C × X. Let Q be a point on G, and let Q′ be the projection of Q in the control space C. We say Q is complete *if any neighbourhood of Q in G projects onto a neighbourhood of Q′ in C.*

Example (i) Any point not on the boundary of G is complete.

Example (ii) The origin Q of the cusp catastrophe is complete, because although Q lies in the boundary F of G (see *Figure 11*), the projection into C of any neighbourhood of Q in G overlaps itself, and wraps round to form a neighbourhood of the cusp point in C.

Example (iii) The origin of the butterfly catastrophe is complete, for the numbers in *Figure 15* show that there is at least one sheet of G over each region.

Example (iv) The fold-point is incomplete. For instance taking Q = A in *Figure 7*, a small neighbourhood of Q in G projects down to only the left hand side of Q′, which is not a neighbourhood of Q′ in C.

We have explained, in Sections 5 and 9 above, the importance of fold-points in initiating catastrophic change; therefore, a classification of only the complete catastrophes might at first sight appear inadequate, because it leaves out fold-points. However we suggest that, in graphs derived from probability functions, fold-points do not appear in their own right, as it were, but only as satellites of the cusp and butterfly. We make this argument precise, as follows.

Define a graph G to have a *centre* Q if G is equivalent to arbitrarily small neighbourhoods of Q. Intuitively, this means the global graph G looks like the local graph at Q. For example, both cusp and butterfly have a centre at the origin; in fact all the elementary catastrophes have a unique centre (Thom 1972). In applications the notion of a centre represents being able to capture the heart of the problem in microcosm at one point. If a graph has a complete centre we call the graph complete.

Lemma 2: Suppose G is the graph of maxima of a probability function. If G has a centre then G is complete.

Proof For each control point c, the probability distribution P_c has at least one maximum. Therefore, G has at least one sheet over each control point. Hence, the projection of G covers C. Given any neighbourhood of the centre Q, we can choose a smaller neighbourhood N equivalent to G, since Q is the centre. Since the projection of G covers C, the projection of N covers a neighbourhood of Q′. Therefore Q is complete. Therefore G is complete.

Having justified the concept of completeness we can now state the classification.

Classification Theorem 2: Let $C=R^4, X=R^n$, with n arbitarary, P be any smooth generic probability function on $C \times X$, and G the resulting graph in R^{4+n}. Then G is a four-dimensional manifold and the only complete singularities of G are cusp-surfaces and butterfly-points. For the proof see (Mather 1969; Trotman and Zeeman 1974).

Remark 1 Compare with Classification Theorem 1 in Section 12 above; had we added the word 'complete' to Theorem 1, this would have ruled out fold-curves. But, just as fold-curves appear as satellites of cusp-points, so do swallow-tail-curves appear as satellites of butterfly-points (see Thom 1972).

Remark 2 Folds are intrinsically co-dimension one, and so in Theorem 1 in a two-dimensional graph they appear as fold-curves. Similarly, cusps are intrinsically co-dimension two, and so in Theorem 1 in a two-dimensional graph they appear as cusp-points, while in Theorem 2 in a four-dimensional graph they appear as cusp-surfaces. Meanwhile, butterflies are intrinsically co-dimension four, and so they cannot appear at all in Theorem 1, while in Theorem 2 they appear as butterfly-points. In general, a catastrophe of co-dimension c appears over k controls as a (k–c)-dimensional sub-manifold of the k–dimensional graph.

Remark 3 For more than four controls a new complete cuspoid appears in each even dimension. In dimension eight another phenomenon appears, the *double-cusp*, which is complete and requires two behaviour modes, and has a wealth of incomplete satellites of lower co-dimension including the umbilics (Siersma 1973; Thom 1972). Although the umbilics have co-dimensions three and four, they do not appear in four-dimensional central probability graphs.

14 COMPROMISE OPINION

Just as our knowledge of the uniqueness of the cusp over two controls gives confidence to postulate the cusp whenever discontinuous or divergent behaviour appears, so the uniqueness of the butterfly over four controls gives confidence to postulate the butterfly whenever compromise opinion appears. We shall now generalize our previous model in this direction. Previously, we deduced the cusp from simpler hypotheses, in order not only to usher our readers more gently into the ideas of catastrophe theory, but also to provide a template for them to manufacture their own applications. This time, we go with confidence straight to the heart of the matter, and take the butterfly as hypothesis.

Hypothesis 6
Threat is a normal factor
Cost is a splitting factor
Invulnerability is a bias factor
Time is a butterfly factor
} *influencing the level of military action.*

First, observe that with average vulnerability ($c = 0$), and at the beginning of a war ($d < 0$), we obtain the top central picture of *Figure 15*, which is the ordinary cusp, the same as in *Figures 11 and 13*. Therefore, in these circumstances, our new model reduces to the old model, and so is a strict generalization or modification of the latter.

Next vulnerability. Why choose vulnerability? Vulnerability is in fact one of the strongest influences modifying public opinion. For example, if an industrial nation feels dangerously threatened, its population may call for strong action; however, if its enemy possesses overwhelming air superiority, then strong action may not be feasible due to the vulnerability of its cities. The public will be aware of this vulnerability, and may consequently modify its opinion in favour of appeasement. By contrast a predominantly agricultural community in suitable terrain may feel no such inhibition, due to the feasibility of guerrilla warfare. The more invulnerable the terrain, the more aggressively the population will modify its opinion. In other words, by Lemma 1 of Section 14, invulnerability behaves like a bias factor. Therefore, let c be some index or scale measuring invulnerability.

Now time. Public opinion does modify with time, especially in a stalemate war of moderate threat ($a = 0$), moderate cost ($b=0$), and moderate vulnerability ($c=0$). People are liable to become weary of the war, and a compromise opinion may emerge in favour of a negotiated cease-fire, an opinion in between, and possibly sharply divided from, both hawks, who demand victory, and doves, who counsel appeasement or withdrawal. Therefore, time behaves qualitatively like a butterfly factor, d, and for $d>0$ the V-shaped pocket of the lower centre picture of *Figure 15* begins to appear. Moreover, the longer the stalemate, the more of the population who adopt the compromise opinion, the higher grows the centre peak of the probability distribution, and the larger grows the compromise pocket in the threat-cost plane. Eventually the inner-V of the pocket crosses the particular point of that plane representing the current threat+cost, and at that moment the administration fighting the war will make the (catastrophic) switch to the compromise policy, and begin to negotiate for peace. It might save many lives if administrations understood sufficiently to begin negotiation at the earlier moment, when the outer-V of the pocket crossed the point, instead of delaying to the last possible moment.

15 OPPOSITION TO A GOVERNMENT

In our first model, we studied the opinion of a population opposing an external threat. We now study a second model of the opinion of a population opposing its own government, which is quite different. In our first model, we assumed that some local maximum of opinion was actually *realized* by an administration obeying the Delay rule. In the second model, the opinion is not realized, because it only represents what the population would like to do if it had the chance. If an election happened to take place, then the population might be able to realize its majority opinion, by the Voting rule; but most of the time no election is in the offing, either because the election rules may only allow for an election every four or five years, or because elections may have been abolished altogether, and so any antagonistic majority of opinion may only represent a vague threat against the government. Therefore, for perhaps economic reasons, a government may find itself in the position of operating policies against the wishes of most of those governed, and for this reason, in this model, we prefer to use the word *government* rather than administration.

Let x be some index or scale measuring the opposition to the government. In a sample survey of the population, in order to discover the probability distribution of x, one might design a *questionnaire*, showing a *continuous* scale, with varying degrees of support or opposition written against various points on the scale, and ask each person surveyed to position himself approximately on this scale. For instance, the scale might read:

Prepared to donate money to re-election fund.
Would canvas for government.
Would vote for government.
Would vote against other parties.
x_N ● Neutral.
Would vote against the government.
Would vote for another party.
Would canvas for another party.
x_S ● Prepared to strike against the government.
Prepared to join a civil disobedience campaign.
↓ Prepared to wage guerrilla war against the government.
x

From the government's point of view, the two critical points on this scale are the neutral point, x_N, and the strike point, x_S. For imagine a government that is enjoying a unified opinion in its favour, in other words the distribution of opinion has a single maximum at x_0, where $x_0 < x_N$. Suppose that the government now runs into economic difficulties, which we shall later assume to be a normal factor influencing opposition. Then x_0 will begin to move in the direction of x increasing. As x_0 crosses x_N the government knows that it has lost majority support, and might lose the next election, but nevertheless it may hopefully pursue economic policies in order to remedy the situation. However if x_0 crosses x_S then the majority of the population may be prepared to strike against the government, thereby wrecking its economic plans, and possibly ruining its chances of re-election.

Some readers may protest against the inclusion of industrial action on a political scale, but there are reasons for doing so. First, this is a model, as we shall see, primarily about the government's reactions; and, looking through government eyes, although the industrial action may be directed towards higher pay, or against industrial management, nevertheless the government may see the importance of such action primarily as wrecking its own economic policies. Indeed, for this very reason, many governments in the world today have ruled strike action to be illegal.

Second, admittedly it might seem a more precise procedure to separate industrial and political action as two different modes of behaviour, in other words use a two-dimensional[15] behaviour space X rather than a single scale. But if we did so, then qualitatively we could arrive back at *exactly the same* graph G over C, or more precisely, an equivalent graph, by the definition of equivalence in Section 11, and the statement of Classification Theorem 2 in Section 14. This is one of the remarkable features of catastrophe theory, that enables us to *implicitly* allow for as complicated a modality of behaviour as we wish, and yet *explicitly* worry only about the control factors. We are now ready to state the main hypothesis of the model, after which we explain the meaning of the controls.

Hypothesis 7

Economic malaise is a normal factor
Promise of reform is a splitting factor
Failure of reform is a bias factor
Pressure is a butterfly factor
} *influencing the opposition to a government.*

Economic malaise is caused by such things as chronic inflation, unemployment, depressions, industrial strife, strains of development, shortages and balance of payment problems. If the government fails to cure these ailments, then malaise will erode confidence, and the majority of opinion x_0 will begin to drift towards opposition. Thus, malaise acts as a normal factor influencing opposition.

To stop the drift the government may promise reforms. But such promises have a splitting effect, between those who approve and disapprove of the reforms. For example, promise of land reform may appeal to peasants but not to landlords, and promise of industrial reform may appeal to management but not to unions. Thus, the single maximum of opinion x_0 may split into two maxima x_1, x_2, where $x_1 < x_N < x_2$. Therefore, initially we have the cusp catastrophe by Theorem 1.

If the malaise persists, the government may, as the control point approaches the cusp, desperately promise more and more reforms, in the hope of at least retaining some local maximum of support,

$x_1 < x_N$, staving off the moment when x_1 disappears, and opposition is unified at $x_2 > x_N$, as illustrated by the point B in *Figure 18*. But, alas, the greater the promise of reform, the greater the opposition, and the greater the eventual downfall of government.

Eventually, the population may agree to suspend the electoral rules, so that a unified opposition $x_2 > x_N$ does not require the resignation of a government, and so that at least some government may be given sufficient breathing space to tackle the economic problems on a long-term basis.

FIGURE 18 Government trying to avoid catastrophe

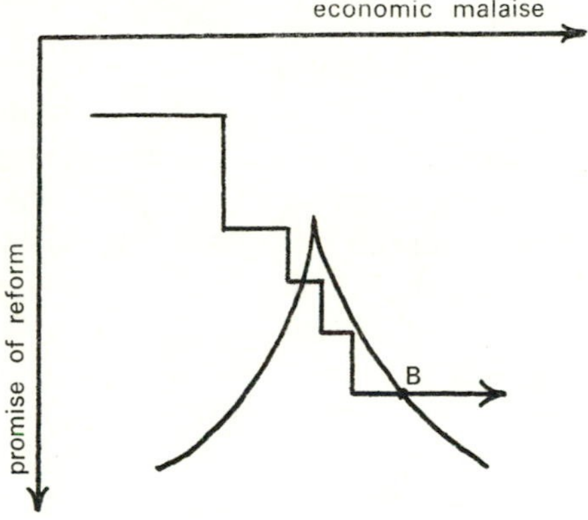

However, this may take a long time. The apparent initial failure of promised reform may act as a bias factor, biasing public opinion yet further against the government. The critical moment occurs when x_2 approaches x_S, because the resulting strike action may have the potential to wreck the long term plans for economic recovery. It is then that the government may feel obliged to exert pressure upon the population, in order to bring the majority opinion back, $x_2 < x_s$. But this in turn may have the effect of splitting off an extremist wing, with opinion centred at a new maximum, $x_3 > x_s$. Thus, we are liable to reach a three-peak probability distribution as shown in *Figure 19*.

By Theorem 2 we must have the butterfly catastrophe, and the butterfly factor that caused the middle peak to appear was the pressure. This time the middle point x_2 does not represent compromise opinion, but rather the opinion of the silent majority, in silent opposition, $x_N < x_2 < x_s$. Eventually, if the economy picks up

FIGURE 19 Public opposition to the government

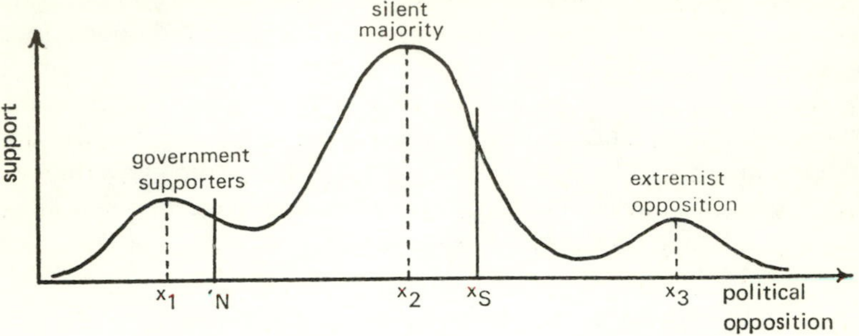

and the malaise subsides, the majority may move back to supporting the government, sufficient for the latter to restore the electoral rules.

Summarizing, the single hypothesis 7, supported by the uniqueness of the butterfly catastrophe, synthesizes a complex behavioural response, and lends itself to the design of many experiments to test it. One of the interesting features of this example is that, while two of the control factors, a and c, depend upon external forces outside the government's jurisdiction, the other two, b and d, are actually under government control, and behave as responses to the stimulus of the first two: a stimulates response b, and c stimulates response d. It is an interesting question as to whether the mathematical ordering of the factors, indicated by the alphabetical ordering, and induced by the Taylor expansion of the canonical probability function, whether or not this ordering can be given a more general interpretation of stimulus and response, beyond the confines of this particular application.

16 CENSORSHIP

To introduce our last example we quote the title of an article by John Wilson. 'The pendulum of censorship or anti-censorship fashions may swing to and fro; but it is not clear that any serious advance in the topic has been made since the days of Plato and Aristotle' (Wilson 1970). In the article Wilson lays his finger on the two criteria that are involved in deciding whether or not to censor a book or a work of art, namely *erotic content* and *aesthetic value*, and he concludes by suggesting: 'But before striking attitudes, and even before collecting more statistics, we need a better conceptual understanding of just how either effect operates; otherwise we shall not know what sort of facts to look for' (Wilson 1970). We suggest that the problem is not how either effect operates by itself, but how the two effects together interfere with one another. By now, the reader will have recognized them as control factors, and have guessed that the cusp catastrophe is going to be involved. But first we must identify the behaviour mode.

The key to the problem is to replace the two states 'censored' and 'uncensored' by a continuous scale of behaviour. Many problems in the social sciences can be unlocked by the same key: the problem may seem to present a finite set of states, giving the appearance of discreteness, but in fact the apparent discreteness may result from discontinuities of an underlying continuous phenomenon, in other words from an elementary catastrophe. The elementary catastrophe may impart to the discrete set a subtlety that escapes description unless one uses the new qualitative language. A typical example is the 'attack' or 'flight' behaviour of an animal (Lorenz 1966; Zeeman 1971).

Here we approach the problem of censorship by designing a simple experiment, which we hope we might tempt one of our readers to perform. Design a *questionnaire* similar to that in the last model. We take the book or work of art into the market-place and ask a sample of passers-by whether it should be censored; we ask each person to place the work on the following continuous scale:

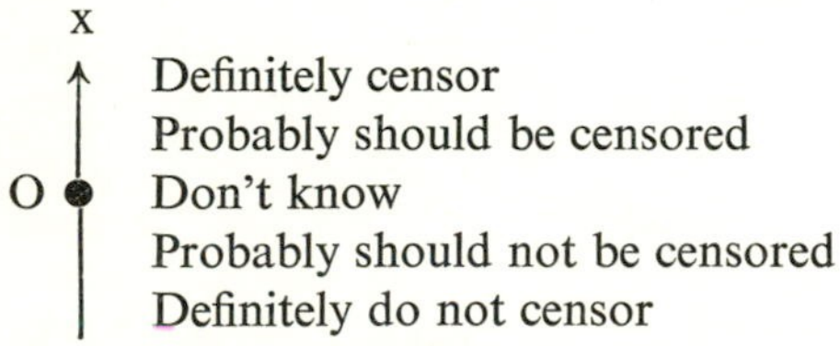

x

↑ Definitely censor
Probably should be censored
O ● Don't know
Probably should not be censored
Definitely do not censor

A probability distribution is obtained for this particular work. Plot the resulting maxima of probability on a three-dimensional graph, as behaviour against control scales measuring erotic content and aesthetic value. Now, do this for many works of art and we obtain a cloud of points, which we conjecture will cluster about a surface equivalent to the cusp catastrophe. More precisely:

Hypothesis 8. Erotic content is a normal factor and aesthetic value a splitting factor influencing opinion about censorship (see Figure 20).

If the work is of little aesthetic value then opinion is likely to be unified, that is to say, that probability distribution is likely to have a single peak, which is likely to give a good judgment of the erotic content relative to the prevailing norm in the market-place at that time. In other words, erotic content acts as a normal factor.

On the other hand, a work of high aesthetic value may well give rise to a double-peak distribution. Some people may feel it should be uncensored because of its high aesthetic value, even though its erotic content may transgress the prevailing norm; others may feel it should be censored because its very aesthetic value endows it with too dangerous an influence, even though its erotic content may be within the prevailing norm. In other words, aesthetic value acts as a splitting factor. The resulting graph is illustrated in the top picture of *Figure 20*; notice that in this picture we only draw the graph G, and omit the middle sheet M – G of *Figure 11*.

For simplicity of discussion let us now assume the graph is not only equivalent to, but actually equal to, the canonical cusp catastrophe. Also, suppose the prevailing censorship-norm is $x = 0$, in other words $x = 0$ is the 'Don't know' position on the *questionnaire* scale. Consider the task of a censor, who is trying to adhere to the prevailing norm.

Define the *type* of a work to be its control point, in other words, the point in the control space that represents its particular erotic content and aesthetic value. Admittedly, it may be difficult to get critics to agree on the type of a work, but for simplicity of discussion suppose that we can. In the control space there is a cusp, as a consequence of Hypothesis 8. If the type of work lies outside the cusp the censor's job is easy; opinion is unified with maximum at x_1, say, and he can censor it if $x_1 > 0$, and uncensor it if $x_1 < 0$. On the other hand, if the type lies inside the cusp he has a problem of choice, because opinion is split, with two maxima x_1, x_2 such that $x_1 < 0 < x_2$, justifying either choice (see *Figure 22* below).

The censorship-norm, $x = 0$, separates the graph G into two regions which we label 'censor', $x > 0$, and 'uncensor', $x < 0$, as shown in the top picture of *Figure 20*. The lower picture shows the projections of these two regions in the control space. This simple diagram helps to explain much of the confusion surrounding censorship. For works of low aesthetic content, $b < 0$, the regions do not overlap, and so their frontier gives a clear delineation of the eroticism-norm, $a = 0$, permitted by the prevailing censorship-norm, $x = 0$. On the other hand, for works of high aesthetic content, $b > 0$, the regions overlap, and so anachronisms can arise, because some works

FIGURE 20 Cusp catastrophe model of censorship

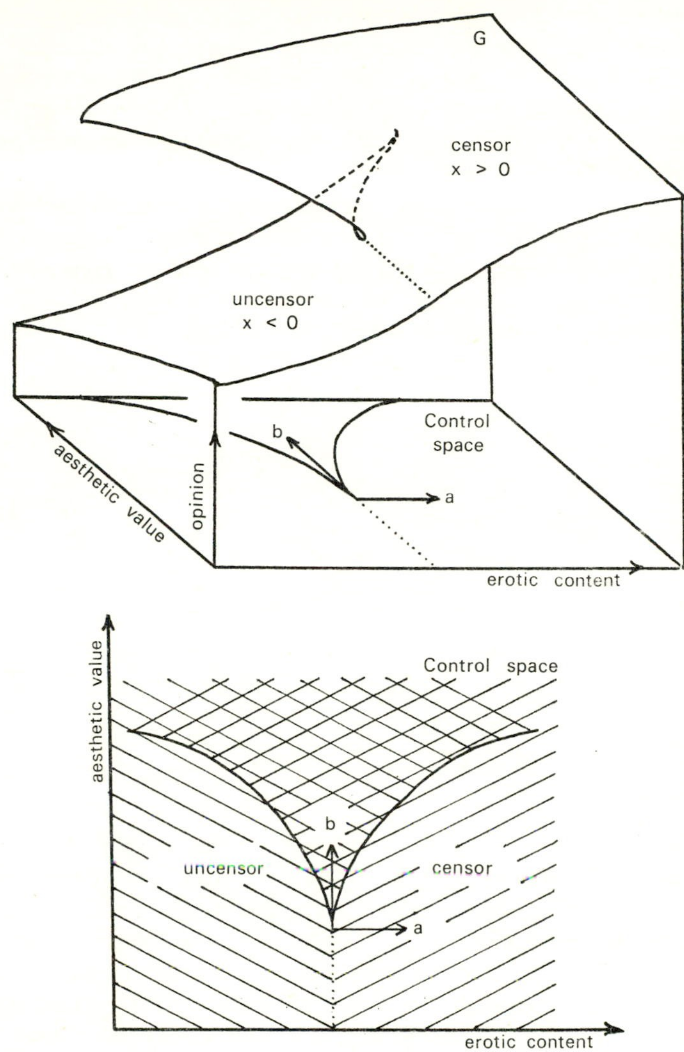

of low eroticism, $a < 0$, can be censored, $x > 0$, while others of high eroticism, $a > 0$, can be uncensored, $x < 0$.

What further confuses the issue is that the phenomena merge smoothly into one another. For example, a new work may 'move up' the aesthetic value scale as it gains recognition amongst the critics.

Two very similar works, on the borderline of the eroticism norm, may experience very close paths as types (like paths 4 and 5 in *Figure 13*), but at the same time, they may undergo divergent treatment at the hands of the censor, one becoming firmly censored and the other firmly uncensored.

Consider now what happens when the market-place becomes more permissive. The censhorship norm moves from $x=0$ to $x=x_N$, say, where $x_N>0$. The probability distribution of opinion for each work does not change, but rather the origin of the scale is shifted (see *Figure 22*). *Figure 21* shows the resulting change from *Figure 20*.

FIGURE 21 Censorship in a permissive society

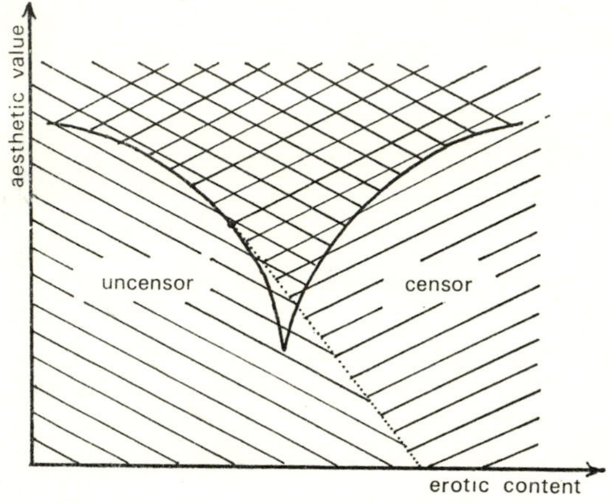

The new frontier between the two regions is the tangent to the cusp at the point $(a,b) = (-2x_N^3, 3x_N^2)$. As a result we should expect the following characteristics of a permissive society.

First, the most noticeable change is a tolerance towards works of low aesthetic value and high erotic content, and the lower the value, the higher the tolerated eroticism. Second, in the neighbourhood of the cusp point, where the debate used to begin, works of modest aesthetic value have all been quietly uncensored. This is not a catastrophic process, because there is no jump from one maximum to the other, but merely a shifting of the norm so that both peaks now lie in the uncensored region. If anything, the debate has moved higher up the aesthetic scale.

Third, there is no qualitative change amongst works of high

aesthetic value, $b > 3x_N^2$, in the sense that types inside the cusp still have one peak either side of the norm as in *Figure 22*, $x_1 < 0 < x_N < x_2$. However, there is a quantitative change in the shift of weight of public opinion which leads to a modified form of the Voting rule as follows. Define the *weight* W by some such formula, as:

$$W = \int_{-\infty}^{x_N} P(x)dx - \int_{x_N}^{\infty} P(x)dx.$$

FIGURE 22 Movement of the norm in a permissive society

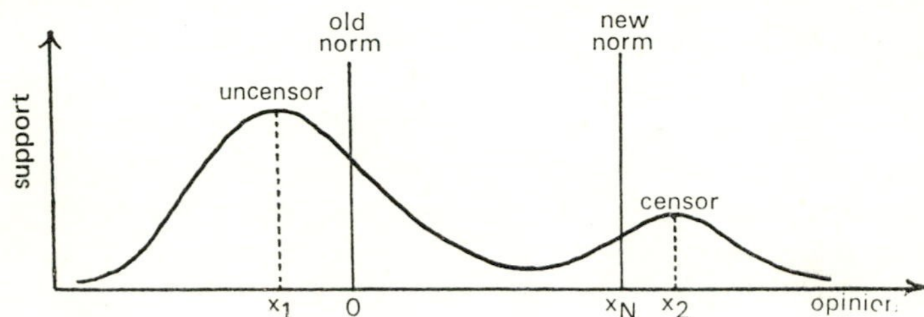

As x_N increases, if W achieves a threshold, $W > W_0$ say, then the weight of opinion should be sufficient to persuade the censor to uncensor a work that had been previously censored. But this time the change is catastrophic, because it is represented by a jump from x_2 to x_1. Consequently, such events are usually accompanied by much ceremony, such as the trial of Lady Chatterley (Rolph 1961).

FIGURE 23 The pendulum of fashion

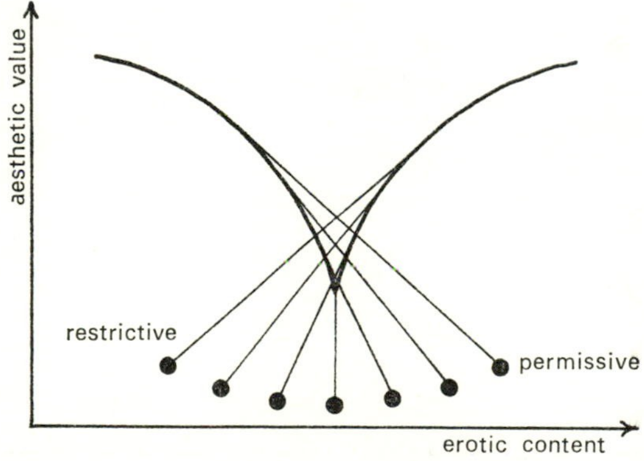

Returning to the metaphor of the 'pendulum of fashion' used in the title of Wilson's article, we can now see this beautifully illustrated by the tangent rolling along the cusp, as shown in *Figure 23.*

Each position of the pendulum gives clear instructions to the censor about the prevailing norm amongst works of low aesthetic value, but the confusion over works of high aesthetic value remains more or less the same, independent of the permissiveness of the particular society or particular age.

Let us look at the metaphor of the pendulum more closely. Thom would probably argue (1970; 1972; 1973b) that since the dynamics of the brain are stable, they are also governed by the same elementary catastrophes, and so intuition would naturally perceive this analogy before reason could explain it; that is why the metaphor appeals to us. Now, a pendulum has not only a swinging bob, but also a fixed pivot. In our case, the fixed pivot manages not only to be a point, the cusp point, but also manages to broaden out so as to include the best of our literature and art, thus providing exactly that fixed backdrop for fashion to swing against.

If, as it seems in Western society today, the pendulum has swung to the permissive side, then our model would predict the presence of a hidden cusp amongst uncensored works of moderate value. It would be very interesting if the experiment described above could reveal so curious a phenomenon. The same model can be applied to a variety of situations where the pendulum of fashion swings.

We conclude with one more short application, to the censorship of facts by governments, because this model links together all three previous models in the paper. The two main reasons for censoring facts are military and political: first, the government is concerned to protect the country against possible external threats, and therefore the military importance of a fact may deem it worthy of censorship. Second, the government is concerned to protect itself against possible internal opposition amongst the population, and therefore the political importance of a fact may deem it worthy of censorship.

Hypothesis 9. Political importance is a normal factor, and military importance a splitting factor, influencing the censorship of facts by governments.

As in the case of pornography, there are variations of censorship amongst different governments and at different times. The most noticeable difference between a permissive and a restrictive regime occurs at low values of the splitting factor, that is to say, in the government attitude towards facts of no military importance, but possibly of political significance. Meanwhile, the attitude of both countries towards facts of high military importance is almost identical. Military weapons, for example, will be either hidden with great secrecy or flamboyantly displayed, and the catastrophic switch from secrecy to display is usually accompanied by much ceremony.

NOTES

1 For the mathematicians: *smooth* means that P, regarded as a function of the three variables a, b, x, is differentiable to all orders. *Generic* means that P, regarded as a map from C to the space of probability distributions on X, is transversal to the natural stratification (Mather 1969; Thom 1972; Trotman and Zeeman 1974); in other words, P is in general position. Smooth generic Ps are open-dense in the space of all smooth Ps, which are dense in the space of all continuous Ps. Therefore, any continuous P can be approximated arbitrarily closely by a smooth generic P, justifying the use of smooth generic models. Furthermore, the latter are stable under sufficiently small, smooth perturbations (Trotman and Zeeman 1974).

2 The combined graph has equation $\frac{\partial P}{\partial x} = 0$, which is a smooth curve by Hypothesis 1. The fold-points are given by the equations $\frac{\partial P}{\partial x} = \frac{\partial^2 P}{\partial^2 x} = 0.$

3 Throughout the paper, and in this section in particular, we use the word 'sociological' to mean pertaining to the social sciences, rather than pertaining just to sociology.

4 In other words, the map $X \rightarrow X'$ is an orientation-preserving diffeomorphism (where a *diffeomorphism* is a one-to-one map that is smooth and has smooth inverse).

5 For an application of catastrophe theory in psychology, involving the fitting of experimental data, and leading to predictions, and the design of new experiments, see Zeeman (1974d; 1975).

6 Indeed, in some cases the change of scale may not even be qualitative, and may only be order-preserving up to some tolerance, in which case the conclusions can only be rigorous up to that tolerance. However, this would require additional mathematical techniques that we do not consider in this paper.

7 For the mathematician: it is true that more sophisticated invariants

such as Betti numbers, homology, and homotopy groups, etc., have been known for a long time, but in most cases these appear to be useless for describing graphs of experimental data. Where they have proved useful, they also tend to be translatable into everyday language, such as 'connected', 'single-valued', etc.

8 For example 'more haste, less speed'. A resolution of this paradox can be made using the language of Section 11 below: skill is a normal factor, and haste a splitting factor, for speed. But of course, a paradox is always more attractive than its resolution, because it gives the mind more pause.

9 A *diffeomorphism of the plane* is a one-to-one map of the plane onto itself that is smooth and has smooth inverse.

10 But not conversely. An example of a qualitative property that is *not* invariant under equivalence is *increasingness* in an ordinary single-valued two-dimensional graph. However, more subtly, in the cusp catastrophe, which is the three-dimensional graph described in the next section, near the cusp point increasingness with respect to a normal factor *is* an invariant property.

11 Thom (1972) calls it the *Riemann-Hugoniot catastrophe* in honour of its first application to shock waves in the middle of the nineteenth century. Of course, it was not realized at that time as being part of the family of elementary catastrophes.

12 For example let $P_c(x) = \left[\frac{x^4}{4} - \frac{bx^2}{2} - ax + f(c)\right]^{-1}$, where $c = (a,b)$ and f is the unique function of c such that for each c, the bracket is positive and $\int_{-\infty}^{\infty} P(x)\,dx = 1$.

13 *Locally-equivalent* means there is a neighbourhood that is equivalent.

14 *Dual* means that maxima and minima are interchanged and so the roles of G and S – G are reversed. See *Figure 16*.

15 Mathematically, we could equally well use a 1000-dimensional behaviour space and the graph would still be a two-dimensional surface. However, this surface might then have so many folds and cusps that it could obscure the very phenomenon that we wish to elucidate. Sometimes, an approximate description of behaviour using only a few dimensions can be more effective than a detailed description using many dimensions, in the same way that, in order to study the flow of water over a dam, for instance, it is more effective to pretend that water is a continuous medium, than to analyse the detailed mechanics of all the water molecules.

REFERENCES

FOWLER, D. H. 1972. The Riemann-Hugoniot Catastrophe and Van der Waals's Equation. In C. H. Waddington (ed.), *Towards a Theoretical Biology, 4.* London: English Universities Press.

HARRISON, P. J. and ZEEMAN, E. C. 1973. Applications of Catastrophe Theory to Macroeconomics. Symposium on Applications of Global Analysis. Utrecht University, Utrecht.

LORENZ, K. 1966. *On Aggression.* London: Methuen.

MATHER, J. N. 1969. Right Equivalence. Warwick University reprint.

POSTON, T. and WOODCOCK, A. E. R. 1974. *The Geometry of the Elementary Catastrophes.* Lecture Notes in Mathematics. Berlin and New York: Springer Verlag.

ROLPH, C. H. 1961. *The Trial of Lady Chatterley.* Harmondsworth: Penguin.

SHULMAN, L. S. and REVZON, M. 1972. Phase Transitions as Catastrophes. *Collective Phenomena,* **1**: 43–7.

SIERSMA, D. 1973. Singularities of C∞ functions of right-codimension smaller or equal than eight. *Indag* **25**: 31–37.

THOM, R. 1972. *Stabilité structurelle et morphogénèse.* New York: Benjamin. English translation by D. H. Fowler forthcoming 1975.

——1969. Topological Models in Biology. *Topology* **8**: 313–35.

——1970. Topologie et linguistique. *Essays on Topology.* Vol. dedicated to G. de Rham. Berlin and New York: Springer Verlag.

——1971a. A Global Dynamical Scheme for Vertebrate Embryology. *AAAS* Some Mathematical Questions in Biology, Symposium V, *Lectures on Mathematics in the Life Sciences* **5**: 3–45. Providence: American Mathematical Society.

——1971b. Phase-transitions as Catastrophes. Conference on Statistical Mechanics. Chicago: Chicago University Press.

——1973a. La théorie des catastrophes: État présent et perspectives. *Manifold* **14** 16–23. Mathematics Institute, University of Warwick.

——1973b. Langage et catastrophes: Eléments pour une sémantique topologique. In M. M. Peixoto (ed.), *Dynamical Systems.* New York and London: Academic Press.

TOLSTOY, L. 1970. *War and Peace.* Vol. III. Trans. by L. and M. Maude, revised and reprinted. London: Oxford University Press.

TROTMAN, D. J. A. and ZEEMAN, E. C. 1974. Classification of Elementary Catastrophes. Warwick University reprint.

WILSON, J. 1970. Censorship. *Guardian,* November 9.

ZEEMAN, E. C. 1971. Geometry of Catastrophe. *Times Literary Supplement,* December 10.

——1972a. Differential Equations for the Heartbeat and Nerve Impulse. In C. H. Waddington (ed.), *Towards a Theoretical Biology, 4*. London: English Universities Press.

——1972b. A Catastrophe Machine. In C. H. Waddington (ed.), *Towards a Theoretical Biology, 4*. London: English Universities Press.

——1973. Applications of Catastrophe Theory. Tokyo International Conference on Manifolds. Tokyo: Tokyo University.

——1974a. Primary and Secondary Waves in Developmental Biology. *AAAS*. Some Mathematical Questions in Biology Symposium VIII. *Lectures on Mathematics in the Life Sciences* 7. Providence: American Mathematical Society.

——1974b. On the Unstable Behaviour of Stock Exchanges. *Journal of Mathematical Economics* **1**: 39–49.

——1974c. Catastrophe Theory: A reply to Thom. *Manifold* **15**: 4–15. Mathematical Institute, University of Warwick.

——1974d. Conflicting Judgements Caused by Stress. Forthcoming.

ZEEMAN, E. C., HALL, C. S., HARRISON, P. J., MARRIAGE, G. H., and SHAPLAND, P. H. 1975. A Model for Prison Riots. Forthcoming.

Life with intelligent machines

DONALD MICHIE

There is a sense in which the study of machine intelligence can be described as the application of philosophy to technology. From mathematical logic insights into processes of reasoning are obtained, and from epistemology ways of representing symbolically what we know about the world. The machine intelligence practitioner is a 'knowledge engineer', who needs to find ways of representing symbolically what his computing system should 'know', and thus equip it to handle the intelligent tasks which he has in mind for it.

Let us consider an intelligent task, that of interpreting mass spectrograms, in order to identify the unknown chemical compounds from which they are obtained. Such a task requires a great deal of sophisticated knowledge about chemistry. E. A. Feigenbaum, J. Lederberg and others at Stanford University, USA, have developed a computer program, DENDRAL, which performs this task. For certain families of organic compounds, identifications are more reliable than those given by experienced human chemists. If we look inside the program we find organized symbolic representations, corresponding to human 'knowledge', of various categories of facts – topological facts about the theoretically possible configurations of atoms to make a molecule of given composition, chemical facts about the stability and non-stability of different configurations, and an entire 'mini-theory' of mass spectrometry. DENDRAL is expected to evolve into a cost-effective tool, able to displace the human chemist over ever-enlarging areas of the mass spectrometry domain. In doing so, it is no more than a forerunner of a 'scientist's aid' type of intelligent computer program which is expected to become commonplace in the years ahead (Michie and Buchanan 1974).

Now, consider a different task – that of picking physical components out of a heap, visually identifying them, and using them to assemble a specified object – say, a toy car. This is undoubtedly an intelligent task. It is performed by our Edinburgh 'hand-eye' robot under the control of a 'flexible assembly' computer program in the following stages (see Ambler *et al.* 1973):

Instruction phase

1 Individual parts are tossed onto the platform and the robot is told, for each possible view of the object, its designation, how to pick it up, and what to do with it (e.g., 'turn it over', or 'put it exactly here in preparation for assembly').
  Approximately five of these training views are needed for each designation (e.g., 'car body on side', 'car body on back') to assure the system can recognize the part; of course it only needs to be told once what to do with it.
2 Starting with the parts laid out in the fixed position, the robot, working blind, is guided through the assembly operation. The instructions developed at this time to guide the robot constitute the assembly program; thenceforth running the assembly program transforms the laid-out parts into the final product.

Execution phase

1 Someone dumps a pile of parts (perhaps with missing or extra parts) onto the platform and starts the inspection and layout process.
2 The robot examines the platform and lays out any recognized parts for assembly.
3 Any unrecognizable pile of parts is pulled apart into its component parts by a set of routines which can deal with arbitrary heaps of arbitrary parts.
4 If all the parts for the assembly are found, extra parts are dumped in a special location. If some parts are missing, the robot appeals for help.
5 The assembly program is run.

The above described performance is based on an elaborate suite of programs which confer a fair degree of flexibility on the system –

it can be taught a new assembly, say a model ship, at a day's notice. How far we still have to go in incorporating 'teachability' into software can be judged from the fact that a three-year-old child can be taught a new assembly in ten minutes! The discovery of better design principles for 'teachable' programming systems is a major goal of most research laboratories in the machine intelligence field.

Over the next decade, what is known as 'software engineering' is expected to develop into one of the world's largest industries. To give an idea of the scale on which the engineering of a single software assignment can be conducted, the writing of one particular program, IBM's OS360 operating system, consumed 3,000 man-years at an estimated cost approaching £30M. Thus, we find that here is a new form of manufacture, the operations of which consist in making marks on paper, with a cost so great that one looks for analogies to such enterprises as the pyramid building of the ancient Egyptians. There is a difference, however. One brick of the Great Pyramid can be out of place, yet the pyramid will still stand. But one binary digit wrong in a complex computer program can cause the whole to malfunction. Such an error did indeed cause the costly failure of one of the unmanned missions of NASA's space program. In software, there is a premium on accuracy which is quite unprecedented.

Techniques of machine intelligence can come in at this point *via* an unconventional interpretation of the principle of redundancy. Classical redundancy operates by replication of *similar* elements. Thus, if a signal is regarded as verified, if, and only if, inputs from three elements all agree, and each of these has an independent error rate of 1 per cent, then the error of the transmitted signal is automatically reduced to one in a million. In a machine intelligence program, as in the case of flexible assembly instanced above, the fundamental design principle is 'if at first you don't succeed, try something else!'. For a given task – say picking a component out of a heap – selection is made from a battery of *dissimilar* strategies – 'grab a protuberant part', 'seek isolated object and identify', 'stir heap and start again', etc. The program is quick to abandon any given strategy if unrewarded by success, and to go back to the strategy-pool. The result is an impressive reliability of eventual goal-accomplishment: sooner or later the program is bound to win through to the given objective. This kind of reliability has not in the past been associated with the behaviour of automatic systems. Rather, opportunistic flitting between alternative strategies in the light of what turns up is more characteristic of the way that a human tackles a skilled task – whether in driving a car, cooking a meal, or proving a theorem.

Several years ago, I discussed the question of 'ripeness of time' with regard to the project to construct an intelligent machine. Although my tentative conclusions were positive, there was nothing then stirring in the world to give them particularly forceful backing. But, less than one year later, in July 1971, the Japanese Government announced their 'PIPS project'. PIPS stands for 'Pattern Information Processing System' and its goals have been characterized in the following terms by an expert American observer, Dr Gilbert Devey of the US National Science Foundation: '. . . an inanimate system capable of sensing a pattern (characters, pictures, 3-D objects), identifying the nature of that pattern, relating that information to a data base of information (scene analysis) to then decide on and take a course of action for the control and manipulation of an output device which performs a useful function, and doing so without human intervention' (Devey 1972:13).

This unprecedented R and D project is to a major extent concentrated on industrial applications of robotics. Whether we like it or not, an internationally competitive program to develop intelligent robots has begun. The United States Government, already investing substantially through its Department of Defence, is responding to the Japanese challenge through additional agencies, notably NASA and the National Science Foundation. Independently of this, activity in robotics research is gathering force in numerous American laboratories, for example, the Draper Laboratories in Cambridge, Massachusetts, and IBM's Thomas J. Watson Research Laboratories at Yorktown Heights. Let us consider what possible consequences to our culture and civilization may ultimately flow from the present world-wide intensification of effort. Whether or not we in Britain decide to go with the wave, it is now unlikely to halt.

Where will it ultimately carry us? Are we, or our children, or our grand-children to share this planet with an alien race of equal, or possibly superior intelligences? If so, is this good or bad? Will new windows of the mind be opened to us, or will we face the ultimate in environmental pollution – pollution with uncomprehended machinery?

An indication that educated people believe that 'it is later than you think' with regard to these questions is given by two recent surveys of opinion which I. J. Good and I made independently of each other. Good (1973) writes:

> 'You asked me to send statistics of the estimates of when a machine would be built with the intelligence of a man. I put the question in the following manner. People were invited to say by which date they thought there was a half chance that the machine would be built, among the eight dates listed below. The answer was to include the belief that it is odds against an intelligent machine's ever being achieved. I asked the question on two occasions. The first occasion was at an after-dinner speech in March at a meeting of Virginia computer users, about half of whom were college men and half were business men . . . The second occasion was at my lecture at the Institute of Contemporary Arts in April. The results were as follows:

		1980	*1990*	*2000*	*2020*	*2050*	*3000*	*5000*	∞
Virginia	(i)	0	6	20	16	5	3	0	4
ICA	(ii)	0	8	24	12	5	3	0	16.'

My own questionnaire was circulated among scientists of several different laboratories in America and Britain working in machine intelligence and in closely related branches of computer science. I reproduce the questions in *Table 1*, and have entered the frequencies with which the various replies were given.

Among the points of significance are:

1 that a majority believed that human intelligence levels will be reached in fifty years or less. Other surveys have given even more optimistic estimates, if that is the right word.

2 that about half the sample believed that the risk of ultimate take-over is at least substantial.

These results could be used to justify unease, expressed by Arthur Clarke in a recent exchange with Good (Clarke 1968:119). The latter remarked that 'If we build an ultraintelligent machine, we will be playing with fire. We have played with fire before, and it helped keep the other animals at bay.' Clarke's reply was 'Well, yes – but when the ultraintelligent machine arrives *we* may be the "other animals"; and look what's happened to them'.

I shall suggest that such prognostications are certainly premature and probably without foundation. It is not that I personally doubt the technical *possibility* within the time-scales here envisaged of constructing

TABLE 1 Aggregate results of a questionnaire completed by sixty-seven computer scientists working in machine intelligence and related fields (Spring 1972)

1 It will have become a technical possibility to construct a computing system exhibiting an all-round intelligence approximating that of adult humans in 5 years *0*, 10 years *1*, 20 years *16*, 50 years *19*, more than 50 years *25*, never *3*, no opinion *3*.
2 Significant industrial spin-off from machine intelligence research can be expected in 5 years *30*, 10 years *28*, 20 years *4*, 50 years *1*, more than 50 years *2*, never *1*, no opinion *1*.
3 Significant contributions to studies of the brain are likely to come from machine intelligence in 5 years *15*, 10 years *20*, 20 years *9*, 50 years *4*, more than 50 years *7*, never *3*, no opinion *9*.
4 Significant contributions to machine intelligence are likely to come from studies of the brain in 5 years *1*, 10 years *14*, 20 years *10*, 50 years *4*, more than 50 years *5*, never *10*, no opinion *13*.
5 'Machine intelligence' (still less the study of intelligence more generally) is not a unitary discipline and is destined to be overgrown by its constituent disciplines: agree *22*, disagree *35*, no opinion *10*.
6 If the goals of machine intelligence are realized, the immediate effect will be that human intellectual and cultural processes will: atrophy *1*, be enhanced *50*, be unaffected *9*, no opinion *7*.
7 The risk of an ultimate 'take-over' of human affairs by intelligent machines is: negligible *30*, substantial *26*, overwhelming *5*, no opinion *6*.

an all-round mechanical intelligence of human or superhuman intellectual power. But I doubt whether human motivation could ever exist for implementing the machine equivalent of an intellectual all-rounder. Under stable social conditions, it is not *undifferentiated potential* which the employer of labour seeks to hire, but *specialist skill* relevant to his current need. Why, one wonders, should the matter stand differently with regard to machines?

As far as a trend can be observed in computer technology, it is a trend towards speciation. Task-specific capability becomes increasingly incorporated into fundamental system design. Scratch-pad calculations for engineering and statistics are moving from the time-shared terminal to the desk-top computer; large-scale number-crunching is being passed to specialized giants such as the CDC7600, and heavy-duty commercial record-handling to the standard IBM ranges. Suspending disbelief for a moment in Good's Ultraintelligent

Machine (Good 1965), can we extrapolate this trend, and envisage populations of machines, each capable within its own narrow repertoire of vast and superhuman powers, but helpless otherwise? The concept is reminiscent of H. G. Wells's vision of functional specialization among the Selenites, the inhabitants of the moon.

> 'The moon is indeed a kind of super-anthill. But in place of the five distinctive types, the worker, soldier, winged male, queen and slave of the ant-world, there are amongst the moon-folk not only hundreds of differentiations, but, within each, and linking one to the other, a whole series of fine gradations. And these Selenites are not only merely colossally superior to ants, but, according to Cavor, colossally, in intelligence morality and social wisdom, higher than man.' (Wells 1956:217–18)

He describes co-operation among lunar beings Phi-oo, Tsi-puff and two other Selenites, in the task of learning Cavor's language. Wells's account is strongly suggestive of the integrated action of three specialized computers: a language processor, a database machine, and a display device:

> 'Phi-oo would attend to Cavor for a space, then point also and say the word he had heard. The first word he mastered was "man", and the second "mooney" – which Cavor on the spur of the moment seems to have used instead of "Selenite" for the moon race. As soon as Phi-oo was assured of the meaning of a word he repeated it to Tsi-puff, who remembered it infallibly . . . Subsequently it seems they brought an artist with them to assist the work of explanation with sketches and diagrams – Cavor's drawings being rather crude. "He was", says Cavor, "a being with an active arm and an arresting eye", and he seemed to draw with incredible swiftness.' (Wells 1956:217)

The analogy with interaction between a suite of special-purpose computing devices is irresistible. Wells's narrative continues: '. . . some adjectives were easy, but when it came to abstract nouns, to prepositions, and the sort of hackneyed figures of speech by means of which so much is expressed on earth, it was like diving in cork jackets. Indeed, these difficulties were insurmountable until to the sixth lesson came a fourth assistant, a being with a huge, football-shaped head, whose forte was clearly the pursuit of intricate analogy' (Wells 1956:217–18).

So might a human scientist of the future, wrestling with a problem of conceptualization, call to his aid some remote and wonderfully elaborated descendant of Pat Winston's computer program for forming analogies which gained its author the PhD degree in 1971 at the Artificial Intelligence Laboratory at MIT.

Here are some questions we must put if we have serious anxiety that intelligent machinery will constitute a threat to man's ego and identity. Should Phi-oo be jealous of Tsi-puff, because of his wonderful memory? Should Tsi-puff be consumed with envy of Phi-oo's linguistic excellence? Should they both feel threatened by the third Selenite's draftsmanship or by the fourth Selenite's grasp of analogy? Surely not. Man is a territorial animal, and his patterns of rivalry and co-operation extend to intellectual territory too. Where skills are complementary and competition pointless, the sense of trespass does not ordinarily arise. When a man has a specialist skill which machine advances render obsolete he may indeed feel resentment. Professor Aitken was the world's most outstanding calculating prodigy and is reported to have felt concern at the growing numerical powers of computers. This distress occurs and will continue to occur, and is part of the general social problem of mechanization. But in each generation the shoe pinches in a different place. Perhaps the only *specialist* skill which human intellectual workers will develop in the world of Good's 'Ultraintelligent Machine' is that of managing and co-ordinating teams of intelligent machines.

Such machine systems may require rather careful and wise management as time goes on, if only to prevent their human beneficiaries becoming helplessly dependent upon them – parasites instead of symbionts. The reality of the problem is underlined by the news, announced in June 1972 by Y. Masuda, director of the Computer Usage Development Institute, that the Japanese Government's £2500M plan for computerization includes the development of a prototype 'computer-controlled city' within the next ten years.

However, such computer-controlled cities belong to the future, and autonomous 'Mars rover' vehicles collecting our garbage or tidying up warehouses, or handling airport luggage will not affect our lives much, for all their science fiction aspect. What *will* begin to colour our existence by the end of this decade is the emergence of the 'home terminal' offering an intelligent 'question-answering' facility as a service.

Not only schools, hospitals, and commercial firms, but also the ordinary householder will be able to tap information and problem-solving power from a national computing grid, rather as he now draws on gas, water, and electricity. Computer-aided self-instruction will have become a hobby of large sectors of the population by the turn of this century. When I look ahead towards the coming symbiosis, I naturally see negative aspects, and dangers which will have to be carefully watched. But the main impression is of a more varied and stimulating world, with prospects of man being culturally and intellectually master in his own house as never before.

REFERENCES

AMBLER, A. P., BARROW, H. G., BROWN, C. M., BURSTALL, R. M., and POPPLESTONE, R. J. 1973. A Versatile Computer-controlled Assembly System. *Third International Joint Conference on Artificial Intelligence.* Stanford: Stanford Research Institute Publications Dept.

CLARKE, A. C. 1968. The Mind of the Machine. *Playboy*, December.

DEVEY, G. 1972. Project Management for Automation Technology. A paper delivered at the Japan Industrial Technology Association (JITA) Symposium on Pattern Information Processing Systems. Tokyo, March 15.

GOOD, I. J. 1965. Speculations Concerning the First Ultraintelligent Machine. *Advances in Computers* **6**: 31–88. New York: Academic Press.

——1973. Personal communication.

MICHIE, D. and BUCHANAN, B. G. 1974. Artificial Intelligence in Mass Spectroscopy: a review of the Heuristic DENDRAL program. *Computers for Spectroscopists.* London: Adam Hilger.

WELLS, H. G. 1956. *The First Men in the Moon.* London: Fontana Books.

The political uses of scientific models: the cybernetic model of government in Soviet social science

DAVID HOLLOWAY

All discussion of politics involves assumptions about the way in which decisions are reached in government, and about the way in which they ought to be reached. This is as true of gossip about politics as it is of systematic study, even if in the latter case the assumptions are supposed to be more carefully scrutinized. It is just because discussion of politics involves assumptions about the activity of politics that it feeds back into that activity by influencing the way in which decisions are made and the extent to which those decisions are regarded as authoritative; hence the temptation for those with political power to censor the modes of political argument. The activity of politics and discussion of that activity are thus inextricably intertwined. For this reason, it is appropriate to ask what assumptions underlie any mode of discussion about politics, and to look for its implications for policy-making and the structure of political authority. These questions are especially important for societies where, as in the Soviet Union, discussion of politics is stringently censored (see Mackenzie 1967:13–20).

With these questions in mind, I shall look in this paper at a new mode of discussion about politics which has emerged in the Soviet Union. This centres on a specific model of political activity: the cybernetic model of government. Cybernetics is commonly defined in the Soviet Union as the general science of the optimal control of complex dynamic systems; and during the 1960s, it came to play an important part in the revival of Soviet social science, in particular by providing a general framework for the emergence of schools of optimal planning and social management. In the words of one group of Soviet authors: '. . . the view of society as a complex cybernetic system with a multidimensional network of direct and feedback links and a mechanism of optimization, functioning towards a set goal, is increasingly gaining prestige as the main theoretical idea of the "technology" of managing society' (Biryukov *et al.* 1967:303). The government of Soviet society has been portrayed in terms of the interaction of two sub-systems within the society – the controlling sub-system (the state and voluntary organizations led by the Communist Party) and the controlled sub-system (the economy, science and other social activities). The essence of governmental activity lies in such conscious, purposive activity by the controlling sub-system as will ensure that social processes develop in an optimal way. Scientific government requires that information about the state of the system be transmitted to the political institutions, that it be processed there into commands or decisions, that these be transmitted to the controlled sub-system, and that the loop be closed by feedback about the effect of the decisions or commands.[1]

I shall examine the assumptions on which this model of government is based, and attempt to assess its implications for policy-making and authority relations in the Soviet Union. It will not be possible to look at these questions comprehensively, much less exhaustively, in a single paper. But this preliminary analysis will, I hope, indicate some of the interesting changes in Soviet politics which lie behind this model of government. It may also throw light on the social functions of social science, and, in particular, on the political uses of social science models; the more so, as the cybernetic model of government bears a close resemblance to the 'administrative' or 'managerial' models of government, which are to be found in societies other than the Soviet Union.

THE CYBERNETIC MODEL OF GOVERNMENT

It may be objected that the cybernetic model of government is not the kind of model that first springs to mind in the context of a seminar on models in the social sciences. Certainly, when Soviet social scientists speak of cybernetic modelling they normally have more specific models in mind (see Sedova 1972:221–67). Nevertheless, the cybernetic model of government is to be seen as a model in the following ways: it draws an analogy between government on the one hand, and biological and engineering control systems on the other; it provides a common language in terms of which the analogy can be elaborated and tested; and finally, in so far as it implies the possibility of improving the processes of government, it both draws an analogy and indicates an ideal (see paper by Harré in this volume).

Each of these claims is implicit in cybernetics itself. Cyberneticians have asserted that their theories of control and communication are, in principle, applicable in the study of social systems. W. Ross Ashby, for example, has written that '. . . cybernetics is likely to reveal a great number of interesting and suggestive parallelisms between machine and brain and society' (Ashby 1956:16). Wiener coined the term 'cybernetics' for the whole field of control and communication theory, in order to emphasize its essential unity. He was concerned primarily with control and communication in biological and engineering systems and thought the social sciences a poor proving ground for the ideas of cybernetics. He did nevertheless assert that '. . . society can only be understood through a study of the messages and communication facilities which belong to it' (Wiener 1954:16). It has been argued that his achievement was not so much that he solved certain complex mathematical problems, but rather that he saw the possibilities opened up by the synthesis of a number of existing theories into a framework, in terms of which the processes of control might be examined in systems of different materiality. However, there is much disagreement about the extent to which cybernetics has been successful in creating such a unified framework. Nevertheless, cybernetics does employ a series of concepts and theories that can be applied, in principle, in the study of control in biological, engineering, and social systems. Chief among them are the concepts of information, message, and channel capacity as defined in information theory; the concepts of control and feedback drawn from the theory of servomechanisms; and the concepts of system, equilibrium, and adaptability from systems theory. It is impossible here to characterize or define cybernetics. But for the purposes of this paper it is important to note the central place of the relationship between control and communication: control can be effected only when there is feedback about the effects of the controlling activity.

Cybernetics is commonly divided into three branches: theoretical cybernetics, which studies problems concerned with the general mathematical description of control processes; technical cybernetics, which works on the technological problems of constructing control systems; and applied cybernetics, which concerns itself with the application of cybernetic concepts and technology in various fields of human activity. Cybernetics may thus be seen as both a scientific and an engineering discipline. The cybernetic model of government is consequently concerned not only with the study, but also with the improvement, of the processes of government.

The claims of cybernetics have not been borne out in a systematic way in Western social science. Several attempts have been made to elaborate a cybernetic analysis of government, but these have not been especially fruitful (see Deutsch 1963 and Easton 1965). On the other hand, certain of the concepts of cybernetics – for example, feedback – and certain of the associated theories – for example, game theory – have been influential. In a more general way, cybernetics may be regarded as part of the intellectual *Zeitgeist*, with its preoccupation with systems and structures. Therefore, any assessment of the influence of cybernetics depends on what is to be understood by that term. It has been pointed out that:

> '. . . in the United States, scientists and engineers working in the theory of self-regulation tend to avoid the term cybernetics which deals to a considerable degree with isomorphisms among various types of self-regulating systems. Since only a very limited range of systems and communications processes are presently amenable to mathematical formalisation and manipulation, there has been a tendency to institutionalise fairly narrow disciplines concerned with limited formal or material applications of these concepts, such as computer engineering, bionics and control systems engineering. In the Soviet Union, on the other hand, the term cybernetics is used quite widely. (Dechert 1966:107)

The same point may be made of the social sciences. Many of the disciplines which in the Soviet Union fall under the rubric of cybernetics – for example, game theory or programming techniques – are rarely called cybernetics in the West. The explanation for this lies both in the internal development of the Soviet school of cybernetics, and in the processes of change in Soviet society. I shall return to the latter point; here I want to sketch briefly the development of the influence of cybernetics in Soviet social science.

In the early 1950s, cybernetics was rejected in the Soviet Union as a bourgeois pseudo-science on both scientific and philosophical grounds. But quite soon the advocates of cybernetics began to press their case, and in 1959 a Science Council for Cybernetics was established at the USSR Academy of Sciences. By the late 1950s, cyberneticians had overcome the obstacles to recognition of cybernetics as a legitimate natural science, and a self-conscious school of cybernetics was formed. This was partly a consequence of the fight to reverse the initial condemnation; and, in the context of Soviet science, organizational recognition made interdisciplinary co-operation easier, and provided a general legitimation for techniques and theories which might otherwise be regarded as unacceptable.

Once cybernetics's legitimacy as a natural science had been established, cyberneticians began to emphasize the possibilities of applying cybernetic concepts and technology in the management of social activity. As a general science of management cybernetics has found its widest application in the fields of defence and economic planning. In defence the primary focus of research has been on command and control, in the attempt to ensure that the immense destructive power of the armed forces can be employed in a controlled way. Command and control entails the making of a decision on the basis of the best information available, the communication of that decision as an order to troops and weapons, and feedback so that the order may be adjusted. Soviet military cybernetics has been engaged in research into the best organizational structures for command and control, and into the improvement of the command decision-making process (see Holloway 1971).

However, the influence of cybernetics on Soviet social science has been most strongly felt in discussions about economic planning and administration. Between 1960 and 1965 a network of institutes, engaging in research into economic cybernetics, was set up: the Central Economic Mathematical Institute of the USSR Academy of Sciences, the Central Research Institute of Management in Minsk, the Institute of Cybernetics of the Ukrainian Academy of Sciences, and the Institute of the Economics and Organization of Industrial Production of the Siberian Division of the USSR Academy of Sciences. It is not possible here to give an account of the wide-ranging, often highly technical, and far from unanimous proposals that have been put forward for an optimal planning system (see Hardt *et al.* 1967; Ellman 1971). But the influence of cybernetic concepts is apparent in the discussions about the structure of information systems and decision-making nodes; and also in the debates about decision-making techniques. It was initially hoped by some economists that computers would make possible a super-centralized planning system, with all decisions taken in Moscow. However, this was a false hope, for it was soon shown that the centre could not conceivably cope with the amount of information which would need to be processed. Consequently, discussion has proceeded to the correct balance between centralized and decentralized decision-making, with most of the optimal planning proposals attempting to combine in a single system elements both of planning and of the market. Planning is required in order to make structural changes in the economy, to determine its basic proportions, and to fix the parameters which regulate the behaviour of the lower-level units. The market mechanism would be used to allocate resources at the micro-level because the huge number of possible plans would overwhelm any central planning agency. Thus, the market mechanism becomes an instrument in the pursuit of optimizing the national-economic objective function that economic cyberneticians assume to exist. It can thus be seen that economic cybernetics is concerned not only with the structures of planning and administration, but also with the techniques whereby scarce resources are allocated. New techniques of decision-making such as linear programming and input-output analysis are assigned a central role within the structural framework.

The recognition that the economic system is part of the wider social system has provided the stimulus for the third major area of cybernetics's influence on Soviet social science: the search for a general theory of the 'scientific management of society' (*nauchnoe upravlenie obshchestvom*) (Afanas'ev 1972: Chapter 8; see also Note 1). This school has emerged later than either military or economic cybernetics; it has indeed developed precisely because an examination of the problems of management or control in defence and the economy leads inevitably to more general problems of social management. It is, for example, a fundamental part of the optimal planning proposals that a rational incentive system be introduced, on the assumption that managers and workers will behave rationally within the structure of a particular incentive system. Again, for a command and control system to work effectively, the human beings involved must function as reliable parts of the overall system. In neither case can behaviour be managed solely within the context of military or economic cybernetics; hence the need for a general model.

The school of the 'scientific management of society' draws out and generalizes the cybernetic model of government which is implicit in the more specialized schools of social management. It provides a framework within which more specific social science models may be employed. It offers a way of looking at organizational structures and decision-making processes. It stresses the hierarchical nature of administrative structures; it points to the possibility of optimal decision-making; it emphasizes the role of information flows in administration; and it assumes that the self-regulation of Soviet society is to be achieved through the interaction of two sub-systems: the controlling and the controlled.

SCIENTIFIC POLICY-MAKING AND THE REVOLUTION IN SCIENCE AND TECHNOLOGY

The existence of a self-conscious Soviet school of cybernetics is perhaps to be explained not so much by the peculiar circumstances of its formation or by the organizational features of Soviet science, but rather by the high value placed by the party and state bureaucracies on the conscious, purposive and scientific government of Soviet society. The advocates of cybernetics have claimed that socialist society offers an especially fruitful environment for the science of optimal control because it develops not anarchically or spontaneously like capitalist society but as a result of the conscious and purposeful activity of the masses led by the Communist Party. Moreover, in a society in which the means of production are owned by the state, and goods and services distributed by an administrative apparatus rather than by the market, the technical problems of resource allocation assume a particular importance at the national level. The claim of cybernetics to be able to improve the management of social and economic processes thus provides an attractive prospect for party and state officials. This claim is the more powerful because, with its natural-scientific credentials, cybernetics carries the promise of making policy-making more scientific.

Marxism–Leninism has always claimed that policy can be, in some sense, scientific. This claim embraces two assertions: that political action can, and should, be guided by analysis of the social and economic situation within which it is to be taken; and that this analysis should be based on Marxist theory. Of course, it is true that the term 'scientific' means different things in different languages, but at the core of Marxism–Leninism's claim to scientific status lies the affirmation of a continuity, resting upon the dialectical method and the materialist interpretation of history, between natural science and Marxist social science. Soviet leaders have insisted that their authority is derived from their ability to use scientific analysis to guide political action.

I shall not discuss here the legitimacy of the claim to scientific status for Marxism–Leninism, nor the various glosses given to it by Soviet writers. But it is important to note that the Leninist tradition stresses the need not only for policies guided by Marxist theory, but also for what may be called the 'technocratic rationalization' of administration. The cyberneticians' appeal to the 'scientific management' movement of the 1920s and to Lenin's interest in Taylorism for legitimation for their proposals. Such an appeal is not surprising, and in this case it draws attention to a sometimes neglected aspect of Lenin's thinking about the state. The texts most often cited are those on administration, in particular those of the early months of 1923 on the need to reform the state apparatus and develop administrative culture among the workers: 'we have so far been able to devote so little thought and attention to the quality of our state apparatus that it would now be quite legitimate if we took special care to secure its thorough organisation, and concentrated in the Workers' and Peasants' Inspection a staff of workers really abreast of the times, i.e. not inferior to the best West European standards' (Lenin 1963: 829). Lenin proposed that a competition be held for a text-book on scientific management, and, during the 1920s, the movement spread in industry and the state apparatus. It had two main aims: to rationalize work and organizational structures, and to inculcate into workers and officials a knowledge of the principles of scientific management and habits of orderly, methodical, systematic, honest, and accountable work (Bendix 1969).[2]

The cyberneticians argue that cybernetics may be seen as the heir to Taylorism, and thus within the Leninist tradition. But they argue also that cybernetics is at a much higher scientific level and that, moreover, the revolution in science and technology has brought important changes in the relationship between science and politics. These changes have been summarized thus: '. . . in connection with the new revolution in science and technology . . . the objective tendency of development of socialist society is such that even the natural sciences are exercising more and more influence on the processes of managing society, on the working out and realisation of the party's political programme' (Kireev 1968:30). There are numerous interpretations of the revolution in science and technology, but its two main characteristics are recognized to be: the development of technologies which replace and augment man's mental activity; and the emergence of natural science as a direct productive force, providing new technologies which can contribute to economic growth, military power, and public welfare. The revolution in science and technology, the origins of which are to be found in the 1950s, has been marked by a rapid expansion in the scale of research and development, and by increasing prominence for science policy as an area of government activity. The influence of natural science on social science lies in the help which cybernetics and mathematics offer in solving the problems of managing society. Thus, natural science is seen to be providing the social sciences with techniques and facilities which enable them to play a more important role in policy-making.

The assertion of such a role for the natural sciences may be viewed with scepticism by those who recall the Lysenko affair. But the revolution in science and technology has been accompanied by a major shift in the relationship between scientific truth and political authority which makes a repetition of that affair unlikely. In the mid-1950s the Central Committee began tacitly to relinquish its claim to authority in natural science, which consequently became depoliticized. Authority in the natural sciences – which may be defined as the right to say what constitutes scientific truth – is now vested in the scientific community: natural scientific truth has come to be defined as that which scientists affirm and believe to be true. Thus, the realization by the party and state bureaucracies that natural scientific research was providing the basis for new industrial and military technologies has been accompanied by a new attitude towards the scientific community, by a recognition of their authority as masters of an autonomous area of esoteric expertise. Of course, greater intellectual autonomy for natural scientists has not meant the abandonment of efforts to ensure that natural science serves political purposes; quite the contrary (see Holloway 1970; Schapiro 1972).

The revival of Soviet social science can be seen in terms of the same shift in the relationship between science and authority, though it is clear that Soviet social scientists do not share the same degree of intellectual autonomy enjoyed by the natural scientists. During the 1950s and 1960s, some natural scientists, in particular mathematicians and computer specialists, played the role of midwife in the rebirth of the social sciences, and thus lent to them some of their own scientific authority. The natural sciences are seen to have provided the social sciences with new decision-making techniques and data-processing facilities, and with a cybernetic model of government which interprets the problems of policy-making in such a way as to encourage the maximum use of those techniques and facilities. In spite of the early claims made on its behalf, cybernetics has not served as a major source of specific models of social behaviour; the intellectual traditions of Soviet social science are more influential in this regard. But the cybernetic model of government does envisage an important role for the social sciences in government, in providing information about the state of society, and in helping to improve decision-making techniques and structures. While the individual scholar may be inspired by curiosity about Soviet society, the party and state bureaucracies look to the social sciences for help in solving the problems of governing that society. Thus, both natural and social sciences are valued by bureaucratic groups primarily for their instrumental uses.

THE CYBERNETIC MODEL: ACCEPTANCE AND CRITICISMS

The attraction of the cybernetic model for the Soviety party and state bureaucracies lies not only in its instrumental uses and the fact that it can be interpreted as part of the Leninist tradition of 'technocratic rationalization'. Also there exists a fundamental congruence between the Marxist–Leninist concept of policy-making as it has developed in the Soviet Union, and the principles of the cybernetic approach to the management of society. In both cases, there is an emphasis on control and management: both are purposive and goal-oriented; both claim to be, in some sense, scientific; both underline the need for a systemic or holistic approach; the one seeks correct policies, the other optimal solutions; the one stresses democratic centralism, the other the hierarchical nature of control systems. Consequently, the cybernetic model matches, in certain important structural respects, the view of policy-making held by the state and party bureaucracies.

Yet mere congruence cannot explain the popularity of cybernetics. It must be asked why, if Marxism-Leninism already provides a scientific guide to political practice, cybernetics should have such a great appeal; and what, if the cybernetic and Marxist–Leninist concepts of policy-making are congruent, cybernetics has to offer that is new. The answer to these questions must be sought at two levels. In the first place, there has been a general recognition within the Soviet bureaucracies that the ideal of scientific policy-making has not always been attained, and that the policy-making process requires to be improved. This recognition was most clearly expressed in the de-Stalinization campaign of the 1950s and early 1960s and in the criticism of Khrushchev's 'hare-brained schemes, hasty and rash decisions' after he had been removed from power. These attacks were more than an attempt to justify changes in policy, for the experience of Stalinist 'voluntarism' and Khrushchev's 'subjectivism' demonstrated – not least to those bureaucratic groups who had suffered – the need to raise the quality of policy-making. During the 1960s cybernetics, systems analysis, and operational research came to be seen as a way of improving the policy-making process, of giving the concept of scientific government a new content. Thus, the Soviet debates parallel those in the United States about planning-programming-budgeting systems, and in Britain about the role of the Public Expenditure Survey Committee and Programme Analysis and Review. Therefore, in one sense, the cybernetic model is related to the systems approach that has influenced thinking about policy-making and government organization in advanced capitalist societies.

But the second and more important reason for the search for new techniques of management and control is to be found not in the acknowledgement of past failings, but in the consciousness of present difficulties. In the mid-1950s the Soviet economic system entered a new phase of development, in which it became clear that the existing arrangements for planning and administration could not cope with the growing complexity of the economy. The growth in the number of economic units – and of the relationships between those units – seemed in the mid-1950s to take on a new significance. Moreover, economic growth was coming to depend less on increases in the labour force than on increases in labour productivity through technological innovation. The complexity is not to be explained by objective factors alone, however, for subjective elements too played an important role. The post-Stalin leadership began, by virtue of their collective nature, to espouse priorities which were more complex than Stalin's. Besides, they were less able – or less willing – to enforce their priorities in the draconian Stalinist manner. Thus the complexity of economic planning and administration became a major preoccupation of the party and state bureaucracies in the mid-1950s; and since that time two major economic reforms – in 1957 and 1965 – have been implemented to cope with it.

Cybernetics, as the science of optimal control of complex dynamic systems, promises a solution to the problem of managing complexity. I have already outlined briefly the way in which the cybernetic model tries to do this: by emphasizing the hierarchical, multi-level nature of control processes, the utility of new decision-making techniques, and the uses of the new data-processing technology. However, at the same time, improved management and control is to be achieved by a shift in emphasis away from administrative methods of control to reliance on social and economic instruments – for example, profit, market prices, interest rates, incentive systems. Control is to be achieved by increasing reliance on instruments which are relevant to the social and economic relationships in the sub-systems to be controlled. Moreover, control from the centre can be strengthened if certain areas of limited self-regulation are permitted – for example, through the market mechanism, or through autonomous social control in the scientific community. Control is seen as the regulation of a system in accordance with its objective laws of development. Thus, within a congruent policy-making concept, important shifts are advocated in the instruments of rule: in general terms an information or 'steering' model is argued for in place of a power and coercion model. This advocacy is clearly relevant to the form of domination exercised by bureaucratic groups in Soviet society, and is therefore a political argument of great importance.

However, the cybernetic model is not unanimously accepted in the Soviet Union, either as a description of the structure of policy-making or as a prescription of how policy ought to be made; moreover, the proposals of the economic and social cyberneticians have not been implemented or endorsed in full. Nevertheless, the cybernetic model reflects and embraces important trends in the development of Soviet organizational structures and instruments of rule: for example, in the rationalization of economic management through the introduction of automated management systems at the sectoral level, and in the shift towards the use of economic instruments of management, as evidenced in the 1965 reform. Although it is difficult to know how influential the cybernetic model is in the party and state bureaucracies, the publicity it has received in the press, at seminars, and in policy discussions suggests widespread acceptance. Thus, at the new Institute of Economic Management which was opened in Moscow in January 1971, to provide three-month courses for Ministers, their deputies and heads of departments, the first lecture was given by the director of the Institute of Cybernetics in Kiev.

Nevertheless, several fundamental criticisms of the cybernetic model have been made by Soviet writers. It has been argued, for example, that the cybernetic model is too abstract and vague to be of any immediate practical value, since it has to be fleshed out with concrete definitions of control and management in specific cases; and cyberneticians are sometimes criticized for making extravagant claims (see Gvishiani 1972: 17ff.). It is certainly true that it is only the general framework, and not the specific models, that cybernetics has provided for the optimal planning school. In fact, cybernetics does not seem to have lived up to its claim of being able to transfer knowledge from one discipline to another, for example, from physiology to economics. But the over-all model is implicit in the partial approaches and provides a general orientation and legitimation for them.

A second, and more fundamental criticism has declared that any scientific approach to managing society requires '. . . full information, unprejudiced thinking and creative freedom. Until these conditions are met (and, moreover, not just for certain individuals, but for the masses) all talk about scientific management will remain just idle chatter' (Sakharov *et al.* 1970: 164). This criticism has been made not in the official, but in the *samizdat*, literature; but there is some evidence to show that at least some of the cyberneticians would share this view. This criticism is often based on an alternative model of scientific politics, which draws its inspiration not from cybernetics or an individual theory, but from a particular conception of the way in which scientists pursue the truth – with reasoned argument and free flows of information. This view of scientific politics is not derived from a high regard for the instrumental uses of science, but from the high respect for the values which are said to be inherent in the activity of research itself.

Further, it has been argued that to define control or management as the regulation of a social system in accordance with its objective laws of development is inadequate for capitalist societies, since management of this kind would entail the destruction of the capitalist state (Burlatskii 1970: 84ff.). Consequently, it is an unsatisfactory definition of management in general. This criticism is fundamental, since it implies that the whole question of management cannot be understood outside the context of a specific social system: thus management or administration in capitalist systems is to be understood in terms of the class system alone. It might be claimed that the same point is valid for Soviet society. But the Soviet cyberneticians are able to argue, in the light of the official Soviet definition of the social system, that Soviet society contains no antagonistic contradictions and that the cybernetic concept of control is thus applicable. The canonization of the Stalinist definition of Soviet society thereby makes possible an acceptance of the cybernetic model without any critical reference to the social and economic system in which it is to be applied.

An objection of quite a different sort has also been made. The cyberneticians have been accused of attempting to undermine the party's leading role in Soviet society. This objection has been made in the military establishment, where the role of the political officer seemed to be threatened by innovations in command and control; and in the discussions about economic planning there has been a running battle between the economic cyberneticians and the political economists. Also, it seems clear that some party and state officials think that party leadership would be weakened if the optimal planning proposals were adopted. However, this kind of conflict should not be overemphasized, for the discussions which have taken place could not have done so without party approval. Nevertheless, it is significant in so far as it reflects institutional and bureaucratic conflicts arising out of generational differences and the greater role now being taken by the scientific-technical intelligentsia in administration, policy-making, and public debate. For the cybernetic model of government not only promises a solution to the problems of managing complexity, but also stresses the role of technical expertise – and of the technically expert – in administration and management.

The cybernetic model of government has thus obtained widespread, but not universal, acceptance in Soviet social science. Within its framework, far-reaching proposals for change have been put forward. The failure to implement the proposed reforms has been seen by some as evidence of the inflexibility of the Soviet system as a whole. But such a judgment under-estimates the importance of the cybernetic model in providing another publicly available mode of discussion about politics and policies. Yet, it is clear that, as a mode of discussion about politics, the cybernetic model has severe limitations. The report of a conference in 1969 describes one of the papers thus:

> 'The speaker based his theses on the fact that there exists a contradiction between the necessity to work out the principles of optimal, or rational from the point of view of society as a whole, decisions, and the fact that the interests of members of society and of various social groups diverse. In this connection he made an attempt to describe several systems regulating the life of society, and enumerated the concepts and categories which, in his opinion, are necessary for the discussion of optimality. Among these the speaker included the democratic mechanism for the self-regulation of social life, the "value" orientation of society, the role of science (i.e. of specialists) and so on.' (Ellman 1971:19)[3]

The paper has not been published, and the questions raised have received little public discussion in the Soviet Union. This means that the new mode of discussion is confined largely to technical problems of management and the possibility of creating new instruments of domination. Moreover, the Leninist tradition has been distorted in so far as one element – that of technocratic rationalization – has been stressed, while that of democratic control over the state apparatus has been neglected (Hegedus 1970:28–56). Thus, the cybernetic model provides a mode of discussion which promises to rationalize and make more efficient the bureaucratic centralist state, but does not allow the question of its democratization to be raised.

CONCLUSION

I have argued in this paper that there exists in Soviet social science a cybernetic model of government that provides an orientation for social science, in the sense of defining its research problems and political role. This model is congruent with the customary Soviet model of policy-making in several important respects, and can be interpreted in terms of the Leninist tradition. However, the explanation for the model's influence lies not in this congruence, nor in its natural-scientific credentials, but in the help it seems to offer the party and state bureaucracies in managing the complexity of Soviet society. The model not only embraces new techniques of decision-making and management, but emphasizes also new instruments of domination, though not necessarily to the exclusion of the state's traditional means of coercion. The cybernetic model has provided a new mode of discussion in Soviet politics, but it is one which excludes the question of democratic control over the exercise of power. I have not discussed the technical adequacy of the various partial models, nor indeed asked whether the cybernetic model as it emerges in Soviet social science is truly cybernetic. But I wish finally to touch on some general issues that arise out of the analysis so far.

Natural and social scientists are being brought more frequently into the processes of policy-making and policy debate, as a result of the increasing contacts between research institutions and government organizations. This phenomenon has been described as a new stage in the rationalization of power, through the extension of rational decision-making criteria and instrumental modes of action into various areas of social life (see Habermas 1968:120). It is clear that this process of relating scientific knowledge to political ends is vastly more complex than is suggested either by the decisionistic model, in which the politician merely uses new knowledge as an instrument, or by the technocratic model, in which the politician becomes a mere agent for the scientific-technical intelligentsia. Habermas points to a pragmatistic model in which expert and policy-maker interact in such a way that the interests of both are reflected in the ensuing decisions (see Habermas 1968:120). In the Soviet Union, the autonomization of scientific authority in the 1950s provided the basis for such an interaction; and it is clear that this interaction has furthered both the purposes of bureaucratic groups and the interests of the scientific community.

Nevertheless, there have been considerable difficulties in institutionalizing this relationship. If the rationalizers are to be effective, they must help to identify problems, criticize existing arrangements and propose reforms. But they must do this within an intellectual and institutional framework which ultimately strengthens the existing system of power relationships and reinforces their legitimacy. The disputes about the revival of economics, sociology, and political science show how difficult it has been to establish this kind of role. The party is extremely jealous of its own prerogatives in organizational and ideological work, and, especially since the Czechoslovak crisis of 1968, it has been wary of proposals for reform. The cybernetic model attempts to define an area of legitimate rationalization in such a way as to make the existing social system more efficient, but not to change its features in a fundamental way. Through its scientific claims, its instrumental approach and its congruence with the Soviet concept of government, the cybernetic model legitimates the Soviet system as a whole, in the very process of carrying through partial reforms, precisely by pointing to the possibilities that the system offers for scientific and rational government. Therefore, the cybernetic model promises to rationalize the existing system of power relationships, not to destroy it, and is thus appropriate to a social system which is regarded by its ruling groups as being in a state of equilibrium.

Therefore, the acceptance of the cybernetic model is to be explained, not merely as a technical response to technical problems, but also in terms of its political functions. It has been argued that Taylorism and Fordism in the 1920s '. . . evoked a European resonance less for their strictly technical features than for their social and political implications' (Maier 1970:28).

The Americanist vision of productivity, expertise, and optimization seemed to provide an escape from class conflict and social division. It offered the hope that power might be sublimated into questions of optimization, thus promising technical solutions to problems of political power and political action. In the same way, it may be said that the cybernetic model is a modern version of this vision, which is attractive to bureaucratic groups precisely because it seems to offer technical solutions to social and economic problems, without entailing major shifts in political power. But the arguments about economic reform, and the proposals for an optimally functioning economic system, have shown that questions of political power and practice arise even in discussions of the technical problems of decision-making and management. These arguments have led inevitably to the questioning of political arrangements and bureaucratic interests. The distinction between technical questions and questions of political power and practice is not clear-cut. Although the cybernetic model is an inadequate mode of discussion from the point of view of democratic control, questions of political power and practice are discussed in its terms, albeit in a veiled, restricted, and unreflexive way.

The Soviet bureaucracies do not appear to have in mind a radical transformation of Soviet society, but seem rather to pursue better management of a stable system. This is reflected in the concept of rationality embodied in the cybernetic model – in particular in the optimal planning proposals – and in the Taylorist movement, which had been revived in the 1960s. This rationality is appropriate to a society which is regarded as being in a state of equilibrium, and hence differs from the rationality of Stalinist rule, with its goal of transforming Soviet society. The Stalinist concept was reflected in the methods of economic planning and in the Stakhanovite movement, with their emphasis on zeal, haste, and enthusiasm. Whether the cybernetic vision of a scientifically managed society can be realized within the present system of power relationships – or indeed at all – is a question that cannot be answered merely by discussing the model itself. The development of Soviet society will not be determined by ideas alone. Nevertheless, an analysis of the cybernetic model reveals some of the changes taking place in Soviet society and politics. The fact that discussion of managerial rationalization leads to at least some questioning of power relationships suggests that no radical rationalization can be carried through without a redistribution of power as either its cause or its effect.

NOTES

1 The fullest statement of this model is to be found in Afanas'ev, V. G. 1967. *Nauchnoe upravlenie obshchestvom.* Moscow: Politizdat. It is also available in English under the title *The Scientific Management of Society.* 1971. Moscow: Progress Publishers. It should be noted that the Russian word *upravlenie* can be translated as control, administration management, or government (in the sense of the activity of government).

2 See the collection of documents from the 1920s in *Nauchnaya organizatsiya truda, proizvodstva i upravleniya.* 1969. Moscow.

3 *Ekonomika i matematicheskie metody*, 1969. No. 5: 791. Quoted by Ellman 1971:19.

REFERENCES

AFANAS'EV, V. G. 1967. *Nauchnoe upravlenie obshchestvom.* Moscow: Politizdat. Translated by L. Ilyitskaya 1971: *The Scientific Management of Society.* Moscow: Progress Publishers.

—1972. *Nauchno-tekhnicheskaya* (see note 2) *revolutsiya, upravlenie, obrazovanie.* Moscow: Politizdat.

ASHBY, W. R. 1956. *An Introduction to Cybernetics.* New York: John Wiley and Sons.

BENDIX, R. 1969. Private and Public Authority in Western Europe and Russia. In *Nation-Building and Citizenship.* New York: Anchor Books Doubleday.

BIRYUKOV, B. V., BRAGINA, L. M., GAVRILETS, YU. N., DOBROV, G. M., LYAKHOV, I. I., NOVIK, I. B., SPIRKIN, A. G., TYUKHTIN, V. S. and

FARBER, V. G. 1967. Filosofskie problemy kibernetiki. In A. I. Berg (ed.), *Kibernetiku – na sluzhbu kommunizmu* Vol. 5. Moscow: Energiya.

BURLATSKII, F. M. 1970. *Lenin, Gosudarstvo, Politika.* Moscow: Nauka.

DECHERT, C. R. 1966. The Development of Cybernetics. In A. Etzioni (ed.), *A Sociological Reader on Complex Organisations* (2nd edition). New York: Holt Rhinehart Winston, Inc.

DEUTSCH, K. 1963. *The Nerves of Government.* New York: The Free Press.

EASTON, D. 1965. *A Systems Analysis of Political Life.* New York: John Wiley and Sons.

ELLMAN, MICHAEL. 1971. *Soviet Planning Today. Proposals for an Optimally Functioning Economic System.* Cambridge: Cambridge University Press.

GVISHIANI, D. 1972. *Organisation and Management.* Moscow: Progress Publishers.

HABERMAS, J. 1968. Verwissenschaftlichte Politik und Öffentliche Meinung. In *Technik und Wissenschaft als 'Ideologie'*. Berlin: Suhrkamp Verlag.

HARDT, J. P., HOFFENBERG, M., KAPLAN, N. and LEVINE, H. S. (eds.) 1967. *Mathematics and Computers in Soviet Economic Planning.* New Haven and London: Yale University Press.

HEGEDUS, A. 1970. Marxist Theories of Leadership and Bureaucracy: A Marxist approach. In R. B. Farrell (ed.), *Political Leadership in Eastern Europe and the Soviet Union.* London: Butterworths.

HOLLOWAY, D. 1970. Scientific Truth and Political Authority in the Soviet Union. *Government and Opposition* **5** (3): 345–67.

——1971. Technology, Management and the Soviet Military Establishment. *Adelphi Papers* No. 76 April. London: Institute for Strategic Studies.

KIREEV, A. V. 1968. Nauchnyi kharakter politiki KPSS. In V. G. Afanas'ev (ed.), *Nauchnoe upravlenie obshchestvom.* No. 2. Moscow: *Mysl'*.

LENIN, V. I. 1963. *Better Fewer, but Better.* Selected Works. Vol. 3. London: Lawrence and Wishart.

MACKENZIE, W. J. M. 1967. *Politics and Social Science.* Harmondsworth: Penguin.

MAIER, C. S. 1970. Between Taylorism and Technocracy: European ideologies and the vision of industrial productivity in the 1920s. *Journal of Contemporary History* **5** (2): 28.

SAKHAROV, A. D., TURCHIN, V. F. and MEDVEDEV, R. A. 1970. From an open letter to the CPSU Central Committee. *Survey,* Summer.

SCHAPIRO, L. (ed.) 1972. *Political Opposition in One-Party States.* London: Macmillan.

SEDOVA, E. L. 1972. Kibernetika i upravlenie obshchestvom. In V. G. Afanas'ev (ed.), *Nauchnoe upravlenie obshchestvom* No. 6. Moscow: Mysl'.

WIENER, N. 1954. *The Human Use of Human Beings.* 2nd edition. New York: Doubleday Anchor Books.

Integrative and disintegrative social structures in decision-making groups

PETER ABELL

INTRODUCTION

In recent years, much ingenuity has been directed towards understanding collective decision processes; given a set of individuals, each with a clearly defined preference ranking over a set of possible policies, the problem of describing a collective decision, under the imposition of different sorts of decision rules, has been studied both by welfare economists and, more recently, by political scientists. The, by now, classical contribution of Arrow (1951), with his general impossibility theorem, has stimulated many subsequent attempts to get around this apparent paradox. Economists and mathematically oriented social psychologists have paid a great deal of attention to decision-making under risk and uncertainty. The area is one which has, for obvious reasons, attracted the attention of mathematically trained social scientists with the consequence that the theoretical structures are some of the most elegant in social science. However, the empirical success of these various formalistic approaches is something less than satisfactory; when faced with 'real live ongoing' collective decision processes, empirical complexity is almost invariably far too rich to be caught by relatively simple models. In so far as any empirical success has been forthcoming, it has usually been at the hands of the experimentalist with comparatively simple group experiments in the laboratory situation.

The sociologist interested in collective decision-making in large complex organizations finds little comfort in the available formal models. This is for many reasons, but in general this discomfort arises from 'empirical complexity'; the salient problems seem to be:

1 In many decision-making contexts there is little reason to suppose that preference rankings are clearly defined or stable over time. This difficulty could be overcome by 'learning theories' and theories of preference dynamics. But the likelihood of developing these sorts of theory, sufficiently rich to embrace the full local complexity residing in each decision-maker's 'consciousness' seems to me, to say the least, remote.
2 It is characteristically the case that decision-making groups face novel situations where established preference patterns are not good predictors. It might be possible to devise preference rankings at a sufficiently abstract level to enable one to embrace apparently novel situations. The sociologists' conception of deep-lying value systems should be helpful here, but as far as I know, has not proved so in practice.
3 Decision-making rarely revolves around some well-defined decision rule (e.g. majority rule). The patterns of influence, power (exercised and potential), compromise, 'playing the waiting game', and so on, all influence the process of decision-making.

At the risk of belabouring the obvious – decision-making groups comprise human beings (albeit playing roles) and thus all the idiosyncrasies and nuances for which they are fortunately renowned. The important question is, can one enter a complex ongoing decision-making process at a sufficiently abstract level to render it amenable to systematic social science?

In this paper I want to adopt an avowedly sociological approach to the group decision-making process. In so doing, I am not rejecting the more traditional approaches, but merely exploring a rather different line of enquiry. What I want to try and show is:

1 That decision-making groups (empirical groups of marketing executives in large industrial enterprises) if they 'exist', for any significant period of time, can fruitfully be studied in terms of their social structures. In particular, the distribution of what I will term *deep-lying integrative and disintegrative functional relations.*
2 That such distributions bear a systematic relation to the 'performance' of the group in making adequate decisions.

3 That environmental novelty is an important consideration in understanding the 'optimal' social structure of decision-making groups.

The paper is intended as a further contribution to an approach I am trying to develop in sociology which, for the want of a better word, I term *globalism* (Abell 1974). The basic idea is to conceptually embrace complex social structures as *total entities* and in so doing establish invariances describing their dynamics and statistics. It is an approach that attempts to move away from the full 'local complexity' residing in individual persons, towards global structure relevance. If I may be permitted a rather loose metaphor – social structures make sense when the parts are put together correctly – rather in the way a jig-saw makes sense. But in general, there are very many ways (equivalences) of designing the jig-saw whilst still preserving the same global picture.

DEFINING SOCIAL STRUCTURES

A closed[1] social structure comprises the following elements:

1 A set of *actors* $P = \{p_i\}$, $i = 1, 2, \ldots, n$. (The actors may be individual persons or social collectivities[2] (Abell 1971).)
2 A set of social relations (5) $R = \{r_i\}$, $i = 1, 2, \ldots, m$, each mapping P into itself. That is, each r_i generates a set of ordered pairs of the form $p_j\, r_i\, p_k$ from $P \times P$.
3 A set of properties $X = \{x_i\}$, $i = 1, 2, \ldots, k$, of the elements of set P. The properties may or may not lend themselves to some sort of measure. Perhaps the most common measure in sociology is a *linear order* of values of the property in question.
4 A set $Y = \{y_i\}$, $i = 1, 2, \ldots, 1$ of ways of parametrizing the social relations – for example 'strength', 'frequency of use', 'length of time in existence', and so on. The elements y_i will lend themselves to various sorts of measure.

MATHEMATICAL DEPICTION OF SOCIAL STRUCTURES

There is a variety of ways in which a social structure, as defined above, can be represented mathematically. If we initially ignore the sets X and Y and concentrate solely on P and R, then the following are some of the alternative mathematical depictions:

1 A set of m *graphs* (di-graphs if any r_i are non-symmetric) of the form $G_i = (P_i; r_i)$ or alternatively as a *multigraph*.
2 A set of m *associated matrices* M_i, $i = 1, 2, \ldots, m$ with entries m_{jk} of unity if $p_j\ r_i\ p_k$ and zero otherwise.
3 A set of *simplicial cluster complexes* of the form $K (P_i; r_i)$ and $K (P_i; r_i^{-1})$ $i = 1, 2, \ldots, m$. $K (P_i; r_i) = K (P_i; r_i^{-1})$ if r_i is symmetric.[3]

Since none of these simple representations takes into account either the properties of the elements of P or the parameters on r_i, we speak of them as *underlying structures*.

If sets X and Y are incorporated into the picture, then the structures can also be represented in a variety of ways:

4 As a set of *vector labelled graphs*[4] $G_i = (P_i; r_i, X, Y)$.
5 Simplicial complexes can be generated in a variety of ways by *filtering* the structure on the values of set Y (see Note 3).

In the present paper, I will make most use of the simplicial complex depiction as this brings out the structural features I wish to focus attention upon.

THE CONCEPT OF SOCIAL RELATION

Our model of social structure rests heavily on the concept of 'social' relation – what is implied by the adjective social? It may help to motivate the discussion if we consider a relationship like 'friendship' and see what is involved in this patently obvious social relation. If we say two persons A and B are in a relation of friendship it seems, at the very least, to imply:

(a) that A will behave in certain ways towards B in certain circumstances. Likewise B will behave towards A in certain ways (not necessarily identical).
(b) that A and B will entertain certain sentiments and beliefs about each other.
(c) that A and B will interpret (attach meanings to) each other's behaviour and their own as appropriate to friendship. Technically the behaviour becomes *action*.
(d) that A will believe that B entertains certain appropriate sentiments and beliefs about A himself – and vice versa.
(e) that A and B will *expect* in the future, other things being equal,

a continuation of the sentiments, beliefs, and action. (Laying the foundation for the relationship to be institutionalized into social roles and the generation of *rules* which govern the exchanges).

(f) that the sets of exchange behaviours/acts will depend on the cultural context of the relation. For example, the word 'friendship' would be used by the actors themselves to describe different sorts of exchanged acts (content) in different contexts. The *content* of a social relation is thus not culturally invariant. This variation may occur even in micro-structural contexts. For instance, in an organization, the content of a friendship relation between 'superior' and 'subordinate' may well be very different to that between subordinates.

(g) *inter-structural interaction:* the content of different social relations, over the same ordered pair of actors may interact, in the sense that the content of each relation mutually modifies the other. This seems to imply that, if one wishes to understand the detailed content of social relations, then one must attempt a study of the *totality* of relations between any two actors.

(h) *intra-structural interaction:* The content of a social relationship between A and B is influenced by the other relationships of the same type that A and B have with other parties.

Even this rather cursory glance at the complexities of the concept of social relation gives some impression of the empirical difficulties associated with a socio-structural analysis. These problems are particularly acute if the structure is changing relatively rapidly, when the time necessary to determine the nature of the structure becomes commensurate with its rate of change.[5] In circumstances like this, it becomes empirically unfeasible to trace out the full local complexity in all but the smallest social structures and one must attempt to embrace the structure at a more global level.[6] The following sections of this paper present a rather meagre attempt in this direction.

INTEGRATIVE AND DISINTEGRATIVE RELATIONS

Returning now to our central concern – the social structure of ongoing decision-making groups. Clearly, in the process of making decisions collectively, a group of individuals will set up a complex pattern of social relationships, and furthermore one would expect with changing preferences, and 'coalitions', etc., some of these to fluctuate over time, especially with groups facing novel situations.[7] In attempting to study such processes, I ran into the problems of complexity mentioned above and came to the conclusion that despite the complexity of the *surface structure* of day-to-day relationships, there was a relatively enduring pattern of deep-structure (deep-lying *functional relations*) which could be handled given reasonable empirical resources. Moreover, I was led to the conclusion that this deep structure bore a systematic relationship to the performance of the groups (as collectivities).

In the particular empirical context under investigation, I want to suggest that it is helpful to concentrate upon two types of deep-lying functional relations between individuals – *integrative* and *disintegrative*. The abstract expressions give a pretty good idea of what I am driving at: integrative relations are those that tend to bind decision-makers together, disintegrative relations the reverse, they imply social estrangement. I cannot pretend that this rather cursory statement is anything less than equivocal, but by integrative relations I mean enduring trust, mutual reliance, positive affectivity, frequent agreement on basic issues and so on. This does not mean that the relationship will be without conflict (Georg Simmel, a very long time ago, noted that one characteristic of really 'close' relationships is that they may permit a high level of conflict without entirely disrupting the relation). Disintegrative relations are associated with a certain level of mistrust, lack of reliance, low affectivity and perhaps disagreement on very basic issues.

The reader might object, at this stage, that these various sorts of orientation should be kept separate, for surely one can trust someone and at the same time dislike them and vice versa. My retort would be couched in terms of my complexity argument, and anyway the proof of the pudding is in the eating – can we explain anything significant using these 'deep-lying' summary relations more effectively than by considering each orientation separately? I wish to suggest that we can.[8]

Before continuing with our basic empirical problem, I will set out in greater detail the methodology of deep-lying functional relation analysis.

If we bear in mind the opening remarks of this paper, concerning the unfeasibility of empirically studying the detailed micro-process of social decision-making, then we can see the present methodology as a response to this problem. The procedure is broken into two stages: (a) establishing the surface lexicon and (b) constructing the functional relation scale.

In order to establish the surface lexicon the researchers established a close and informal contact with a sample of members of the decision-making group and invited them to *ad lib* about 'the problems associated with a group of *colleagues* working together in a department'. There was very little attempt to direct or structure the responses. The subjects were invited not to identify individuals but rather the range of problems and issues that arise. The informal replies were then examined to establish the types of abstract nouns, verbs, adjectives, etc., which the individuals used in responding to the question. A typical sequence was as follows:

> 'It is important to be able to *rely* on your colleagues – life is so complex these days that one must be in a position to *trust* fellows to get on with the job. It's nice, of course, if one can *get on* with people, one needs a *pleasant* atmosphere – a few *friends* help, don't you think!'

The key words are italicized. Characteristically, it was found that in sessions of this sort the same words were used to describe the colleague relationship. This enables us to establish a surface lexicon of typical interpersonal orientations that individuals take up and regard as important to the colleague relationship. The assumption must be made, of course, that the words carry the same connotations for the individuals. There is not, needless to say, universal agreement, but words like 'trust', 'rely', and 'efficient' occurred with great regularity.

Adopting our model of social structure then, it would seem possible to construct a sub-structure for each type of orientation (relation). We could thus speak of 'trust structures', 'friendship structures', and so on. Each structure could be analysed separately. However, it appears that such an approach would fail to take into account what I will term the *functional coherence* of structures in complex ongoing, decision-making situations. The surface structures (derived from the surface lexicon) tend to cluster in the sense that if one is friendly towards another, then one normally trusts him. However, the clustering must be less than perfect, if this were not the case, any one of the surface structures would be analytically as powerful as any other. In a group facing a variety of decisions, the 'trust structure' is 'activated' for some decisions and the 'efficiency structure' for others. The important point being that the different sorts of surface structure integrate the individuals for different decision problems. Thus, for certain decisions one needs 'efficiency', for others some close 'friends' with whom to discuss the issues. What is more, the idea of functional coherence implies a spill-over effect such that if the different orientations are all present between the same ordered pair, effective social interaction is enhanced – when trust is needed, it is easier to interact with a friend you trust, and so on. Thus, we operate with a deep-lying functional relation that provides functional coherence over a variety of decisions and appropriately activated structures.[9] The second stage is to construct a scale of the functional relation from the surface lexicon (see below).

INTEGRATIVE AND DISINTEGRATIVE STRUCTURES

Consider the *underlying structure* generated by two relations A (integrative) and N (disintegrative) over a set P of actors. Furthermore, for the sake of initial simplicity, we will assume that A and N are symmetric relations. Mathematical nicety will also dictate that we treat A as reflexive – i.e., an actor is integratively linked to himself, a not unreasonable assumption (schizophrenics apart!)

Thus, there will be, in an *incomplete* structure, three types of symmetrically ordered pairs, those in A, those in N, and null (O) pairs. Null pairs occur if either p_i does not know p_j (impossible in the chosen empirical context) or if they are indifferent to one another. One could allow a pair to be related both by A and N, which would suggest ambivalence, but since empirically this situation seemed unimportant, we will exclude this complication from our analysis. Thus, in a *complete* structure each pair of actors will be related in A or N, not both.

We will make two further assumptions about the actors:

(i) *Postulate of unsegmented interaction* (Abell 1968); this assumption is intuitively easy to understand but difficult to express precisely. Broadly speaking the idea is that the actors in the ongoing group process do *not* interact in very different contexts. So that interaction between p_i and p_j takes place in the 'felt presence' of p_k.[10] Now, I am not just suggesting a common meeting of the three actors (for example in a committee), so that the relations are all contemporaneously face-to-face. That would be too strong an assumption. What I am suggesting is that over time, the group works sufficiently 'close together' to warrant us assuming that we have a situation where any two actors in their social exchange must take into account the others in the group. This leads to intra-structural interaction (see above).

(ii) Secondly, we assume that each actor perceives not only his relationship with others correctly, but also those between all other pairs of actors.[11]

Closely following developments in balance theory (Abell 1968) we postulate that for any three actors, p_i, p_j, and p_k, the following conditions are *balanced*:

$$p_i \, A \, p_j \wedge p_j \, A \, p_k \Rightarrow p_i \, A \, p_k \vee p_i \, O \, p_k \quad \text{— (1)}$$
$$p_i \, N \, p_j \wedge p_j \, N \, p_k \Rightarrow p_i \, A \, p_k \vee p_i \, O \, p_k \quad \text{— (2)}$$
$$p_i \, N \, p_j \wedge p_j \, A \, p_k \Rightarrow p_i \, N \, p_k \vee p_i \, O \, p_k \quad \text{— (3)}$$

Thus ruling out – as a balanced configuration – any three-cycles with an odd number of N relations. Generalizing to a structure on n-points, we would postulate that all the three cycles in the structure would conform to 'axioms' (1) to (3). If a structure is *complete* in A and N then there will be no null pairs and the first alternant only on the RHS of the axioms applies. In this paper, we confine our attention to such structures.

The basic idea behind the balance axioms is that they represent relatively strain-free states of affairs in contrast to imbalanced three-cycles (i.e., those containing an odd number of N relations) where it is postulated that they produce psychological strain for the actors involved (Taylor 1970). Also it has been suggested that disintegrative relations themselves provide additional strain.[12] In a structure of n-points a measure of global balance β (3) can be obtained by simply taking the ratio of balanced to total number of three-cycles in the structure. Clearly β (3) takes a value of unity when the structure is globally balanced. It is also possible to speak of *point-balance* and *arc-balance* by taking, in the first case, the ratio of balanced to imbalanced three-cycles a particular point is involved in, and in the second case the ratio of balanced to total three-cycles a particular arc (relation) is involved in. We can then define a balanced matrix $[\theta]_{ij}$ —$i, j=1, 2, 3, \ldots, n$, for any structure of n-points where the entries θ_{ij}, $i \neq j$ for all i and j give the value of arc-balance and θ_{ii} give the values of the point balance. Thus, $[\theta]_{ij}$ gives a picture of the distribution of 'strain' in the structure.

Consider a structure $G = (P_i; A, N)$. This will generate simplicial cluster sub-complexes $K(P_i; A) = K(P_i; A^{-1})$ and $K(P_i; N) = K(P_i; N^{-1})$ (Atkin 1974).

Theorem 1 In a complete balanced structure of n-points the sub-complex $K(P_i; A)$ will comprise a (n–1) simplex, if there are no negative relations in the structure and exclusive (unconnected) $(N - \o - 1)$ and $(\o - 1)$ simpleces, if there are two or more negative relations in the structure.[13]

(The reason for expressing the theorem in the language of simplicial complexes rather than the more conventional graph theoretic notions will become evident below.) The theorem clearly follows from the transitivity of A guaranteed by axiom (I) in a complete structure. Thus, we are led to the conclusion that if a complete structure is to eradicate its internal strain (due to imbalanced three-cycles), it will comprise either one 'integrated' group or two exclusive and exhaustive groups. Of course, they are equivalence classes in A. If disintegrative relations themselves lead to strain independently, then only the former condition will be strain-free.

When a complete structure departs from balance then the sub-complex $K(P_i; A)$ will usually have a characteristic pattern of q-connectivity and since we normally expect only moderate departures, a typical complex comprises two 'relatively' high dimension simpleces with relatively low dimension simpleces connecting them. If we are permitted to call the 'high' dimension simpleces cluster groups, then we can distinguish rather informally between three major structural types:[14]

(i) *core members of a cluster group*: those actors in relatively high dimension simpleces with integrative links only to other actors (points) in the same simplex (cluster group).

(ii) *boundary members of a cluster group:* those actors in relatively high dimension simpleces with integrative links outside the simplex. Boundary members may belong to two or more cluster groups.

(iii) *Interstials*: those actors in relatively low dimension simpleces on a path of q-connectivity between two or more simpleces of relatively high dimensions.

So, in general a balanced structure comprises core members only, whereas an imbalanced structure will also have boundary members and interstitials.

It should be noted in passing that boundary members are involved in a greater number of integrative bonds than core members. Indeed, this is also logically possible for interstitials. This implies that simply counting the number of integrative bonds an individual is involved in, is not necessarily a good indicator of over-all social integration of the individual – this depends on 'where the integrative bonds go'.

INTEGRATIVE AND DISINTEGRATIVE STRUCTURES IN DECISION-MAKING GROUPS

The formal theory developed in the preceding section suggests that balanced structures lead to a minimum of psychological tension within the group.[15] In this section I will present some empirical results, pertaining to decision-making groups in large organizations, which call into question the universal tendency for structures to minimize imbalance (i.e., to reduce tension). Basically, what I want to try and demonstrate is that when decision-making groups are faced with novel, non-routine environments, then a relatively unbalanced social structure is positively functional for the group, leading to a high performance. Conversely, with decision-making groups, in highly routine situations, high performance is associated with a balanced state of affairs. However, since the results rest upon observations made on seven decision-making groups only, they must be regarded as tentative, and any extrapolation might be extremely hazardous.

The study centres on seven groups of marketing executives, four operating in relatively stable market situations (by their own estimation) and three not.[16] They varied in size from eleven to fifteen members. Each group was rated as either of above or of below average performance on the testimony of the company senior executives.[17] Each member of the group was asked to score every other member in the group on an integrative–disintegrative scale derived from the surface lexicon, using a modified semantic differential technique.[18] Thus, for any pair of individuals we had A's assessment of B and vice versa. In four cases, it was found that A and B differed radically in their assessment in the sense that A evaluated B integratively whilst B evaluated A in the reverse manner. These were treated as disintegrative relations.[19] The scores were dichotomized into integrative and disintegrative relations.[20]

Table 1 gives the distribution of the seven groups categorized into four types, generated by a cross-classification of environmental stability against performance. Our problem is to see if we can discern any systematic differences between the functional structures of the groups.[21]

TABLE 1 Distribution of decision-making groups

	Stable environment	*Unstable environment*
High performance	A, B, C	D, E
Low performance	F	G

Much of the literature, both formal and informal, on group decision-making seems to rest upon the assumption, often implicit, that a high degree of consensus and social integration is essential to a high performance. Looking at it the other way round – dissensus and poor integration are likely to be unproductive. Concentrating on consensus takes us into the realm of individual preference rankings which we have already noted becomes empirically difficult in ongoing decision processes. Here, we concentrate upon the pair-wise social integration between members of the decision-making groups. Translating these ideas into structural terms, the implication seems inescapable – decision-making groups should not only have a balanced structure, but since balance permits polarization (therefore poor integration) we must go one step further and postulate a complete integration condition. In so far as a structure is unbalanced there is both a reduction in social integration (i.e., the presence of disintegrative relations) and the introduction of 'psychological tension'. Of course, a balanced, polarized structure would not generate tension, but the differentiation into two groups clearly lowers the social integration and permits any strain independently attributable to disintegrative relations. An inspection of *Table 2* shows that in stable, decision-making environments, the high performance groups tend to comprise a single grouping (i.e., they approximate to a complete integration condition). They consist of predominantly core members. However, the low performance group, F, has a very different sort of social structure. It has a low β (3) value, and is not significantly 'integrated' into a cohesive grouping. Thus, for stable environments the results lend tentative support for a theoretical structure depicted in *Figure 1* (*a*).

The interesting comparison is with the decision-making groups facing relatively non-routine, unstable environments. From *Table 2* it can be seen that the high performance groups (D and E) have relatively low β (3) scores whereas the low-performance group is

FIGURE 1 Decision-making, integration, and uncertainty

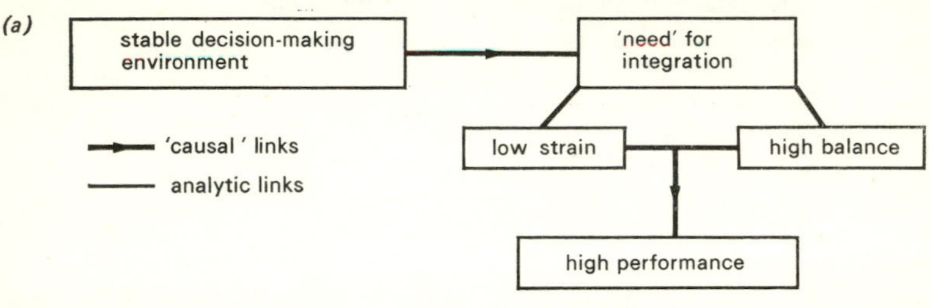

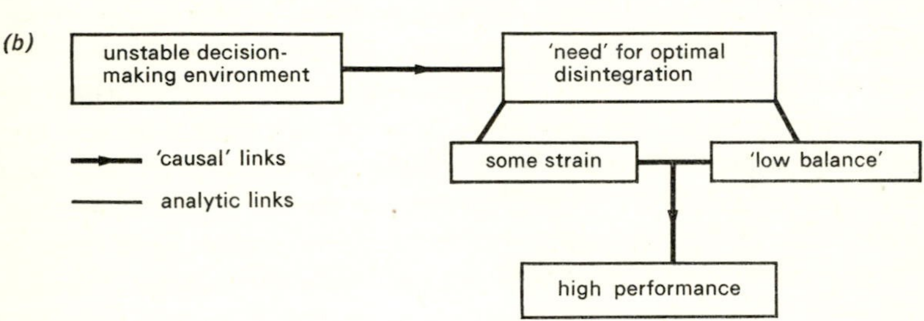

completely integrated, β (3) = 1·0. How can this be explained? It would appear that in unstable, decision-making environments a degree of social disintegration is functional for group performance. This does not seem unreasonable – groups facing non-routine problems must learn to innovate and an 'over' integrated social structure presumably operates against this possibility. In such situations a significant level of psychological tension will also perhaps be functional, and the optimal social structure will thus not be a balanced one. A bi-polarized structure is, of course, a possibility, but this can be ruled out as optimal since if a group is completely divided it will not be able to function at all as a collective entity. This sort of informal reasoning seems to be supported by the data in *Table 2* and the ideas are summarized in Figure 7 (b).

TABLE 2 The social structure of decision-making groups

Groups	β *(3)*	*Description of structure**
A	0·95	Single grouping
B	0·92	Single grouping
C	0·88	Single grouping
D	0·48	Two groupings with interstitials
E	0·59	Two groupings with interstitials
F	0·43	No significant grouping
G	1·00	Single grouping

* These descriptions are approximate.

THE 'CAUSAL' FORCE OF THE INTRA-STRUCTURAL BALANCE EFFECT

In the preceding sections we have repeatedly noted that it is possible to conceive of an individual actor as feeling interpersonal tension due to both the direct effects of disintegrative relations and the intra-structural effect of imbalanced three-cycles. The above results, though interesting, do not in any way establish the relative importance of each effect. Groups A, B, C, and G possess very few disintegrative relations and on either count the strain should be negligible. Group F, on the other hand, is highly imbalanced, possessing many disintegrative relations; any postulated tension could be a consequence of either or both of the direct and imbalance effects; similarly with groups D and E.

The only way to come to grips with this issue is to try and estimate the strength of the separate effects on the level of interpersonal tension felt by individuals. To this end, each executive was given a

TABLE 3 Average felt tension

Group	*Tension*
A	1·5
B	1·3
C	2·0
D	3·8
E	4·2
F	4·5
G	1·3

batch of questions aimed at measuring his 'general feelings of interpersonal tension in the work situation'. A simple index of tension was thus derived which could range from zero to five. The results in *Table 3* show the relative 'average' tension in the different groups.[22] These results are qualitatively entirely in accord with our general hypothesis connecting both imbalance and disintegrative relations with tension.

Let us now concentrate upon the variable 'felt interpersonal tension' (Y). We may postulate that Y is a function of:

(a) the number of A relations in which an actor is involved (X_1) – the direct A effect.
(b) the number of N relations in which an actor is involved (X_2) – the direct N effect.
(c) the number of balanced three-cycles in which an actor is involved (X_3).
(d) the number of imbalanced three-cycles in which an actor is involved (X_4).

Our previous deliberations would lead us to postulate:

$$\frac{\partial Y}{\partial X_1} < 0 \, ; \frac{\partial Y}{\partial X_2} > 0 \, ; \frac{\partial Y}{\partial X_3} < 0 \, ; \frac{\partial Y}{\partial X_4} > 0$$

Variables X_3 and X_4 can be collapsed by postulating that Y is a function of the point balance coefficient (above). Then we postulate:

$$\frac{\partial Y}{\partial \theta} < 0$$

In a similar vein the ratio $Z = X_2/X_1$ was used to measure the disintegrative/integrative ratio,[23] whence we postulate:

$$\frac{\partial Y}{\partial Z} > 0$$

A regression analysis[24] gave the following results:

$$\underset{(0{\cdot}60)}{y = 2{\cdot}5z} \quad + \quad \underset{(0{\cdot}45)}{1{\cdot}3\,\theta}$$

$$R^2 = 0{\cdot}52$$

$$r_{yz.\theta} = 0{\cdot}68 \quad ; \quad r_{y\theta.z} = 0{\cdot}35$$

They suggest that whilst both θ and Z have a significant effect on Y, Z has a stronger influence. Therefore, we may tentatively conclude that the direct 'causal' effect of N relations is greater than that of imbalanced three-cycles in determining the level of felt interpersonal tension.[25] The word 'cause' must, of course, be interpreted with some caution and since θ and Z exhibit multicolinearity the values of the coefficients should be taken as suggestive rather than conclusive.

NOTES

1 I will assume, for the sake of simplicity, that the social structure can be studied without reference to its environment. Of course, this is rarely, if ever the case, but the restriction will not alter the substance of my argument.

2 There are some rather thorny conceptual problems concerning the idea of collectivities as actors, but since in this paper we concentrate upon individuals the problem will be ignored. In fact, much of the complexity of social structures resides in the fact that they comprise units at different levels of abstraction in patterns of interrelatedness (Abell 1971).

3 Simplicial complexes can be generated in other ways, for example, the I-arc connected complex or the path complex see Peter Abell, 'Equivalence and Integration: Analysing Emergent Social Structure', mimeo, Imperial College, London.

4 Merely a graph where each vertex and/or arc has a vector of labels attached to it.

5 See Abell in John Rex (ed.), *Approaches to Sociology* 1974, where I suggest that 'primary cognitive constraint' on the practice of sociology often vitiates a methodological programme that suggests full descriptions of local complexity. See also Peter Abell, *The Ontological Foundations of Sociology: A Global Approach*. Forthcoming.

6 The methodological precept of such an approach is to treat descriptions of local complexity as '*unmeasured*' theoretical concepts, *contingently* leading to exchanged behaviours (or statements concerning these). The distribution of exchanged behaviours then has consequences at the level of the structure *per se*. So one's theoretical postulates (concerning local meaning etc.) can be deductively tested in the classical manner. An important point being that the same 'state' of a total structure is often reasonably *invariant* to changes at the local level. See note 5 for a further treatment of these issues.

7 I will assume that the membership of the decision-making group does not change.

8 This is, in effect, a colloquial way of restating the points alluded to in note 6. The question we have to ask ourselves is: given we wish to

explain the variation or stability of a certain 'group level variable' how much information do we need about the individuals comprising the group to adequately establish an explanation. In the analysis that follows the global pattern of functional relations is, in all cases, clearer cut than any one of the constituent structures and bears a more systematic relationship to the dependent variable performance.

9 The concept of functional coherence will be set out in more detail in a forthcoming publication. There have been many attempts to classify social interactions both empirically and conceptually: Foa, U. G. (1961), Convergences in the Analysis of the Structure of Interaction *Psychological Review* for instance, distinguishes dominance and affiliation. The present analysis is close to the notion of affiliation (and its reverse). Dominance relations, independent of affiliation seemed of little relevance in the basically 'democratic' style of the marketing groups. Although there were small differences in status within the groups (in terms of salary and length of service) they were not seen as important by the executives themselves in terms of internal relationships. The groups may thus be viewed as internally affiliative.

10 It seems to me that the general theory of 'felt or symbolic presence' is a much under-explored area in sociology.

11 This could, of course, be tested empirically.

12 See Taylor 1970. We will explore below the relative importance of the intra-structural effect due to three-cycles and the direct effect due to N links.

13 For a proof of this theorem see Abell 1968 or Taylor 1970 for the graph theoretic equivalent. In fact, the theory can be modified by dropping the stipulation that all N three-cycles are unstable when the analogous theorem suggests multi-polarization rather than bi-polarization. A somewhat similar situation arises in incomplete structures, see Abell 1968.

14 An interesting issue is the extent to which the different structural types generate allegiances to sub-groups as groups. I have explored these issues elsewhere: Abell, *Explorations in the Analysis of Organisational Structure* (mimeo). The definitions of the structural types given here are not mathematically rigorous.

15 If we allow that N links *per se* are strainful, then a situation of completion in A corresponds to a minimum in tension. In a balanced complete structure with some N links the level of strain will be a function of the number of N links and will reach a maximum when the n actors are bi-polarized into approximately equal sized subgroups (see below).

16 The stable market situations were characterized in two ways: a reasonably stable range of products and a fairly constant market

share. There was near universal agreement about stability or instability which seemed to make more elaborate measures superfluous.

17 Once again this relatively unsophisticated measure was given high validity. The two low-performance groups were selected precisely because of their performance. There was universal agreement about their low performance.

18 Each executive was asked to 'score' each of his colleagues on a series of simple polar opposites: reliable – unreliable; trustworthy – untrustworthy; easy to get on with – difficult to get on with; helpful – unhelpful; pleasant – unpleasant; fair – unfair; efficient – inefficient. No attempt was made to scale each polar opposite as in the classical semantic differential technique, because, on the whole, the executives resisted the possibility (meaningfulness) of doing so.

19 Taking them as integrative does not materially alter the global nature of the results.

20 Empirically it was found unnecessary to include null relations (i.e. indifference).

21 Stable and unstable environments are basically a consequence of the sort of technology in which the company is involved. The columns of *Table 1* are, in effect, controlled for technology. Stable environments correspond to a slow rate of technological innovation, unstable environments, a high rate.

22 Five simple yes/no questions were used and scored 0, 1, an additive index was then constructed.

23 Apart from the theoretical sense of taking this ratio, Z maximizes R^2 in the following regression model.

24 Non-linear and interaction models were also tested but the linear additive model maximizes the variance explained. The variables are measured from their means.

25 Unfortunately, our research design did not include an attempt to scale the opposite of 'felt tension' but only low and high tension. It would seem reasonable to think in terms of a bi-polar scale, direct A effects and point balance pushing an individual towards one pole, N effects and imbalance to the other.

REFERENCES

ABELL, P. 1968. Structural Balance in Dynamic Structures. *Sociology* **2** (3): 333–52.

——1971. *Model Building in Sociology.* London: Weidenfeld and Nicholson.

——1974. Mathematics and Sociological Theory. In John Rex (ed.), *Approaches to Sociology.* London: Routledge & Kegan Paul.

ARROW, K. J. 1951. *Social Choice and Individual Values.* New York: Wiley. (2nd edition 1963.)

ATKIN, R. H. 1974. *Mathematical Structure in Human Affairs.* London: Heinemann Educational Books.

TAYLOR, H. 1970. *Balance Processes in Small Groups.* New York: Van Nostrand.

*Development of models for application to conflict problems**

K. C. BOWEN and DAVID G. SMITH

INTRODUCTION

Conflict is not an easy subject to deal with. Like many subjects in the social sciences, it is too easily regarded as something which everyone knows about and has the ability and the right to discuss. The right should not be questioned, but the ability and the knowledge is more difficult to accept. It would generally be agreed that, in the physical sciences, awareness and experience of light, heat, and sound does little to fashion an expert; that, in the natural sciences, an awareness of life does not provide an adequate qualification. Yet, the average well-informed man may readily lay claim to being something of a historian, a psychologist, an observer of international affairs, or a student of industrial unrest; he may see himself as well-versed in bargaining and as having the ability to interpret facts sensibly and come to rational decisions. If we compare the subject of conflict with any equivalent complex physical, as opposed to behavioural, phenomenon, we find that few have studied it deeply and conceptually, and none has yet been able to place it in an adequate and logical systems framework. It is the latter task which we shall discuss, because, without such a framework, even good ideas will themselves generate conflict, the very thing they purport to explain.

Before describing why we decided to tackle so difficult a problem, and where we now stand with regard to potential application of our research, it is worthwhile enlarging on the regression which we have implied; namely, that students of conflict will conflict about the adequacy of 'rival' theories. These theories must therefore be extended to contain a rationale for understanding this conflict, which will in turn engender further conflict, and so on. Conflict is a concept of some kind of inconsistency recognized by an observer, who may or may not be involved directly in the relevant situation. It has a relation to, but is by no means the same thing as, combat.

It will be seen that the study of conflict implies that the student should place himself outside the conflict situations he studies, so as to view the 'facts' impartially. This, of course, he cannot do; but he must consciously accept that he cannot, otherwise he will generate conflict either by interference or by misinterpretation, and perhaps be unaware of the very process he pretends to study. Any problem of this kind must lead to an infinite regression: examples are 'I think that he thinks that I think . . .'; awareness of awareness; and, indeed, observation of any system of which the observer is a part. Dunne (1942), examining time, correctly produced such an infinite regression, but it seems to us that he wrongly extended it outwards in physical (time) dimensions, rather than inwards as a conceptual model. It may well be that regressions of this type pose problems for which there is no final solution in theory. In practice, this may not be serious, since the major gain in understanding may come from examination of the first few stages of the regression; an analogy could be made with infinite series, in which two terms after the first may be enough to give insight into the series as a whole. A more difficult, but very relevant example, is given by Howard (1970: 205–31) in a mathematical examination of a competitive/co-operative game of strategy.

A final point, by way of introduction, is that, while the main themes of our discussion will be the logical structures of interaction, conflict and crisis, the basic elements will be those of defined special languages (metalanguages) and of systems theory. Although some of the examples given will be of a military nature (which is not unnatural since our work is done under the aegis of defence operational research), we do not want to emphasize the military aspects of conflict, although some of these are important even to those who may feel antipathy towards any form of military science. 'The best form of defence is attack' used to be the cry; nowadays, for well-known reasons, this is a risky philosophy: more and more, defence is becoming regarded as the art of avoiding, or at least minimizing, combat. The optimum way of engaging in physical combat is still important, but only when less crude methods of resolving conflict have failed.

THE INITIATION OF RESEARCH

The background to this research is a fairly straightforward story. The opportunity arose for a long-term research programme to be defined and to be carried out independently of the main defence operational analysis programme, albeit linked, potentially, with its eventual needs. The reason for selecting conflict as a research subject was that military operational studies were normally constrained to hypothetical combat situations from a point in time when war was assumed to have started. Consequently, the facilities, which studies had showed were needed for the efficient prosecution of war, did not necessarily include those which might have offered, had they been available, a potential for avoiding war; e.g. by control over events which would be likely precursors to war. Obviously, any military strength may act as a deterrent to war: equally it can act as an incitement to war. Similar remarks apply to political, economic and social behaviour, and it seemed desirable to look at facilities for the control of conflict in a wider framework than the purely military. There was an additional reason for wishing to examine the possibilities for control of conflict, namely that, unless the precursors to war could be examined and understood, the initial premises on which different aspects of combat studies were based would not necessarily be compatible one with another, nor with the assumptions on which parallel political and economic studies would be proceeding. This is not to imply that there is not any proper and reasonable communication and co-ordination: it is simply a statement of belief, based on study and experience, that the adequacy of such communication and co-ordination is severely limited by the absence of suitably explicit models within which assumptions can be more rigorously tested for compatibility.

At an early stage, consideration was given to the sort of techniques which were available and which seemed to have some potential for application to conflict studies. One such technique[1] that seemed to hold promise, was the application of graph theory, in particular, the concept of trees. The branch points would be critical decision events in hypothetical, future situations and the branches would represent courses of action or behaviour. Such a tree needed to be constructed in both directions; the questions to be asked were not only 'where do we go from here?', but 'why did we get here in the first place?'.

Looking backwards to answer the second question, it seemed that one might need to go back, however imprecisely, to issues of socio–economic imbalance in setting a true picture for any recourse to military action.

It was with this in mind that the first account (Bowen 1970) of our research was presented at a NATO Symposium under the title of Operational Research on Social Problems and the Roots of Conflict. Its purpose was to urge that there should be close links between the NATO Science Committee's Advisory Panel on Operational Research and the then newly formed NATO Committee on the Challenges of Modern Society. Both these bodies, whose work is widely published, were set up to advise on and study basic scientific problems of general concern to the welfare of nations, NATO or non-NATO. The subject of conflict seen from a sociological, rather than a purely military, viewpoint seemed to be of proper concern to both committees.

The work reported to that Symposium was the early stage of some fundamental conceptual modelling which has since been more completely described in two informal papers (Smith 1971a; 1971b) and is repeated in slightly different form below. The models provide the central logic and framework for our continuing development of methods for the study of conflict. If they appear to be simple and to state what is already known, so much the better. To the best of our knowledge the diagrammatic notation is new and it lends itself naturally to mathematical set description, a not inconsiderable advantage which we have already put to use in small ways. Further, the full process of interaction does not seem to have been described before by a systems approach.

As a further benefit of 'restating the obvious', if that is what we seem to be doing, we would suggest that a good diagram helps to overcome language problems, particularly misinterpretations, which are basic ingredients of conflict. It is perhaps the replacement of a number of linked, but complex, ideas by a 'single' piece of information that achieves this – 'single' here implies a pattern that can readily be held and used by the conscious mind. Subjectively, we have found our models of great value both to our understanding of conflict problems and to our communication with each other during our research. We do not apologize for such a subjective statement: the concept with which we are dealing is at present essentially subjective, and it is only through an agreed framework that its study and understanding can achieve any objectivity.

A MODEL OF INTERACTION

If there is to be conflict there must be an interaction; the reverse is likely to be true, if only in a minor way, but interaction is a more basic concept and must be studied.

We structure inwards from a simple box which represents the total environment – there is nothing outside (*Figure 1*). Importantly therefore, the observer (researcher, analyst, experimenter) is represented by a box inside. The diagram is a representation (model) and the *actual* observer is outside, the model being an external manifestation of a concept within his mind. The observer may thus be helped to study how he, as a system, is capable of interaction with the interaction he is studying. The latter system is represented by a box which encloses the immediate environment of the interaction, within which are representations of the two interacting systems, X and Y.

FIGURE 1 A model of interaction

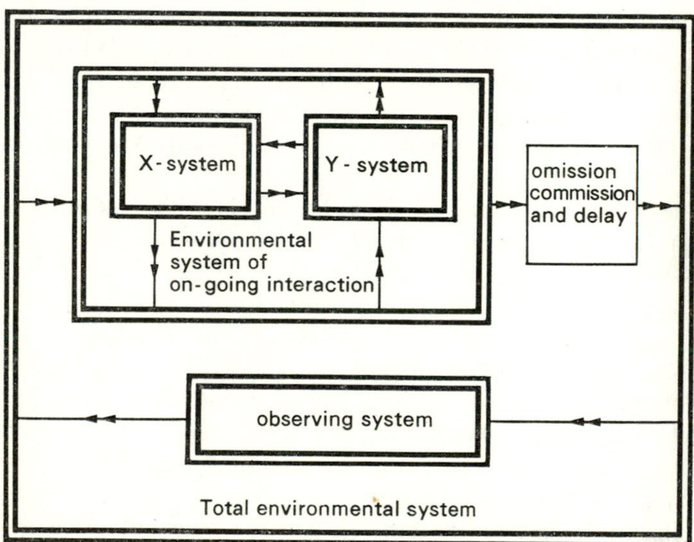

The double-arrowed lines represent the modification of one system (box) by another: self-modification takes place through the immediate environment. Modification lines must exist between any system enclosed within another; they may or may not exist strongly, and directly at any moment of time between disjoint sets (systems), although each must modify a common environment. The environment of any system is understood as including the system itself. Finally, the box which is labelled omission, commission and delay, shown, for simplicity, in one position only, indicates that information describing the state of any system may be subject to some kind of distortion. The flow of information which is part of system modification is communication in the broadest sense, and is a central factor in any conflict situation.

We shall return to the subject of the wider usefulness of the type of structuring used here, but we now go on to a more detailed description of the X-system.

A MODEL OF AN ADAPTIVE SYSTEM

Figure 2 shows the four essential sub-system components of the X-system. These are the receptors, the representation, the director and the effectors.

The receptors, as illustrated, are classified according to the origin of information from the environment. For simplicity, we have omitted similar sub-systems in other boxes, although these sub-systems must exist. For our purposes, the receptors of the interacting systems are of particular importance, especially the one which deals with information about the system itself.

The X-representation describes the way in which information is held prior to processing, which is done by the X-director according to rules which are subject to modification (these rules would be a subset of the director-set). The processed information is fed back to the representation. Together, these two sub-systems form an important sub-set, labelled X-brain in *Figure 2*.

For our purposes, we classify the effectors into two groups. Type 1 effectors are responsible for modifications, the relevant immediate consequences of which are manifested externally to the X-system, i.e. in direct interaction with other systems. Type 2 effectors produce modifications, the relevant immediate consequences of which are not manifested externally: these sometimes act to close the effector-receptor–representation–director loop. This is shown by the hatched modification line in the X-brain box which is the feedback referred to above. It is responsible for the consciousness and the internal adaptive behaviour of the X-system. The Type 1 effectors similarly provide for

FIGURE 2 A model of an adaptive system

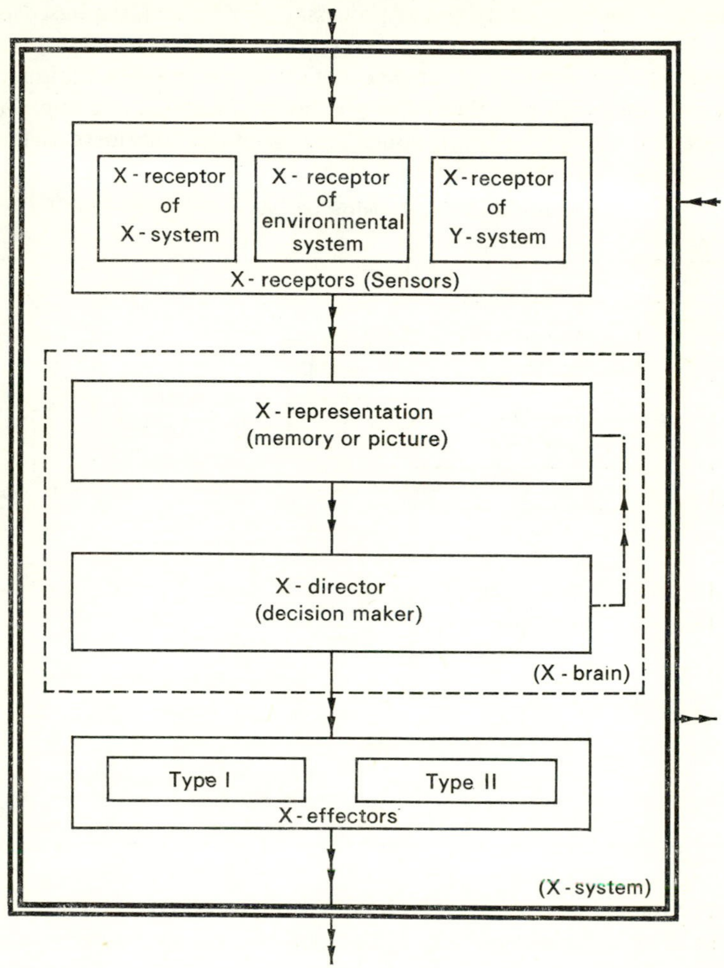

external adaptive behaviour. Only the more important modification lines are illustrated in *Figure 2*.

A MODEL OF THE DECISION PROCESS

Figure 3 gives a far from complete, and perhaps far from accurate, impression of the decision process. It shows sub-sets of the director and of the representation which cannot be regarded, even theoretically, as modelling physical components. In the case of the director, they represent logical processes or formulations based on the information held by the representation, and, in the case of the representation, one important aspect of the information held is identified. All these sub-sets are ill-defined both as to what is being processed and how this is being done. Because of this 'fuzziness' (which

FIGURE 3 A model of the decision process

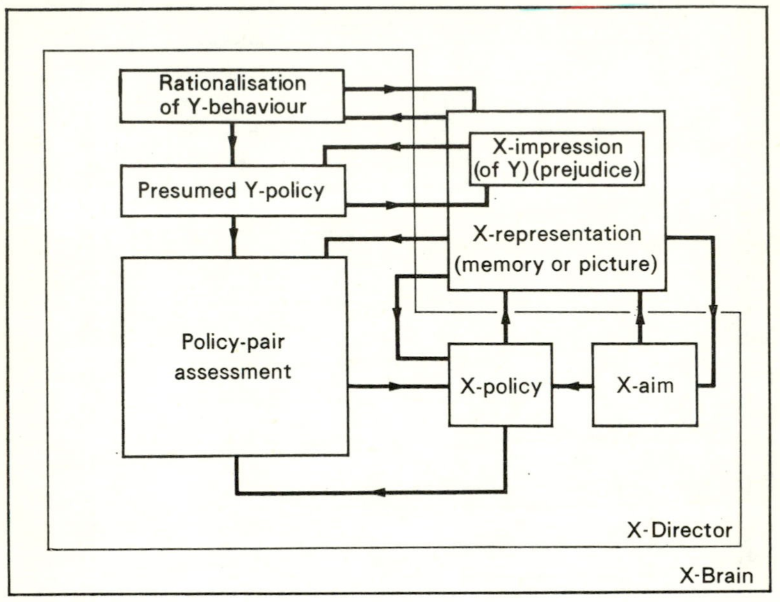

can be theoretically defined (Bellman and Zadeh 1970: 141–69)), they are shown as being connected in a loop process by single-arrowed lines which represent information-flow lines between the logical process boxes and between these and the representation. Essentially, they are no different to the modification lines, but they draw attention to the special type of uncertainty attached to the sub-sets specified. The loops are shown as closed and theoretically the whole process is continuously re-cycled as information reaches the representation. In practice (see comments on *Figure 1*), distortion will occur and there will be inefficiencies in these processes: it is important to note that they are still essentially logical even though performing an inadequate selection, with inappropriate rules, and even incorrect or incorrectly correlated information. We can, arbitrarily, use the words illogical or irrational to imply that, given the same information, we would not think or act in stated ways, but, unless we can define the representation and processing being used by another person, we cannot infer anything other than some unspecified dissimilarity to us.

The X-aim is the desired future state of the X-environment, including the X-system itself. It is formulated by using the X-representation which will contain information on feasibility, risks, and constraints. The X-policy is a similar selection process to define potential behaviour which will result in the achievement of the X-aim.

The assessment of Y, the other main interacting system, is also necessarily obtained from the X-representation. Information about Y is rationalized and his presumed policy is deduced. This last process uses a special (and fuzzy) sub-set of the X-representation which we have called X-impression of Y. In *Figure 3* it is labelled prejudice: this strictly means pre-judgment but we use the more emotive term as a warning that this process of assessing someone else's policy is often distorted by our prior judgments of him. It is typified by the feelings of suspicion when an apparently reasonable proposition is put forward by an 'enemy' – 'what is the devil up to' – and the last idea to be examined may be that he is truly trying to be reasonable. It is in the face of such barriers to communication that conflict has to be handled.

It will be noted that presumed Y-aim is not included. All that is needed to test the adequacy of X-policy is presumed Y-policy. The process as carried out by X for X is reversed in the case of his observation of Y. Any processing of presumed Y-aim in the cycling of the logical processing can be assumed to take place in the loop that associates X-impression of Y with presumed Y-policy.

THE CONCEPTS OF CONFLICT AND CRISIS

The models of interaction, adaptation, and decision are, and are intended to be, generic. They have potential application to all adaptive systems, whether machine or human, whether one be dealing with interactions between individuals or groups of people,[2] whether the interaction is in a business, social or political environment, and whether one is talking about industrial bargaining or international conflict. It is clear from these models that interaction will generally involve conflict, although this conflict can be benevolent as well as malevolent. The most benevolent form of conflict leads to co-operation; in other words, the interaction promotes conflict which generates new ideas but, more importantly, is studied with a view to arriving at mutually satisfactory and consistent aims and policies.

Competition accepts that aims and policies conflict, but assumes, within limits, that it is beneficial for ability and for eventual aims and policies that they be tested the hard way. There may exist both written and unwritten rules for ending the conflict by moving to new aims and policies which are part of a pre-planned set. However, it is true that competition can span the benevolent and malevolent range of conflict: that interacting systems can be forced to consider aims and policies outside that *a priori* acceptable set. This moment of choice we define as the onset of crisis and crisis continues until achievable aims and policies can be accepted. Crisis can be overcome by one system changing its concept of what is acceptable and either moving away from conflict or moving more deeply into it: one might call the new policies weak or strong, but this does not tell whether they are sound or unsound, wise or unwise. All depends upon the adequacies of both the representation and the interpretation by the director. As with chess, strategy must look many moves ahead but unlike chess, the full information and rules are not available. Nevertheless, decision-trees must be formulated in some way (e.g. if I do A, he will do B or C: if he does B etc.) and any system will be conditioned, with regard to the decisions it considers, by the facilities and information that it has or that it is accustomed to using. It is interesting that even in long term planning, major innovations are rare, because the acceptable decision set tends to be a conventional choice. Such planning problems are investigated by Friend and Jessop (1969).

Crisis is a subjective concept. Both parties to an interaction may not both be faced with crisis; on the other hand, they may both be faced with crisis seen in quite different ways. They may not recognize crisis at all, whereas another system in the mutual environment may do so, correctly or incorrectly, because its representation is different. An extreme form of this is seen in news-reporting, since crisis is news and is therefore necessary: it may be noted that such reporting causes a three-system interaction and may induce or exacerbate major conflict between the initially interacting systems. What has been structured above has been a two-system interaction, but there is no barrier, in principle, to extending the system structure to more complex interactions. However, there is good reason to isolate two-system interactions wherever possible, since there is already enough complexity for initial study.

A SUBJECTIVE APPLICATION

The concepts of information, conflict, and crisis described above have been found useful in achieving constructive discussion of conflict situations which we debated in developing our models. However, it was necessary to test their usefulness by a more complete analysis. We chose a situation, for which there was considerable documented information available to us, as a vehicle for testing our ideas. Because some of the material used in our study came from confidential sources it is not possible to summarize the study in detail, and it was, in any case, too complex to describe adequately in the limited space available to us. Therefore, we will confine our attention to the main points which arose, and which we believe to be of general relevance.

Large quantities of data in the form of messages and reports were available from many different sources. Each piece of information was subject to distortion of various kinds. Without a precise understanding of the system under study it was impossible to estimate the nature and extent of this distortion. Therefore, it was necessary to compare every piece of information with every other relevant piece, allowing for possible lack of dependence between them, in order to identify where distortion might be occurring. Hence, inconsistency was a prime source of new insights, while consistency often merely reflected hidden dependence. This kind of problem must be experienced by many other researchers, for example by historians in trying to build up a picture of a developing situation. To a lesser extent the same problem would be (or should be) experienced by the participants in the actual situation. There is a clear parallel between the picture-building taking place in such a situation and the theory-building process carried out by a physical scientist. The major difference is that the metalinguistic description of the situation is very much more precisely defined in the latter case because of the control that the physical scientist has over his experiments.

The conceptual models described above were used as a framework of 'labels' and concepts. This framework was employed in reading through the information available, and two readings were necessary.

The first was to establish the main elements of the dynamic situation and their more obvious relationships. The second reading filled in the detailed description of these elements and relationships. The processing of information in messages could usefully have employed a kind of content analysis (Lasswell and Leites 1968). We say 'a kind of' because the messages were very short, yielding only a very small sample for such analysis. Moreover, the environment and background knowledge of the communicants were changing so rapidly that the kind of inferences which could be validly drawn would have been extremely weak. Content analysis, in a form suitable for the detailed semantic analysis of diplomatic and military messages, or similar communications in a fast moving political/industrial conflict, does not seem to have been developed. We had to rely on careful reading and re-reading of the messages in order to build up our picture, while attempting to analyse and check our own prejudices. In this sense, it was a very subjective process. However, it did produce a reasonable picture, which we were able to check with an independent description of and comment on the same over-all situation which became available to us after our study.

Certain general points which emerged from our study are worth noting, although they are not, in principle, very surprising.

1 It was neither possible nor useful to say that certain actions or beliefs were right or wrong. However, it was possible to point to alternative interpretations of behaviour, and question whether these appeared to have been considered, or whether the facilities for making it likely that they would be considered were organizationally available.
2 The extent to which communication between individuals and groups appeared to be affected by the very different representations, against which the communication was interpreted, was amenable to limited analysis.
3 In particular, it was possible to adduce reasons why and how prejudgments of attitude might have limited interpretations of both events and acceptable sets of decisions. (Prior patterns of presumed Y-policy affect the analysis of new pieces of information by forcing a 'fit' within an existing 'theory'. They also affect the search for and acceptance of information.)

The most important finding was the extent to which it was necessary for the analyst to criticize his own behaviour in interacting with the available data, along the same lines as his attempts, through criticism, to comment usefully, for the future, on the behaviours of parties to the real-world interaction. It is most apparent that a structure which would allow individuals to monitor their own behavioural patterns, in however limited a way, would be a potentially powerful tool for crisis management, an idea which has been used in the specific context of controlled communication (Burton 1969).

Further, it is required that the lessons of the past be described in generic ways, so that these can be used as references within such a monitoring process. We believe that a taxonomy is needed to describe the basic elements within past conflicts and crises, both for information retrieval and for the application of 'lessons learnt' in situations which may well be described in very different languages, e.g. relationships between tribal disputes and industrial unrest, or between the latter and international conflict.

PLANS FOR OBJECTIVE APPLICATION

The difficulties we experienced in this case-history analysis were accentuated by the lack of control which we had over the type, quality, and quantity of data available to us. We intend to overcome this by setting up experiments (games) within which we can study the broader aspects of decision-making in a crisis situation under controlled conditions. In the field of war gaming, and comparable work on civil problems, much experience is available (Shubik 1972:20–36).

It will first be necessary to define the decision-maker with whose role we are concerned. This, in itself, is not an easy task. Then we have to describe the system in which he operates. We intend, first of all, to replace the decision-maker's 'opponent' by an automaton, which behaves deterministically in accordance with our prior logical instructions, some of which may be conditional. The process of building up the crisis situation will be performed iteratively with successive games representing single-decision situations, along lines suggested elsewhere for command and control games (Bowen 1971). Therefore, our games will differ markedly from games in which whole sequences of conditional decisions and actions are represented.[3]

By this systematic gaming process it will be possible, we hope, to build up a decision tree for the situation 'played'. The early games will not place any measures of likelihood of utilizing the various branches of the decision tree. Later games will allow multiple decisions in order to obtain information on likely paths through the decision tree. Critical points in the tree may then be identified – points at which certain decisions ought to be taken in order to ensure a satisfactory outcome. The question of the facilities that are required in a real situation in order to assist our decision-maker in this task can then be tackled.

The next stage of gaming will be to try and 'grow' the decision tree backwards (beyond the initial starting-point) in order to see what decisions might cause such a situation to develop. This will enable us to investigate how such situations might be avoided, or, if this is not possible, how to steer the development towards more satisfactory outcomes.

As occurs in a real situation, our decision-maker will be asked to take into account many factors in coming to his decision. Since the real-world decision-makers, like our experimental subjects, are expected to have widely differing backgrounds of experience, training, and knowledge, they may make, when presented with the same information, quite different decisions. Therefore, it will be necessary, in our experiments, to investigate the behaviour of different decision-makers under identical experimental conditions. In a similar way, we must also investigate the sensitivity of their behaviour to the experimental situation. Since much of the information coming to the decision-makers must be in the form of messages, telephone calls, telegrams, reports, etc., we must pay very special attention to the style, format, and other linguistic factors which are basic to the situation in the real world. Even so, we cannot avoid the fact that the decision-maker is not making his decisions in a *real* situation. However, experience in war gaming and other game situations has shown that, provided great care is taken in the experimental design, the participants can become so involved that the difference between the real and the experimental situation can be reduced to acceptable proportions, provided that the output required from the game is not too elaborate.

EXTENSION OF THE CONCEPTUAL MODELLING

One of the difficulties experienced by analysts is that the statement of the problem which they are asked to tackle is in normal, everyday language, although it may well be a technical description, using a special sub-set of that language. Problems are usually complex and often ill-defined because of uncertainties. Natural language lacks the precision necessary to define and agree what is to be measured and how to measure in ways suited to mathematical or computer modelling. To overcome this difficulty, the analyst and the person he serves must establish a common language or conceptual framework through which the problem can be discussed systematically.

There is a similar difficulty in trying to relate the result of a number of distinct studies which are all nominally concerned with the same problems. Because the approaches to the problems, the assumptions made,[4] and the data used, depend so much on the nature of the separate studies, there is usually no way of checking the consistency between studies. The final results of the studies may be easier to compare, but discrepancies at such a late stage are decidedly unwelcome.

Because the conceptual modelling we have described is relevant not only to studies of conflict and of crisis management, but, indeed, to any situation in which adaptive systems are interacting, it is not unreasonable to try to use this to create a conceptual framework which can embrace many large-scale dynamic system studies. What follows gives some indication of the kind of approach which is possible in defence studies.

The National System can be thought of as an adaptive, decision-making system with a number of effectors, e.g., trade, economic, diplomatic, and military systems. The political system represents the highest level brain, or decision-making system. The political system will deploy its effectors in ways in which its aims (however loose and ill-defined, and whether positive or negative) may be pursued. Further, these effector systems deploy their own effectors in order to pursue the aims set to them by the political system. For example, the military system can be thought of as having two main effectors, land-air and maritime systems, controlled by the military decision-making system, e.g., Chiefs of Staff. Each system can be further sub-divided in a similar way into sensors, brain and effectors, throughout the normal military hierarchy.

Therefore, the National System can also be thought of as a hierarchy of nested systems. The functional structure so produced can be used to describe the roles of the various levels in this hierarchy. For example, a platoon commander is one level of brain or decision-maker, while a corps commander plays a similar role at a much higher level. Similarly, a single soldier with binoculars is acting in the role of sensor for a low level system, while a reconnaissance patrol will be acting as a sensor at a higher level.

It is interesting to consider the effectors in more detail. As we stated earlier, there are two kinds of effectors – those that modify the system itself (i.e. their immediate environment) and those that modify the 'enemy' system or any non-X part of the environment. The first category refers to the 'support' arms (catering, logistics, field hospital, etc.) while the second refers to the 'teeth' or fighting arms. Some units, e.g., engineers, may appear in either category, depending on their immediate role. The second category has a role that is specifically 'countering' the enemy. If the enemy system is assumed to be capable of similar description, this role can be further sub-divided into categories according to what they are countering, e.g. counter-sensors, counter-logistics, and so on. The regression can be continued further (it is theoretically infinite) by considering the role of countering enemy teeth arms. This role can be sub-divided into counter-counter-sensors, counter-counter-logistics, and so on. Roles may not always be defined explicitly enough to enable such a detailed description to be used immediately. Nevertheless, the attempt to structure roles in this way can lead to a useful appreciation of the extent to which facilities have been related to clearly perceived roles.

Within the national hierarchy, there will be a hierarchy of aims of the corresponding systems. As discussed above, failure to achieve aims and inability to adapt will cause a system, at any level, to experience crisis. In some cases the crisis may be transmitted upwards to the very top of the hierarchy, and we would call this political crisis. The aim of our defence forces, we postulate, is to avoid political crisis by resolving crisis at the lowest possible level.

We are therefore trying to relate this national structure to the nature and level of conflict as measured by political/military response, from peace (no conflict), through cold war, tension, impedition (harassment or blockade), sub-belligerent confrontation (tit-for-tat impedition) to Limited War, General War, and various stages of Nuclear War. This sub-division intentionally expands the lower levels as compared to Kahn's (1969) scale. The decision to initiate a transition up the scale might be one means of resolving a political crisis, in the same way that a lock-out or strike resolves an industrial crisis by altering the situation and forcing a complete reconsideration of aims and policies.[5] Of course, new crises may develop rapidly, although, ideally, this will have been assessed in deciding to implement a potentially dangerous policy.

The conceptual framework allows us to relate a detailed study, at any level, to the broad concept of a defence force. It also enables us to suggest the appropriate measures of effectiveness at any level of study. These are not always the obvious ones; ships with guns could be more effective in times of tension than ships with missiles irrespective of any other considerations of cost, accuracy, lethality, etc., which might be the more obvious measures of effectiveness. This is because it is somewhat easier to signal intent with guns than with missiles, and, as we have argued earlier, communication in the broadest sense, is at the heart of conflict/crisis problems.

APPLICATION TO THE ADVISORY FUNCTION

Anyone who is advising on a problem has to choose suitable methods by which he defines, interprets, and models the problem and provides information in a suitable form for ultimate decision and implementation. The fact that there is a problem, means that there is conflict; in a very simple case this could be conflict in the mind of an individual, based on uncertainty about the facts relating to the problem and about the way in which they should be balanced. In the more complex, and more frequent cases, there are several parties involved. In these cases, the way in which conflicting interests are to be balanced, and the extent to which prior judgments may have become a part of the problem, have to be taken into account.

An advisor who is content to say what he thinks is right and adopts a 'take it or leave it' attitude is in danger of being regarded as another party to the conflict. It is important that the pattern of processed information that he provides be related to the possible policy sets of the decision-maker he serves, and also to the conflict between parties directly affected by the decision that is to be taken.

The models which have been described are useful, not only for the purposes of problem definition, but also for structuring and enquiring into the interaction both between the analyst (in his subsequent advisory role) and the decision-maker, and between the decision-maker, when advised, and those whom his decision affects. An understanding of these processes will help to avoid the giving of irrelevant advice, relevant advice in irrelevant form, or advice which, although fully relevant as far as it goes, does not help as soon as further polemics are introduced. In the last case, it is impossible to crystal-gaze so deeply as to prepare advice for all contingencies, but at least the process that provides the advice can be planned to be adaptable to possible further queries, which cast doubt on the assumptions, approximations, and aggregations that are essential to model-building.

The choice of methodology used by the advisor, the sum total of his analysis of the problem, his techniques for processing information, and his final presentation should themselves be as objective as possible. On analysis the reasons for choice will be found to be varied. They may include such things as personal preferences related to personal skills, influence of time constraints, and limitations or opportunities open depending on the available supporting staff and facilities. These are all relevant to subsidiary aims; the question is whether they are fully appropriate to the main aim. If they are not, then the subsidiary aims are not well understood and are probably wrongly chosen, or, if essential, are associated with a poor policy choice.

As far as the work on conflict has been described and developed, we are far from being able to make systematic use of it in planning the advisory process. This does not imply that such planning is not attempted or that such attempts are not well executed. The simple fact is that it would be valuable, even to those experienced as advisors, to have some type of logic to apply directly and systematically to any new problem. To act by analogy from one problem to another, or to work out afresh for each problem, in its own language, a procedure which may in principle already be known, is a wasteful and an inefficient way of doing business.

THE DANGER OF A NEW APPROACH

What has been referred to in the last section is basic to the methodology of decision theory (White 1969) which, apart from specific aspects such as statistical decision theory which seems to us to have very limited practical application, is still undeveloped. It is apparent that what we are putting forward could be considered as a new approach to some of these decision-theoretic issues. This is not surprising since we have already commented on the fact that conflict is ever-present and is a normal and probably benevolent precursor to many, if not most, decision processes.

We have also drawn attention to the need for a systems approach and there is of course a large literature on Systems Theory and Systems Analysis (Emery 1969). At an early stage in our structuring, we found it necessary to develop in a set diagrammatic direction in order to meet the logic of the task we analysed. This appears to provide facilities for more complete descriptions of systems, and it points to ways of bringing mathematical logic to bear. It has now become second nature in our approach to problem structuring. Nevertheless, we find ourselves in very good agreement with what is said elsewhere by Ackoff (1971) and others who have studied the theory of systems.

Our models are essentially cybernetic (Ashby 1956), since we are considering adaptive systems. They also have great similarity to ones developed in the area of control theory (Bellman and Kalaba 1965), and in the study of information processes (Tou 1965).

In the studies we have made of the literature on conflict (Boulding 1962; Nicholson 1970; Forward 1971), on politics (Easton 1965; Deutsch 1966; Rosenau 1971), and on social systems (Galtung 1966), we have found ideas which we recognize and which seems logically consistent with our models. Of course, we have since the initial development stage, when we formulated our own ideas without having made any detailed literature survey, borrowed a great deal to ensure that we were not going against the common sense and theories of those whom we recognized as experts, both in the social sciences generally, and in the specialized areas of psychology, communication, linguistics, and the various subjects discussed above. In some cases, we have found ourselves able to accept descriptive 'theories' which appeared to conflict.[6] We have found, in some cases, similar diagrammatic structures, but used only for specific illustration and not as a general logic.

There is clearly a danger in making a new approach to a problem, namely that one can easily be working in isolation, creating a new language and a new mystique and communicating with only those few who are inclined to prefer the new format. A new approach is only justifiable if the intention is to integrate what is at present separate, to offer a framework for a coalescing of otherwise independent disciplines, and to suggest reasons why the proposed new approach has advantages.

FINAL COMMENTS

At this early stage, reasons for our optimism can only be tentative and we put them forward for debate and not as a rigorous and fully developed basis for future work. Briefly they are as follows:

1 An interaction between systems, as we have described it, seems to be a fundamental building block. A total systems logic can be developed in detail, with the same logical units, both outside and within the systems on which attention is first focused.

2 Any adaptive system which can interact with another can usefully be described in terms of receptors, representation, director, and effectors. It is not always necessary to show these in the structures developed, although the logic may demand that their existence is recognized.

3 The diagrammatic logic we have developed is a useful general language which concentrates ideas and provides a uniformity of approach. We have found that, within the research team and to a lesser extent outside, we are achieving more rapid and less ambiguous communication. We are also beginning to discern more clearly why certain words and concepts are being interpreted differently by different people because of their different perspective. It has impressed upon us the importance of linguistics as an essential supporting discipline, if new 'theories' are to be firmly established (MacCormac 1971:145–59; Parsons 1971:131–44).

4 The logic has two very important characteristics. First, it insists on a clear distinction between systems which are separate and systems which are contained within others. Second, it offers a pattern to which mathematical set-theoretic ideas can be applied, and we have made some tentative progress in this direction. We believe this to be a necessary stage in the development of the sort of metalanguage we seek, but we accept that, ultimately, we must aim at some defined sub-set of ordinary language and diagrammatic aids.

5 The logic also focuses attention on the dimensional cross-section of the systems being discussed. The same diagram is often found to be unsatisfactory for description of a situation at different levels of decision and control, because the systems involved and their relationships are differently perceived. The same differ-

ences and difficulties are observed in trying to place in a single framework the physical descriptions of systems and the concepts of their roles.

However, there are major difficulties in studying the subject of conflict, in the broad sense we have chosen, which must not be overlooked.

1 We are dealing with dynamic adaptive systems which change continuously in both physical and psychological ways. We have to find ways of representing time changes which will extend, both logically and mathematically, the capability of the models we have described.
2 We need to develop experimental (gaming) techniques so as to be able to use our models objectively; in other words, we must learn how to analyse the reactions of people to conflict and crisis situations, within the framework we have proposed.
3 We require more understanding of the nature of 'fuzzy' concepts (Bellman and Zadeh 1970) and how to define and manipulate them.
4 We need to acquire, or borrow, the skills and experience of many disciplines, and specialized areas within disciplines, so as not to repeat work already done, but to re-interpret it within a more fundamental and integrated framework.

Finally, to reiterate the last point in a different way, we must not appear to be claiming to understand other people's expertises better than they do themselves. For by doing that we should merely prove that we cannot ourselves use what we purport to offer. A theoretical model of conflict, that could not be expressed or used without creating non-benevolent conflict, would prove its own inadequacy.

NOTES

* This paper is presented by permission of Dr A. Stratton, Director of the Defence Operational Analysis Establishment, to whom the authors are grateful for his encouragement of their research and for his suggestion of a measurement scale, related specifically to political/military conflict studies.

1 Others examined, and still believed to be very relevant were the linked

use of gaming and game theory (behavioural decision studies); historical surveys and analyses; and various aspects of taxonomy.

2 The extent to which psychological conflict, within an individual, can be looked at in the same way needs expert judgment and study. One associated type of problem is mentioned in a later section: Application to the Advisory Function.

3 There is some question as to whether games of this wider scope have been useful for research, although they do provide a valuable vehicle for learning (Thomas and McNicholls 1969).

4 This point has been made earlier, specifically in relation to assumptions about the precursors to war in military combat and associated political/economic studies (see section on the Initiation of Research).

5 This idea stemmed from comments made by D. Gowler, Manchester Business School, in a BIM seminar on The Management of Change, August 1971.

6 One example is given by the 'opposing' philosophies of the policy-making process which Hirschmann and Lindblom (1962: 211–22) have expounded, and the more conventional theory of 'rational' decision-making. The 'conflict' appears to be due to concentration on different features of the logical processes and to incomplete definitions of their interrelationships. Another example is given by the views on conflict of Galtung and Burton, which are contrasted in a book on the Northern Ireland situation (Elliot and Hickie 1971). Again, different dimensional perspectives of a multi-dimensional problem are being viewed.

REFERENCES

ACKOFF, R. L. 1971. Towards a System of Systems Concepts. *Management Science* **17** (11): 661–71.

ASHBY, W. R. 1956. *Introduction to Cybernetics*. London: Chapman and Hall.

BELLMAN, R. and KALABA, R. (eds.) 1965. *Dynamic Programming and Modern Control Theory*. London: Academic Press Inc. (London) Ltd.

BELLMAN, R. R. and ZADEH, L. A. 1970. Decision-Making in a Fuzzy Environment. *Management Science* **17** (4): 141–64.

BOULDING, K. E. 1962. *Conflict and Defence: A General Theory*. New York: Harper and Row.

BOWEN, K. C. 1970. Operational Research on Social Problems and the Roots of Conflict. Paper presented at a NATO Symposium on Past and Future Contributions of Operational Research to NATO. Brussels.

——1971. The Structure and Classification of Operational Research Games. *DOAE Memorandum* 7117. Defence Operational Analysis Establishment, Ministry of Defence.

BURTON, J. W. 1969. *Conflict and Communication.* London: Macmillan.

DEUTSCH, K. W. 1966. *The Nerves of Government: Models of political communicaton and control.* New York: The Free Press; London: Collier-Macmillan.

DUNNE, J. W. 1942. *The Serial Universe.* London: Faber and Faber.

EASTON, D. 1965. *A Framework for Political Analysis.* Englewood Cliffs. N.J.: Prentice-Hall.

ELLIOT, R. S. P. and HICKIE, J. 1971. *Ulster: A Case Study in Conflict Theory.* London: Longman.

EMERY, F. E. (ed.) 1969. *Systems Thinking.* Penguin Modern Management Readings. Harmondsworth: Penguin.

FORWARD, N. 1971. *The Field of Nations: An Account of Some New Approaches to International Relations.* London: Macmillan.

FRIEND, J. K. and JESSOP, W. N. 1969. *Local Government and Strategic Choice.* London: Tavistock.

GALTUNG, J. 1966. *International Relations and International Conflicts: A sociological approach.* 6th Trans World Congress of Sociology.

HIRSCHMANN, A. O. and LINDBLOM, C. E. 1962. Economic Development, Research and Development, Policy Making: Some converging views. *Behavioural Science* (7): 211–22. (See also Emery 1969.)

HOWARD, N. 1970. Some Developments in the Theory and Application of Metagames. *General Systems* Vol. 15. Ann Arbor, Mich.: Society for General Systems Research.

KAHN, H. 1965. *On Escalation: Metaphors and scenarios.* London: New York and Pall Mall Press.

LASSWELL, H. D., LEITES, N., Fadner, R., Gobdsen, J. M., Grey, A., Janis, I. L., Kaplan, A., Kaplan, D., Mintz, A., De Sola Pool, I., and Yakobsen, S. 1968. *Language of Politics: Studies in quantitative semantics.* Cambridge Mass.: MIT Press.

MACCORMAC, E. R. 1971. Meaning Variance and Metaphor. *British Journal for the Philosophy of Science* **22** (2): 145–59.

NICHOLSON, M. 1970. *Conflict Analysis.* London: English Universities Press.

PARSONS, K. P. 1971. On Criteria of Meaning Change. *British Journal for the Philosophy of Science* **22** (2): 131–44.

ROSENAU, J. N. 1971. *The Scientific Study of Foreign Policy.* New York: The Free Press; London: Collier-Macmillan.

SHUBIK, M. 1972. On the Scope of Gaming. *Management Science* Part 2. *18* (5): 20–36. January. (See also references quoted by Shubik and those quoted by Bowen 1971.)

SMITH, D. G. 1971a. Crisis Management. Paper presented at the 1971 Annual Conference of the Operational Research Society of Great Britain, held at the University of Lancaster. Birmingham: The Operational Research Society.

——1971b. A Framework for Research into Crisis-Management: The concept of the interaction between adaptive decision-making systems. *DOAE Memorandum* 7122. Defence Operational Analysis Establishment, Ministry of Defence.

THOMAS, J. C. and MCNICHOLLS, G. 1969. *Why People Play Games: Report of a survey*. Denver: Joint National Meeting of The American Aeronautical and Operational Research Societies.

TOU, J. T. (ed.) 1965. *Advances in Information Systems Sciences*. Vols. 1 and 2. New York: Plenum Press.

WHITE, D. J. 1969. *Decision Theory*. London: George Allen and Unwin.

The use of models in linguistics

JOHN LYONS

For the purposes of this paper, the field of linguistics may be conveniently sub-classified in terms of the following four distinctions: theoretical versus applied, general versus descriptive, synchronic versus diachronic, microlinguistics versus macrolinguistics.

1 By theoretical linguistics is meant the scientific study of language for its own sake; by applied linguistics, the application of the concepts, techniques, and results of either theoretical or descriptive linguistics to such practical tasks as language-teaching, speech-therapy, the design of literacy programmes, the standardisation of national languages for emergent states, and so on. We shall not be concerned with applied linguistics at all in what follows.

2 'General linguistics is not normally distinguished from theoretical linguistics; and we will not insist upon the difference here. It will be convenient, however, to reserve the term 'general' as the complement of 'descriptive'. General linguistics, then, sets itself the goal of establishing a theory of the structure of language (i.e., of language in general), whereas descriptive linguistics deals with the analysis of particular languages (English, Amharic, Navaho, etc.). In both cases, it should be noted we can talk appropriately in terms of model-construction: the general linguist sets out to construct a model of language, and the descriptive linguist to construct a model of some particular language. How the general model is related to particular descriptive models is an important question, which we will take up briefly at the end of this paper.

3 Synchronic linguistics deals with languages considered as static

systems, without reference to their previous or subsequent historical development and without reference to their so-called genetic relationships; diachronic (or historical) linguistics is concerned with the changes that take place, or have taken place, in languages between successive points in time. The distinction between general and descriptive linguistics, it should be observed, is independent of the distinction between synchronic and diachronic linguistics. If our aim is to construct a theory, or model, of language change, then we are engaged in general diachronic linguistics. If we are dealing with the historical development of some particular language, we are doing descriptive diachronic linguistics. Just as synchronic models may be either general or descriptive, so also may diachronic models.

4 The terms 'microlinguistics' and 'macrolinguistics' are here being used to refer to a relatively narrow or relatively broad conception of the scope of linguistics. The microlinguistic view of languages deliberately abstracts from their social context and social function, from the manner in which they are acquired in infancy, from the psychological mechanisms which underly the production and reception of speech, from the aesthetic and literary function of language, and so on. These, and other aspects, of language are dealt with in such branches of macrolinguistics as sociolinguistics, psycholinguistics, neurolinguistics and stylistics. A particular instance of the distinction between the subject matter of microlinguistics and of macrolinguistics – and one of central concern to us in the present connection, as we shall see – is the distinction between competence and performance. Microlinguistics is commonly referred to as structural linguistics (cf. Lyons 1970:8).

Before moving into the subject proper, I should perhaps say something about the term 'model' and the way in which it is, or has been, employed by linguists. As Chao (1962) pointed out in his article on this very topic, it is a term that is used in somewhat different senses in different disciplines. For the mathematician and mathematical logician, a model is a formal system considered from the point of view of its interpretation, or application to some practical problem, rather than abstractly for its own sake. However, when the social scientist or physical scientist employs the term 'model', he usually means some deliberately restricted and abstract representation of the phenomena whose structure or behaviour is being studied. Typical examples of models, in this sense of the term, are a physicist's representation of atomic structure or an economist's analysis of monopolistic competition. Since any model of this kind is necessarily based upon an idealization of the data that it is designed to describe or explain, how one decides which variations in the data are of significance and which variations can be discounted becomes a question of crucial importance; and the answer to this question will depend upon the nature of the correspondence that is assumed to hold between the data and the model, and upon a fairly precise prior specification of what it is that the model is intended to explain or describe.

I will come back to the problem of idealization later. Here it may be worth mentioning that, as Chao points out in the same article, there are conflicting senses in the everyday use of the term 'model', and these can affect our intuitive interpretation of its more technical senses. Sometimes we think of a model as a norm to which actually existent objects or actually occurrent patterns of behaviour merely approximate; at other times, we talk as if the model were but an imperfect and purely derivative representation of independently existing objects. One is reminded of the age-old philosophical problem of universals: which are more 'real', the variable phenomena of experience or the unvarying ideas, or universals, manifest in these phenomena? And what is the nature of their 'manifestation'? Chomsky's (1962:531) attitude, as reflected in the following quotation from his paper delivered at the same conference as Chao's paper, is representative of one standpoint: 'Actual discourse consists of interrupted fragments, false starts, lapses, slurring, and other phenomena that can only be understood as distortions of an underlying idealised pattern . . .'. Against this, one could cite passages from other linguists who point out, correctly, that many sentences allowed as grammatical by Chomsky's model of English would never occur in any normal context of use and, on the basis of what Chomsky calls 'distortions of an underlying idealised pattern', condemn the model itself, saying that it forces the data into an arbitrarily restricted and confining mould.

The two senses of 'model' that have been distinguished above are not of course incompatible. Moreover, since the term tends to be used by those who favour formalization of a mathematical kind in the interests of rigour and explicitness, in linguistics, as in other sciences, the two senses are frequently merged or conflated. There are occasions, however, when it is important to emphasize one aspect of model construction rather than the other and in doing so to use the term in one sense rather than the other. In linguistics, the distinction between the two senses is most clearly seen perhaps in relation to the distinction between general and descriptive linguistics that has already been drawn. The phrase 'a model of language' is more naturally construed in the mathematician's sense of the term than is the phrase 'a model of English' or 'a model of Amharic'.

Both of the senses of the term 'model' referred to so far might be described as relatively strict, or technical, senses. In the linguistic literature of the last fifteen or twenty years, the term has often been employed rather more loosely – most notably perhaps in the title of Hockett's (1954) important paper on 'Two Models of Grammatical Description, which contrasts in this respect with Chomsky's (1956) Three Models for the Description of Language. For Hockett (1954: 210), a model is 'a frame of reference within which an analyst approaches the grammatical phase of the language and states the results of his investigations'; and in his paper he is concerned with two such 'archetypical frames of reference'. In much the same vein, linguists commonly talk about the generative, or 'Chomskyan', model and contrast this with the tagmemic, stratificational, system-structure, Prague School, or glossematic models of description. Whether these various frames of reference should all be regarded as distinct general models of language, in the stricter sense of the term 'model', is a question that I will not go into in detail. However, I will say something about the general question of comparing different theoretical frames of reference after they have been formalized as mathematical models. Here I merely draw attention to the fact that the term 'model' is often used more loosely in linguistics than it will henceforth be employed in this paper.

According to Bar-Hillel (1962:551), 'Linguistics is a complex mixture of theory and observation. The precise nature of this mixture is still not too well understood, and in this respect the difference between linguistics and, say, physics is probably at most one of degree.' How theory and observation are, and should be, related in both general and descriptive linguistics is, in fact, a matter of considerable controversy among linguists. Here I can do no more than state one view of this relationship (cf. Lyons 1972:55ff.).

I will begin by drawing a distinction between *language-behaviour* and the *language-system* which underlies it. When we say that someone is speaking a particular language, English for example, we imply that he is engaged in a certain kind of behaviour, or activity, in the course of which he produces vocal signals, or *utterances*. Native speakers of English will recognize these utterances as belonging to the language, we assume, and as being, for the most part at least, acceptable, appropriate to their situation of utterance and interpretable. So much is a matter of pre-theoretical observation (in a somewhat extended, but surely legitimate, sense of 'observation', which allows us to include under this head the questioning of informants about the acceptability, appropriateness, and meaning of utterances). What the linguist does when he describes a language is to construct a model, not of actual language-behaviour, but of the system of regularities which underly, or are manifest in, that behaviour – a model of the language-system. The distinction between language-behaviour and an underlying language-system was drawn by de Saussure (1916) in terms of the opposition between *parole* and *langue*; and, in Europe, if not in America, it was widely accepted and became the foundation stone of twentieth-century microlinguistics. The same, or a very similar distinction has been drawn by Chomsky (1965:4), in terms of performance and competence. When we say that someone can speak English, we imply that he has acquired, normally in infancy, the mastery of a system of rules or regularities underlying the behaviour which we refer to as speaking English: he has acquired a certain *competence*, and it is this which makes possible, and is manifest in, his *performance*. (Note in passing that 'He speaks English but he never speaks English' is not necessarily contradictory. The first clause may be referring to competence; the second to performance.)

Throughout this paper, we will restrict our attention to models of competence (and, more narrowly, to models known as *sentence generating grammars*); and we will make a certain number of simplifying assumptions. None of these are in fact unchallengeable; and to certain of them we will come back presently; for the moment, however, we will let them stand unchallenged. We will define a language to be a set of *sentences*; and we will assume that, prior to the construction of a descriptive model for any particular language, we know or can discover that certain utterances, actual or potential, are sentences of the language and that certain other utterances, actual or potential, are not. We will assume that each sentence is composed of a finite and determinate number of *words*; that, in general, words can be readily identified as tokens of the same type (on different occasions of their utterance and in different sentences); that they are discrete and, as far as we are concerned, internally unstructured; that their sequential order in sentences is significant (in the sense that every distinct permutation of the same set of words is a different sentence). One final important assumption we will make is that, although every sentence of the language must consist of a finite number of words, no determinate upper bound can be set to the length of sentences (i.e., there is no longest sentence). Confronted with any sentence consisting of n words, speakers of the language will be able to produce an equally acceptable sentence consisting of $n + 1$ words (for all finite values of n): this being so, we can define the language to be an infinite set of finite sequences of words. This assumption has been challenged (e.g., by Reich 1969) but it is accepted by most linguists.

We can now apply these assumptions and considerations to English and attempt to make them more precise. Let W be a finite set of elements each of which can be put into correspondence (either one-to-one or many-to-one) with the set of all English words. W may be thought of as modelling the vocabulary of English. Henceforth, we will refer to the members of W as words. Now, let U be the set of all finite sequences, or *strings*, that can be formed from the members of W by means of the binary operation of concatenation. If α is a string and if β is a string, then $\alpha + \beta$ (i.e., the result of concatenating α with β) is also a string: that is to say, U is closed under concatenation. It is convenient, for ease of formalization and for the purpose of achieving greater generality, to let single words count as strings (i.e., $W \subset U$), and also to introduce, as a distinguished member of U, the empty string ø (i.e., the string of zero length) to serve as an identity element with respect to concatenation: thus, $\alpha + ø = ø + \alpha = \alpha$. Concatenation is associative: $(\alpha + \beta) + \gamma = \alpha + (\beta + \gamma)$. However, it is not commutative: $\alpha + \beta \neq \beta + \alpha$. Any system with the mathematical properties just described (closure, associativity, and having an identity element) is a semi-group, or monoid; and if the operation under which it is closed is concatenation, it is called a *free monoid*. In our example, U is the free monoid on W; and the elements of W are the generators of U (cf. Gross and Lentin 1970:4).

If there are m words in the vocabulary (i.e., $W = \{W_1, W_2, W_3 \ldots, W_m\}$), there are just m strings of length 1 (or degree 1), m^2 strings of length 2, and in general m^l strings of length l in U. (The empty string represents the case where l is zero: $m^0 = 1$.) The total of the number of strings in U is given by the formula $m\ (m - 1)/(m - 1)$. If m is finite, and if no upper bound is set to *l*, there is an infinite, but denumerably infinite, number of strings in U (cf. Chomsky and Miller 1958). Every finite or infinite subset of U, we will say, is a *formal language* (and there is a non-denumerable infinity of them). Using 'L' to refer to the set of all the subsets of U, we can distinguish each subset by means of a subscript: $L = \{L_a, L_6, L_c, \ldots\}$. Any string in L_x (where 'L_x' is a variable ranging over the members of L) may be described as a sentence of L_x. But how do we select from L some particular member, which we will refer to as L_e and for the moment assume to be unique, to serve as a descriptive model for English? Of all the strings in U, some can be put into correspondence (in an intuitively obvious and quite readily formalizable way) with acceptable sentences of English (e.g. *there is a conference going on*); others cannot (e.g., *is conference a chicken an of not*). Ideally, we want L_e to contain as sentences all the former, but none of the latter, strings. In addition to the clearly acceptable (i.e., pre-theoretically grammatical) and clearly unacceptable (i.e., pre-theoretically ungrammatical) sequences of English words, there is a third set whose status pre-theoretically, is uncertain (e.g., *this book has been being read, that the book that the boy that that girl goes out with is reading should be so abstruse surprises me, she doesn't astonish easily*). With respect to this third set of sequences, which we will call *pre-theoretically indeterminate*, and the strings corresponding to them in U, there are alternative courses of action open to us. But let us leave this for the moment.

Any set of rules for selecting L_x from U is a *grammar* of L_x: it *generates* L_x, and will be symbolized as $G(L_x)$. In principle, the grammar might be finite or infinite. As linguists, we are interested in using formal grammars as descriptive or general models for natural language. All natural languages, including English, are learned and used by human beings; and human beings can hold in store only a finite number of units (of whatever kind). Therefore, we will restrict ourselves to a consideration of formal grammars with a finite number of rules (operating upon a finite vocabulary). What grammar, or set of rules, will generate L_e? Are there different grammars – G_1, G_2, $G_3, \ldots, G_n$ – each of which generates L_e? If so, what are the formal properties which differentiate them? Can any of these properties be said to reflect, or model, properties of the sentences of English? It is questions of this kind which engaged the interest of Chomsky in his early work on models of linguistic description.

None of these questions, it should be noted, is purely empirical. Even the first of them depends quite strongly upon formal considerations. For, as we have been careful to emphasize throughout, the model does not directly generate the set of acceptable English utterances, but a set of theoretical constructs which can be put into correspondence with (a subset of) acceptable English utterances. The members of L_e may be described as *system-sentences* (of English); and the utterances actual or potential, in correspondence with them as *text-sentences* (of English). It is in principle conceivable that there is no grammar that will generate all and only the strings in U that correspond (in the intuitively obvious way) with the pre-theoretically determinate text-sentences of English ('. . . the set of all subsets of U is non-denumerably infinite). Thus, the set of possible languages in a given vocabulary is non-denumerable. However, a grammar is of finite length, so the set of all grammars is denumerable. Therefore, not all languages can have grammars that generate them' (Chomsky and Miller 1958). So far it has not been proved that this is or is not the case. What has been proved is that there are certain classes of strings in U in correspondence with classes of pre-theoretically determinate text-sentences of English which cannot be generated by grammars of a particular type: we will come back to this presently.

But first we must take up the question of the pre-theoretically indeterminate text-sentences of English. One way of resolving the issue (if we can do so) is first to formulate the rules of G (L_e) so that they generate system-sentences in correspondence with the pre-theoretically determinate text-sentences of English but fail to generate system-sentences corresponding to the pre-theoretically determinate non-sentences of English and then, to decide that all and only the sequences of English words in correspondence with system-sentences of L_e are thereby defined to be grammatical. This is the simpler, and perhaps the more satisfactory way, of handling the problem (cf. Chomsky 1956:114). Alternatively, one might attempt to generate system-sentences corresponding to all the pre-theoretically indeterminate text-sentences as well as to the pre-theoretically determinate text-sentences, but to do so in a way which distinguishes between them and thus formalizes some notion of a degree of grammaticalness. In either case, it should be noted, the descriptive model can be interpreted as a theory of the grammatical structure of English. The sentences which it generates can be regarded as theorems derivable, or 'provable', within G (L_e) in so far as G(L_e) is treated as an abstract system, but empirically verifiable as 'predictions', by means of observation and the questioning of informants, when G (L_e) is interpreted as a model of English. From this point of view, the formal grammar is an axiomatic system which recursively defines the extension of the predicate 'grammatical in English'; alternatively and equivalently, as a theory of the grammatical structure of English sentences.

So much for the general framework. There can be no question in the space available, of discussing the details of the different kinds of linguistic models that have been constructed within the framework of assumptions and definitions outlined above. For such discussion reference may be made to the works in the list of references (especially to Chapters 11–13 of Luce, Bush, and Galanter 1963, and Part 2 of Luce, Bush, and Galanter 1965). Let me just mention some of the more important conclusions that have been drawn from the theoretical investigation of linguistic models and their application to the task of describing the grammatical structure of natural languages in recent years. In the mid-1950s, linguistics, like a number of other disciplines, was quite strongly influenced by information-theory (cf. Shannon and Weaver 1949); and proposals were made for the construction of *stochastic* models for the representation of grammatical structure. Since then, the interest of linguists in probabilistic models has waned (at least as far as competence models are concerned; the situation with respect to performance models is rather different). Nowadays, most linguists seem to be of the opinion that grammaticality is not a statistical concept; and the focus of attention has shifted to *algebraic* models.

In his early works, Chomsky (1956; 1959), drawing upon the ideas of such linguists as Harris (1951; 1952) and of mathematicians and logicians like Post (1944), Kleene (1956) and Davis (1958), investigated the formal properties of different kinds of algebraic models and compared them in terms of their *adequacy* for the representation of the grammatical structure of the sentences of natural languages. Adequacy, in the context of Chomsky's discussion, splits into two parts: weak and strong. *Weak adequacy* (or weak generative capacity) has to do with whether a given set of system-sentences is or is not generated by a grammar; strong adequacy is a more complex and controversial notion, which we will take up presently. Chomsky considered a variety of different types of model with respect to their weak generative capacity: notably, finite state grammars (FSG), context-free phrase-structure grammars (CFG), context-sensitive phrase-structure grammars (CSG) and, in a more limited way, transformational grammars. He showed that, from this point of view, they could be arranged in a hierarchy: finite-state languages (i.e., languages generated by FSG) constitute a proper sub-set of CF languages; and CF languages constitute a proper sub-set of both CS languages and languages generated by transformational grammars. Furthermore, he demonstrated that there are certain system-sentences of English (i.e., strings that we should wish to include in L_e) which grammars of the lowest type are intrinsically incapable of generating. But he left open the question whether there are any system-sentences of English beyond the generative capacity of grammars of the next highest type. (It was for other reasons that he decided in favour of transformational grammars.)

If different grammars – G_1, G_2, G_3, . . . , G_n – generate exactly the same language, they are said to be *weakly equivalent*; and various equivalences of this kind have been proved, by Chomsky and others. In particular, it has been demonstrated that a number of formally distinct grammars (dependency grammars, categorial grammars, pushdown-store grammars, etc.) are all weakly equivalent to CF phrase-structure grammars. The fact that different grammars can be weakly equivalent raises the important question, how, if at all, one might decide between them in the selection of a descriptive model for a particular natural language; and this brings us to the notion of strong adequacy.

Linguists are not interested simply in deciding whether a given string of words is or is not a grammatically well-formed sentence of the language that they are analysing. They are much more concerned with saying, granted that it is well-formed, what its grammatical structure is; that is to say, with assigning to it a certain *structural description.* Now, certain formal grammars (though not all) are capable of assigning a categorial classification (roughly speaking, a classification in terms of the parts of speech) to the words in the strings that they generate and grouping these words into phrases; and this is part at least of the information that a linguist would wish to have represented in the structural description of the sentences of natural languages. He would no doubt wish to say of a sentence *My friend has just died* that the first two words go together and constitute a single phrase, as do the last three words; and that *my* falls into the same category as *your, his,* etc., *friend* into the same category as *boy, father*, etc., and so on. A grammar that is capable of assigning a structural description incorporating information of this kind to the sentences that it generates is clearly more strongly adequate than one that is not.

Strong adequacy, as I have already mentioned, is more controversial than weak adequacy; and it is, in practice and perhaps also in principle, a comparative notion. For certain types of grammars at least, it is a decidable question whether they generate or fail to generate a given set of sentences. It is arguable that there is no similarly absolute measure of strong adequacy and that the most we can hope to demonstrate is that one descriptive model is more strongly adequate than another, not that it is, without qualification, strongly adequate. What then are the criteria of evaluation? Unfortunately, there is no clear answer to this question. In general, we can say that the structural descriptions assigned to the system-sentences generated by the grammar should be such as to provide us with insights into the way in which the corresponding text-sentences are used and understood. Two criteria of strong adequacy which satisfy this general requirement may be mentioned here.

In English, as in other languages, there are many instances of syntactic ambiguity; that is to say, ambiguity which depends not upon the ambiguity of particular words, but rather upon the way in which words are grouped or combined in sentences and phrases. A simple example is the phrase *beautiful girl's hat.* We would expect a formal grammar of English to model the ambiguity of this phrase by assigning to it at least two non-equivalent structural descriptions; and furthermore to show in these alternative structural descriptions that under one interpretation *beautiful* is taken with, or modifies, *girl's hat*, but that under the other interpretation *beautiful* modifies *girl* and the phrase *beautiful girl's* modifies *hat.* (There is yet a third interpretation according to which both *beautiful* and *girl's* simultaneously, as it were, modify *hat.*) Syntactic ambiguity then, yields one criterion of strong adequacy.

Just as the same sequence of words may, in different contexts or on different occasions of its use, have more than one meaning, so more than one sequence of words may have the same meaning. This fact yields another, though less generally accepted and less clear-cut, criterion of strong adequacy. (It is less clear-cut because people will differ about what counts as sameness of meaning.) It can be argued that different sentences that have the same meaning and whose sameness of meaning does not depend upon their containing synonymous words (e.g., corresponding active and passive sentences, *John opened the door* and *The door was opened by John*) should be shown as grammatically related by deriving the one from the other or both from some common underlying more abstract structure. This is what is done in a transformational grammar; and it is primarily for this reason, rather than for anything having to do with weak generative capacity, that transformational grammars, as formalized by Chomsky are widely regarded as being more satisfactory than CF grammars as models of the grammatical structure of English and other natural languages.

It is difficult to say much more than this about the notion of strong adequacy without getting embroiled in controversy; and even the little that has been said here would be regarded by some linguists as tendentious. The weak generative capacity, and consequently the weak equivalence, of formal grammars can be subjected to precise mathematical investigation; and the results that are obtained are, generally speaking, incontrovertible. The problem with strong adequacy is that it rests rather heavily upon the subjective judgment of native speakers of the language that is being described, on the one hand, and of linguists, on the other. Even the native speaker's judgments of acceptability and semantic equivalence are, in many cases, uncertain; and little progress has yet been made in devising reliable operational tests (but see Quirk and Svartvik 1966; Greenbaum and Quirk, 1970). Intuitions of grammatical relatedness (on the assumption that native speakers do have such intuitions) would seem to be far less amenable to observation or controlled experiment; and yet much of the argumentation that goes on in linguistics about the relative merits of alternative analyses depends upon the pre-theoretical assumption that certain grammatical constructions are related and others are not (or not so closely). Even when linguists are in agreement about the data to be accounted for by their descriptive models, they may still disagree on the question whether alternative descriptions are strongly equivalent. For example, the assertion by Lyons (1968:231) that categorial grammars and CF grammars are weakly but not strongly, equivalent is denied (without argument) by Bar-Hillel (1970:372). More strikingly, in the current controversy centering upon the status of 'generative semantics' (cf. Lakoff 1971; Chomsky 1971) has claimed that the difference between the way in which the relationship between syntax and semantics is handled in the 'standard theory' of transformational grammar and the way in which it is represented in 'generative semantics' is purely 'notational';

that is to say, that the two models are strongly equivalent. In so far as the dispute between the protagonists turns upon the interpretation of formal properties of the two models, as in part at least it seems to, it is insoluble. Whether there is anything of empirical consequence at stake is as yet unclear.

In view of what has just been said about strong adequacy (and it must be emphasized that the weak generative capacity of different formal systems is of only limited interest to the linguist), it might well be asked what is the point of using mathematical models at all. The answer is that a mathematical model makes precise and explicit, in a way that it is almost impossible to do without formalization, just what is being said about the object of description and, provided that the nature of the correspondence between the model and the data is clarified to the satisfaction of those using it, it is suggestive of empirically testable hypotheses. It is unlikely, for example, that scholars would have thought of trying to determine by experiment the relative acceptability or comprehensibility of sentences containing different kinds of embedded structures (cf. Wales and Marshall 1966), if the differences between these structures had not first been made explicit in a formal model.

It has been argued by Hockett (1968) that the whole enterprise of constructing linguistic models is misbegotten, on the grounds that a natural language is not a well-defined system (i.e., a system 'that can be completely and exactly characterised by deterministic functions'). This brings up the whole question of *idealization*. I have suggested elsewhere that this can be thought of as comprising three stages, or phases (cf. Lyons 1972:58 ff.): regularization, standardization, and what I will here call abstraction. By *regularization* I mean the elimination from utterances used as data of all such performance errors as 'slips of the tongue', mispronunciations, hesitation pauses, stuttering and stammering, etc. By *standardization* I refer to the deliberate discounting of all the purely idiosyncratic features in the speech of any particular informant and all but the major systematic variations of style and dialect in the speech-community whose language is being described. And by *abstraction* (by far the most controversial of these three phases of idealization), I mean the isolation of utterances and parts of utterances from their context and their conversion to what are regarded, pre-theoretically, as grammatically complete and independent text-sentences. If this is what the descriptive linguist does when he idealizes the data, it is clear that he cannot reasonably claim to be describing the language-system as this is stored, neurophysiologically, in the brain of any one individual at any one time. The language-system that the linguist is describing, no less than his model of it, is a theoretical construct. It may even be the case that the language-system underlying the language-behaviour of any one individual is in part indeterminate and unstable through even short periods of time, so that it is, in Hockett's sense of the term, in part ill-defined. But it surely does not follow that because not everything is determinate, everything must be indeterminate and beyond the scope of description by means of a system of rules. As Palmer puts it, 'it is difficult to see how serious linguistics could be undertaken without some form of' the assumption that underlying language-behaviour there is 'a limited set of rules or structures that is (a) valid for a period of time, (b) shared by a community, and (c) exemplified by a select number and not the totality of actual utterances' (Palmer 1969:621). The important thing is not to be misled by this methodological assumption into thinking that for every string of words it is in principle decidable, if we could but devise a satisfactory operational test, whether it is or is not generated by the language-system internalized by any or all speakers of the language.

One final point. At the beginning of this paper I drew a distinction between general and descriptive models. So far, in the body of the paper, I have talked only of descriptive models. What then is the relationship between the one and the other? It should be noticed, first of all, that, in defining the aim of general linguistics to be the construction of a model of language, I am presupposing that there is such a thing as language; that is to say, that all natural languages have certain common properties which distinguish them from other behavioural systems. Most linguists nowadays would probably agree that there is good reason to believe that this is the case (cf. Lyons 1972). Just how much is universal in the grammatical structure of different natural languages is, however a matter of considerable dispute. It is in principle possible that within the class of formally distinct sentence-generating grammars there are those that are more adequate as descriptive models for certain natural languages than they are for others. At present, there is no clear evidence that this is so. It seems reasonable therefore, to work towards the construction of a unitary general model of grammatical structure. Of course, this will not be a sentence-generating grammar of the same kind as the formal grammars used as descriptive models. Unlike them, it will not consist of a system of rules for the recursive enumeration of well-formed strings on a set of entities which can be put into correspondence with the words of natural languages. Its relationship to different descriptive models would be that of metalanguage to object language; and its function would be to define the class of possible grammars, and thus, at once remove, the class of possible natural languages, by specifying what kind of theoretical constructs are permissible in descriptive grammatical models and the nature of the rules by means of which they are combined or otherwise manipulated. Needless to say, linguistics is still a long way from having constructed such a model, but some progress has been made.

REFERENCES

BAR-HILLEL, Y. 1962. Some Recent Results in Linguistics. In E. Nagel, P. Suppes, and A. Tarski: Reprinted in Bar-Hillel (1964: 185–94).

——1964. *Language and Information.* Reading, Mass.: Addison-Wesley.

——1970. *Aspects of Language.* Jerusalem: Magnes.

CHAO, Y. R. 1962. Models in Linguistics and Models in General. In E. Nagel, P. Suppes and A. Tarski.

CHOMSKY, N. 1956. Three Models for the Description of Language. *IRE Transactions on Information Theory, IT*-2. 113–24. Reprinted in R. D. Luce, R. R. Bush, and E. Galanter (1963: 269–321).

——1959. On Certain Formal Properties of Grammars. *Information and Control* (**1**): 91–112.

——1962. Explanatory Models in Linguistics. In E. Nagel, P. Suppes, and A. Tarski.

——1963. Introduction to the Formal Analysis of Natural Languages. In R. D. Luce, R. R. Bush, and E. Galanter *Handbook of Mathematical Psychology.* Vol. 2. New York, London and Sydney: Wiley.

——1965. *Aspects of the Theory of Syntax.* Cambridge, Mass.: MIT Press.

——1971. Deep Structure, Surface Structure and Semantic Interpretation In D. D. Steinberg and L. A. Jakobovits.

CHOMSKY, N. and MILLER, G. A. 1958. Finite State Languages. *Information and Control* **1**: 91–112. Reprinted in R. D. Luce, R. R. Bush, and E. Galanter 1965: 156–171.

DAVIS, M. 1958. *Computability and Unsolvability.* New York: McGraw Hill.

GREENBAUM, S. and QUIRK, R. 1970. *Elicitation Experiments in English.* London: Longman.

GROSS, M. 1972. *Mathematical Models in Linguistics.* Englewood Cliffs, N.J.: Prentice Hall.

GROSS, M. and LENTIN, A. 1970. *Introduction to Formal Grammars.* New York: Springer.

HARRIS, Z. 1951. *Methods in Structural Linguistics.* Chicago: University of Chicago Press.

——1952. Discourse analysis. *Language* **28**: 18–23; 474–94.

HOCKETT, C. F. 1954. Two Models of Grammatical Description. *Word* **10**: 210–33. Reprinted in Joos, M. *Readings in Linguistics.* Washington: ACLS, 1957; and Chicago: University of Chicago Press, 1966.

——1968. *The State of the Art.* The Hague: Mouton.

KLEENE, S. C. 1956. Representation of Events in Nerve Nets. In Shannon, C. E. and McCarthy, J. *Automata Studies.* Princeton, N.J.: Princeton University Press.

LAKOFF, G. 1971. On Generative Semantics. In O. D. Steinberg and L. A. Jakobovits.

LUCE, R. D., BUSH, R. R., and GALANTER, E. 1963. *Handbook of Mathematical Psychology,* Vol. 2 New York: Wiley.

——1965. *Readings in Mathematical Psychology.* New York: Wiley.

LYONS, J. 1968. *Introduction to Theoretical Linguistics.* London: Cambridge University Press.

——1970. *New Horizons in Linguistics.* Harmondsworth: Penguin.

——1972. Human Language. In R. A. Hinde, *Non-Verbal Communication.* London: Royal Society and Cambridge University Press.

NAGEL, E., SUPPES, P. and TARSKI, A. 1962. *Logic, Methodology and Philosophy of Science.* Stanford: Stanford University Press.

PALMER, F. R. 1969. Review of Hockett (1968). In *Language* **45**: 616–21.

POST, E. C. 1944. Recursively Enumerable Sets of Positive Integers and their Decision Problems. *Bulletin of American Mathematic Society* **50**: 285–316.

QUIRK, R. and SVARTVIK, J. 1966. *Investigating Linguistic Acceptability.* The Hague: Mouton.

REICH, P. A. 1969. The Finiteness of Natural Language. *Language* **45**: 831–43.

SAUSSURE, F. DE 1916. *Course de linguistique generale.* Paris: Payot.

SHANNON, C. E. and WEAVER, W. 1948. *The Mathematical Model of Communication.* Urbana, Ill.: University of Illinois Press.

STEINBERG, D. D. and JAKOBOVITS, L. A. (eds.) 1971. *Semantics.* London: Cambridge University Press.

WALES, R. J. and MARSHALL, J. C. 1966. The Organisation of Linguistic Performance. In Lyons, J. and Wales, R.J. *Psycholinguistics Papers.* Edinburgh: Edinburgh University Press.

WALL, R. 1972. *Introduction to Mathematical Linguistics.* Englewood Cliffs, N.J.: Prentice Hall.

*The application of a stochastic process model to geographical analysis**

LYNDHURST COLLINS

INTRODUCTION

The use of models in geography, though widespread, has tended to lag behind their use in several other social sciences. The use of Markov chain analysis – the simplest form of stochastic process model – was not, for example, introduced to the geographic literature until the early 1960s (Brown 1963). However, during the last decade, numerous studies, both in 'human' and 'physical' geography, have adopted Markovian frameworks. Most of these studies have employed concepts relating to regular, finite Markov chains, though a limited number have been concerned with absorbing chains and a few with continuous and semi-continuous Markov processes. Much progress has been made, but since most applications have been concerned with empirically based Markov chains, data deficiencies (insufficient number of observations, or inadequate time series) have limited the scope and goals of many research designs. For example, most studies have used Markov chains for descriptive purposes only and very few have used the concept as a model of geographic process. Although data deficiencies created difficulties the overriding geographical problem is the classification of a system of spatial states. In all approaches of our discipline, geographers have discovered that there is no unique causal ordering device for spatial series and as yet all attempts at a comprehensive definition have proved to be fruitless. Many of the more successful applications in geography have employed aspatial systems of states. This paper will show how both aspatial and spatial systems of states for a regular finite Markov chain can be used in a geographic study.

The study is concerned with describing and predicting the structural and spatial dynamics of manufacturing activity in the Province of Ontario. Although there is little formal theory to suggest which general approach would be the most appropriate the philosophies elaborated by Dacey, Curry, Simon, and Steindl in the social sciences suggest a probabilistic framework. Conceptually, the requisite operational forecasting model should accommodate not only processes of birth, growth, and death but also of migration. For instance, several studies have indicated that an important factor influencing the differential growth patterns of urban-industrial areas is their interdependency which in terms of manufacturing activity can manifest itself in the form of industrial migration, involving the relocation of plants from one urban area to another. The simplest stochastic model, amenable to migration research, is Markov chain analysis.

Technically, there are several advantages to a Markov chain model though it is not within the scope of this short paper to demonstrate that a Markovian framework is the best approach. One critical assumption of Markov models, as with most other models, is that of constant parameters or 'stationarity' but in Markov chain analysis statistical procedures are available for testing this and other underlying assumptions. The stochastic properties of Markov models allow a multiplicity of variables to be embraced by a random component, thereby considerably simplifying the computational procedures. Moreover, the basic matrix structure of a Markov model avoids the necessity of replicating the analysis over as many spatial units as comprise the study area so that in generalizing the processes involved the technique provides insight which may not be so readily attainable by conventional methods of analysis (Rogers 1968).

For computational simplicity two sets of Markovian matrices are developed. One set is aspatial in that the Markov 'states' comprise establishment size categories; such structural matrices are used to predict changes in the size distribution of establishments for the selected area, in this case the Province of Ontario, individual towns, and industrial categories. Therefore, this model analyses the internal structures of selected areal units on a disaggregated basis since frequency distributions are used as input parameters. These parameters are analysed within the conceptual framework of two hypotheses – the Pareto and the lognormal distributions. Both hypotheses embody Gibrat's Law of Proportionate Growth which postulates that the proportional change in the size of a plant in any single time interval is independent of its absolute size; this implies that large and small plants have the same proportionate rates of growth. Changes in the configurations of these probability distributions are generally assumed to be generated by a simple stochastic or Markov process (Simon 1954).

Spatial states comprise the second set of Markovian matrices. Ideally, any system of spatial states should cover completely the study area so that all movement is included in the model. For example, the basic first-order Markov property provides that the future location of an observation unit at time, t + 1, will be dependent upon its location at time t but not on previous locations. Conceivably, then, a system of states can be adopted, whereby all movement is masked because the 'size' of the state, in terms of geographical area, effectively excludes movement out of that state. Thus, a ten state Markov matrix representing the Canadian provinces may not be appropriate for predicting provincial establishments if interprovincial relocations do not occur; in this event the provincial increase in number of establishments would be independent of events elsewhere. It is for this reason, therefore, that it is necessary in the first instance to determine as accurately as possible the nature of industrial movement so as to select a meaningful descriptive set of spatial states.

THE DATA AND THEIR ORGANIZATION

All the data have been extracted from information collected by Statistics Canada for its annual census of manufacturing industries. This information has been recorded on computer tapes since 1961 but the analyses, because of time constraints, have been confined to the 1961–66 period. The data include all manufacturing establishments as defined by Statistics Canada with individual total employments ranging from zero to the size of the largest plant. Each establishment on the computer tape is assigned a code for its province, county, municipality, industry (at the 4– digit level), and establishment number. Thus a plant (013), manufacturing coffins (S.I.C.=2580), in Gravenhurst (13), Muskoka County (30) in the province of Ontario (05) is identified as 05–30–13–2580–013. This unique number enables the data with some minor exceptions, to be organized into four homogeneous groups which for convenience are assigned demographic terms. A *resident* or *permanent* plant is one which appears with the same location code on each of the five annual tapes 1961–65. (Only the 1961–65 period is used for analysis. The data for 1966 are used for testing the model's predictive accuracy.) A plant is 'born' when its unique number appears on a tape for the first time and is described as a *birth*; similarly, a plant 'dies' when its unique number disappears for the first time and is termed a *death*. Those plants that appear on two successive tapes but with different location codes are termed *migrants* or *relocations*. In each year there is approximately a total of twelve thousand establishments.

THE PARETO AND LOGNORMAL DISTRIBUTIONS

The application of many statistical model techniques to social science data is, or should be, contingent on the verification of particular underlying assumptions. For instance, on what basis can we justify the adoption of Markovian theory developed for studying the processes of classical mechanics to geographical analysis? This question can be answered in part with reference to the pioneering works of Kapteyn (1903) and Gibrat (1931). For instance, Gibrat in his analyses of industrial size distributions postulated a process in which growth in proportion to size is a random variable with a given distribution that is considered constant in time. Two of the most common probability distributions that approximate the observed distributions, the Pareto and the lognormal, can both be generated by a simple stochastic process.

Gibrat referred to this process as the Law of Proportionate Growth. In its strongest form, this proposes that temporal changes in firm sizes are governed by a simple Markov process in which the probability of specified percentage increments are independent of a firm's absolute size. Therefore, Gibrat's model bears a strong resemblance to an unrestricted random walk on a line in which the length of the steps taken at each time interval is a random variable relating to its position on the line. Theoretically, if the law of proportionate growth is valid and the process is allowed to continue unhampered for an identical sample of firms, their variance would continue to increase and the sample would exhibit Brownian movement. But as subsumed by Simon and Bonini (1958:607–17) the increase in the 'population' of firms would be offset by a stream of new firms entering and of old firms dying. Although the time period is short the

TABLE 1 Regression of variance of log employment on time for a constant sample of plants in twenty 2-Digit industries 1961–65

	1961		*1962*		*1963*		*1964*		*1965*			
Ind.	Mean	Var.	Mean	Var.	Mean	Var.	Mean	Var.	Mean	Var.	Corr. Coef.	Regr. Coef.
1	·96	·459	·96	·469	·95	·485	·95	·493	9·6	·499	·9859	·0104
2	2·13	·422	2·12	·555	1·12	·525	2·08	·510	2·03	·536	·5624	·0184
3	1·95	·605	1·99	·545	2·02	·587	2·03	·502	2·07	·536	—·6949	0181
4	1·45	·583	1·46	·610	1·46	·601	1·47	·605	1·46	·596	·3217	·0021
5	1·24	·547	1·25	·570	1·27	·569	1·28	·586	1·27	·604	·9655	·0130
6	1·56	·422	1·60	·380	1·61	·339	1·63	·320	1·62	·357	—·7630	—·0190
7	1·25	·370	1·23	·403	1·24	·414	1·26	·412	1·25	·425	·9104	·0119
8	·93	·524	·94	·555	·96	·564	·97	·583	·98	·574	·8929	·0127
9	·69	·542	·70	·549	·72	·558	·72	·567	·73	·575	·9998	·0084
10	1·67	·380	1·68	·380	1·67	·412	1·69	·411	1·72	·389	·4791	·0048
11	·84	·450	·83	·461	·84	·456	·85	·455	·86	·464	·6229	·0022
12	1·60	·690	1·63	·685	1·65	·703	1·65	·731	1·69	·737	·9355	·0139
13	1·16	·438	1·21	·448	1·23	·449	1·26	·453	1·28	·465	·9588	·0060
14	1·60	·395	1·63	·406	1·66	·414	1·68	·422	1·72	·435	·9955	·0096
15	1·60	·732	1·64	·776	1·69	·769	1·73	·801	1·74	·819	·9465	·0198
16	1·81	·463	1·86	·458	1·88	·468	1·89	·482	1·92	·474	·7902	·0047
17	1·18	·406	1·20	·421	1·20	·426	1·21	·437	1·23	·448	·9919	·0100
18	1·73	·656	1·76	·606	1·81	·625	1·83	·617	1·83	·635	—·2488	—·0030
19	1·32	·531	1·34	·529	1·34	·532	1·36	·527	1·37	·535	·3385	·0006
20	·94	·518	·95	·530	·97	·537	·99	·545	1·00	·551	·9922	·0081
All inds.	1·11	·563	1·13	·581	1·14	·590	1·15	·598	1·16	·609	·9890	·0109

figures in *Table 1* indicate the tendency towards Brownian movement for nine of the twenty 2–digit categories whose variance of the logarithm of size increases proportionately with time; for 'all industries' the correlation coefficient between variance and time covered is 0·989, but the best examples are furniture and fixtures (9) and machinery industries (17).

This partial verification of Gibrat's law is upheld further by analysing the actual size distributions. In accordance with Gibrat's law, frequency distributions should be calibrated with constant size intervals. Champernowne (1953) for example, adopted a common logarithmic scale whereas Hart and Prais (1956), and Archer and McGuire (1965) set the upper limit of their intervals as twice that of the lower limit (i.e., an interval progression factor of two). Most other studies have adopted an arbitrary classification (Adelman 1958). Since the goodness of fit of the observed frequencies to the lognormal distribution depends on the size of the class intervals selected, and since individual size observations are available for this study, an iterative search procedure is used to derive the best interval classification scheme for approximating the lognormal distribution. The computed progression factor is 1·55 with $r = 0{\cdot}9624$ and slope of $-1{\cdot}01$ for the constant sample of permanent establishments; the derived size categories are listed in *Table 2*.

When plotted as a Pareto curve on logarithmic paper the distribution for the constant sample of Ontario establishments takes the

TABLE 2 Establishment size categories by number of employees

1	2–3
2	4–6
3	7–10
4	11–17
5	18–27
6	28–43
7	44–67
8	68–105
9	106–165
10	166–256
11	257–398
12	399–618
13	619–960
14	961–

form shown in *Figure 1*. Only the large plants – those with over 400 employees – fall within the range of the Pareto tail with a slope of −1·06; the number of medium and small plants – those below 150 – is grossly unpredicted. When the observations for the same sample

FIGURE 1 Cumulative size distributions (Pareto Curves) for permanent establishments in selected industries for Ontario, 1965

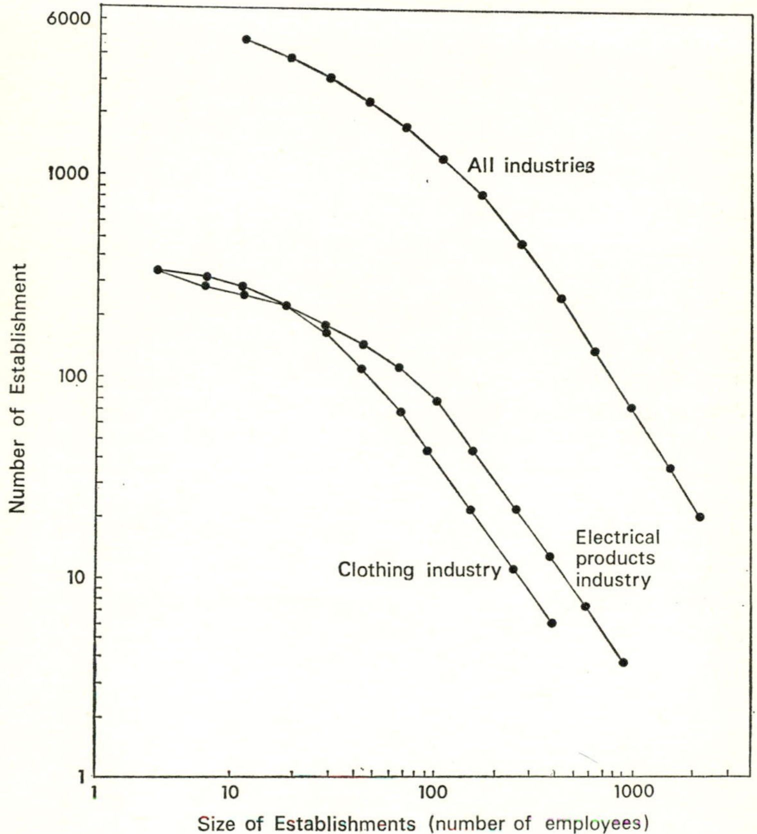

are plotted on logarithmic probability paper the distribution assumes an almost linear form *Figure 2* and endorses Gibrat's notion that the lognormal is a more appropriate model for industrial plants than is the Pareto curve. Also, the almost parallel upward movement of the curve from the 1961 position to that of 1965 confirms in graphic form the dispersive tendency or Brownian movement. Usually the log-

FIGURE 2 Cumulative size distributions (Lognormal Probability Curves) for permanent plants in all industries, 1961–65

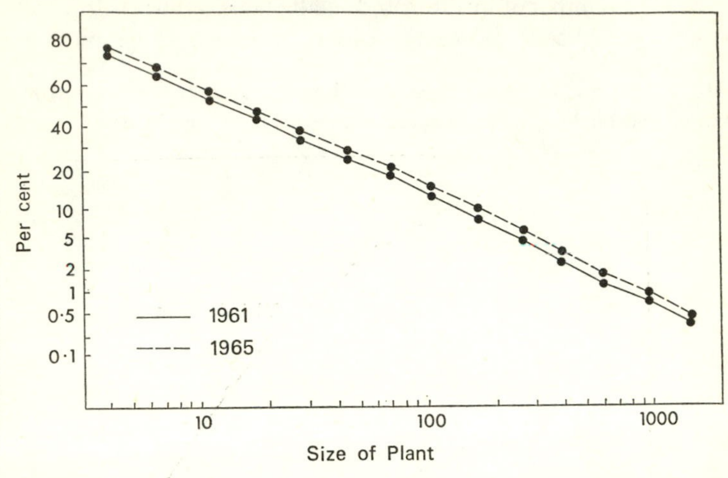

FIGURE 3 Lognormal probability curves for permanent establishments in selected industries, Ontario, 1965

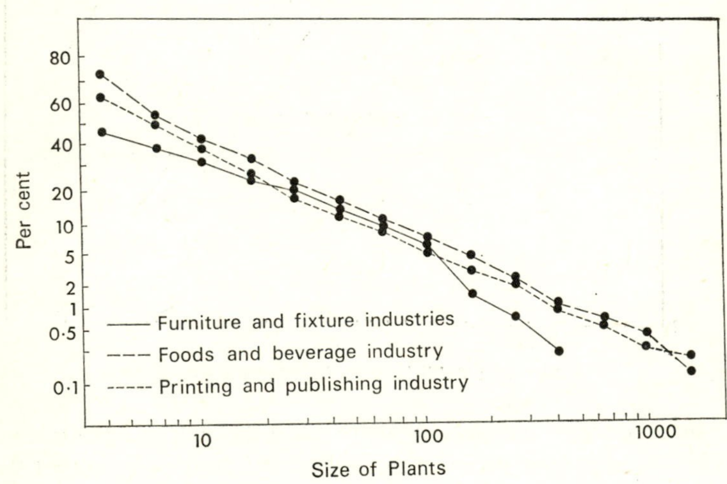

normal and Pareto distributions are only fitted to aggregate industries because a '. . . neat division of firms, if it goes beyond the broad division of manufacturing, trade etc., is artificial . . .' (Steindl 1965:

194). Nevertheless, in Ontario, industrial categories do conform quite closely to the lognormal distribution (*Figure 3*) as do the distributions for 'all industries' in industrial agglomerations (*Figure 4*).

These preliminary analyses indicate the relevance of interpreting Gibrat's law as a mechanism of change for the observed size distributions and suggest therefore, the suitability of Markov theory for further analysis.

FIGURE 4 Lognormal probability curves for permanent establishments in the cities of Toronto and Hamilton, 1965

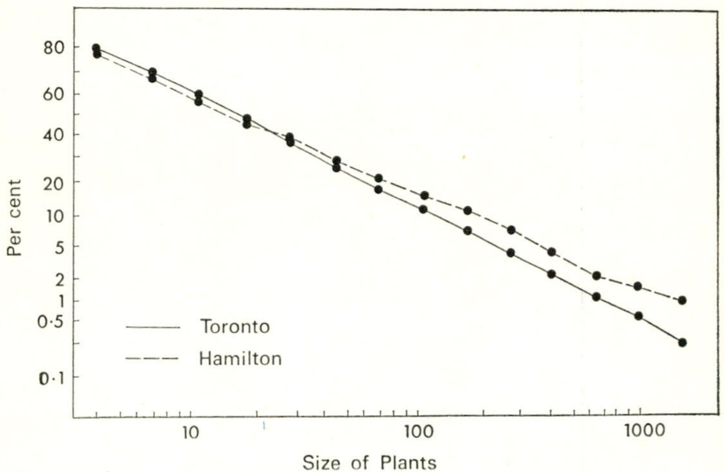

GIBRAT'S LAW AND STRUCTURAL MARKOV MATRICES

The structural matrices comprise, as states, establishment size categories derived for analysing the data in the context of the Pareto and lognormal distributions. Thus, the rationale for the adopted system of structural states rests on an optimum classification derived for analysing the lognormal distribution which is assumed to be generated by a simple stochastic process. When arranged into Markov matrices the observed frequencies lend further support to Gibrat's law of proportionate growth. The transition probabilities (*Tables 3–6*) of the Markov matrices are obtained from the original tally matrices by maximum likelihood techniques. Similar matrices for individual

TABLE 3 1961–62 Structural probability matrix for permanent establishments

	1	*2*	*3*	*4*	*5*	*6*	*7*	*8*	*9*	*10*	*11*	*12*	*13*	*14*
1	·7375	·2228	·0294	·0086	·0017									
2	·1475	·6530	·1674	·0244	·0055		·0011	·0011						
3	·0085	·1681	·5883	·2132	·0183	·0024	·0012							
3	·0011	·0157	·1265	·6585	·1825	·0090	·0045	·0022						
5		·0025	·0038	·1648	·6388	·1660	·0203	·0038						
6		·0014	·0027	·0096	·0984	·6940	·1803	·0123	·0014					
7					·0052	·0873	·7068	·1867	·0140					
8			·0020			·0061	·1086	·6967	·1160	·0184	·0020			
9							·0052	·1016	·7318	·1484	·0130			
10								·0034	·1092	·7201	·1638	·0034		
11								·0059	·0059	·0941	·7588	·1235	·0118	
12							·0101			·0101	·1111	·7071	·1515	·0101
13												·0755	·8491	·0755
14												·0169	·0847	·8983

TABLE 4 1962–63 Structural probability matrix for permanent establishments

	1	*2*	*3*	*4*	*5*	*6*	*7*	*8*	*9*	*10*	*11*	*12*	*13*	*14*
1	·7641	·2095	·0211	·0053										
2	·1283	·6861	·1627	·0195	·0011	·0023								
3	·0104	·1545	·6610	·1623	·0104	·0013								
4		·0097	·1122	·7077	·1552	·0108	·0022	·0011	·0011					
5			·0062	·1324	·6894	·1586	·0144							
6				·0085	·0897	·7422	·1538	·0057						
7					·0098	·1187	·6992	·1610	·0081	·0016			·0016	
8						·0119	·1074	·7316	·1412	·0060	·0020			
9							·0050	·0693	·7748	·1485	·0025			
10							·0034	·0034	·0850	·8027	·0986	·0068		
11							·0052			·1082	·7526	·1340		
12											·1031	·7835	·1031	·0103
13												·1343	·7463	·1194
14													·0345	·9655

TABLE 5 1963–64 Structural probability matrix for permanent establishments

	1	*2*	*3*	*4*	*5*	*6*	*7*	*8*	*9*	*10*	*11*	*12*	*13*	*14*
1	·7996	·1787	·0162	·0054										
2	·0898	·7423	·1560	·0106	·0102									
3	·0078	·1089	·7134	·1530	·0104	·0052	·0013							
4		·0055	·0837	·7434	·1564	·0088	·0022							
5		·0013	·0053	·1043	·7233	·1631	·0013	·0013						
6		·0027		·0041	·1076	·7262	·1553	·0041						
7				·0016	·0099	·0755	·7373	·1691	·0049	·0016				
8				·0020		·0100	·0778	·7784	·1257	·0020	·0040			
9								·0699	·7831	·1470				
10								·0031	·0748	·7913	·1308			
11									·0053	·0535	·7968	·1390	·0053	
12											·0796	·7965	·1150	·0088
13								·0159				·0476	·8413	·0952
14												·0154		·9846

TABLE 6 1964–65 Structural probability matrix for permanent establishments

	1	*2*	*3*	*4*	*5*	*6*	*7*	*8*	*9*	*10*	*11*	*12*	*13*	*14*
1	·8533	·1390	·0076											
2	·1074	·7228	·1538	·0134	·0024									
3	·0052	·1310	·7004	·1543	·0078	·0013								
4	·0023	·0079	·1160	·7061	·1554	·0090	·0023	·0011						
5			·0051	·1120	·7001	·1686	·0116	·0026						
6				·0139	·0099	·7396	·1407	·0111	·0014					
7			·0033	·0050	·0076	·0924	·7310	·1535	·0050					
8						·0152	·1042	·7235	·1439	·0038				·0019
9				·0024		·0048	·0048	·0697	·7716	·1370	·0096			
10								·0031	·0948	·7768	·1254			
11						·0050		·0050	·0050	·0693	·7723	·1436		
12											·1000	·7917	·1000	·0083
13												·0746	·8060	·1194
14												·0141	·0282	·9577

industrial categories and selected areas and towns are also computed.

The growth mechanism postulated by Gibrat requires only that the probability of moving to the next higher interval is the same for all intervals. If Gibrat's law is valid, we can expect a similar distribution of proportionate growth among size classes in the off-diagonals of each stochastic matrix. It is reasonable to hypothesize also that such similarities will be greater at the end of the 1961–65 period than at the beginning because many of the constant sample will be those recently established before 1961, thus exhibiting greater probabilities of decline or growth at the beginning than at the end of the period. The null hypothesis – that the proportions of growth along the first off-diagonal elements do not deviate from some average value – is tested by means of Chi-square, and the computed statistics for twelve degrees of freedom are listed in *Table 7*. Thus, the longer the period covered by the constant sample, the greater our confidence in accepting Gibrat's law of proportionate growth.

A SYSTEM OF SPATIAL STATES

Ideally, the most appropriate system would be one comprising as states the smallest areal units for which data are available, in this case the individual municipalities (townships and urban centres), but they are two numerous (> 500) for computational feasibility. Therefore, operationally, it is necessary to aggregate the municipalities into spatial groups. Conceptually, for the analysis of manufacturing activity, several alternative methods of grouping can be proposed though the combinations of the number and size of states within any one system are innumerable. One alternative is the 'regionalization' of contiguous municipalities on the basis of their economic viability

TABLE 7 Chi-square statistics for hypothesis of equidistribution

Transition period	*Chi-square statistics*
1961–62	10·23
1962–63	6·76
1963–64	4·40
1964–65	2·71
1961–65	4·46

measured in terms of a variety of factors. A second alternative, and one that is implicitly suggested by several Canadian studies stressing the increasing tendency towards decentralization, is a system of states, based on a series of concentric distance bands radiating outwards from the core area of industrial activity. Another alternative is the grouping of locations according to their industrial attractiveness or 'similarities' in which case the system need not be spatially continuous as it would be in the first two alternatives. The particular system adopted for this study emerged from detailed analyses of recent changes in the spatial pattern of Ontario's manufacturing activity.

This activity is completely dominated by Metropolitan Toronto which in 1961 accounted for 4584 or 37 per cent of Ontario's manufacturing establishments. During the 1961–66 period, Ontario increased its number of establishments by 4·5 per cent, but the dominant trend was towards the development of an 'industrial doughnut' around the city of Toronto. Between 1961 and 1966 the city suffered a net loss of 314 establishments, representing a net decrease of 11 per cent. Therefore, in five years, Toronto lost more establishments than were located in any other centre except Hamilton.

But far more spectacular were the gains that occurred in Toronto's suburbs and fringe areas which more than offset the loss in the city. Consequently, the whole metropolitan area increased its number of establishments by 10 per cent and its share of Ontario's total by 1·6 per cent. Altogether, the suburban areas experienced a net increase of 769 plants or 42 per cent of their 1961 total.

Beyond the limits of this ring of intense industrial development, change was less marked except for the increasing concentration in the Kitchener–Waterloo–Preston–Guelph complex of urban centres which increased its 1961 total number of establishments by 20 per cent in the five-year period. In eastern Ontario, 75 per cent of the urban centres (greater than 10,000 population in 1961) had a net loss of establishments for the five-year period.

These net changes in the number of establishments is a function of two processes: a birth-death differential which may result in either a 'natural increase' or 'decrease'; and a 'migration' process. The impact of both processes between 1961 and 1965 had marked, spatial variations. For example, during the 1961–65 period, the city of Toronto lost 300 establishments but the average annual death-rate was only 0·2 per cent higher than the birth-rate; between 1961 and 1965

MAP 1 Proportional selection of relocations in Metropolitan Toronto 1961–62

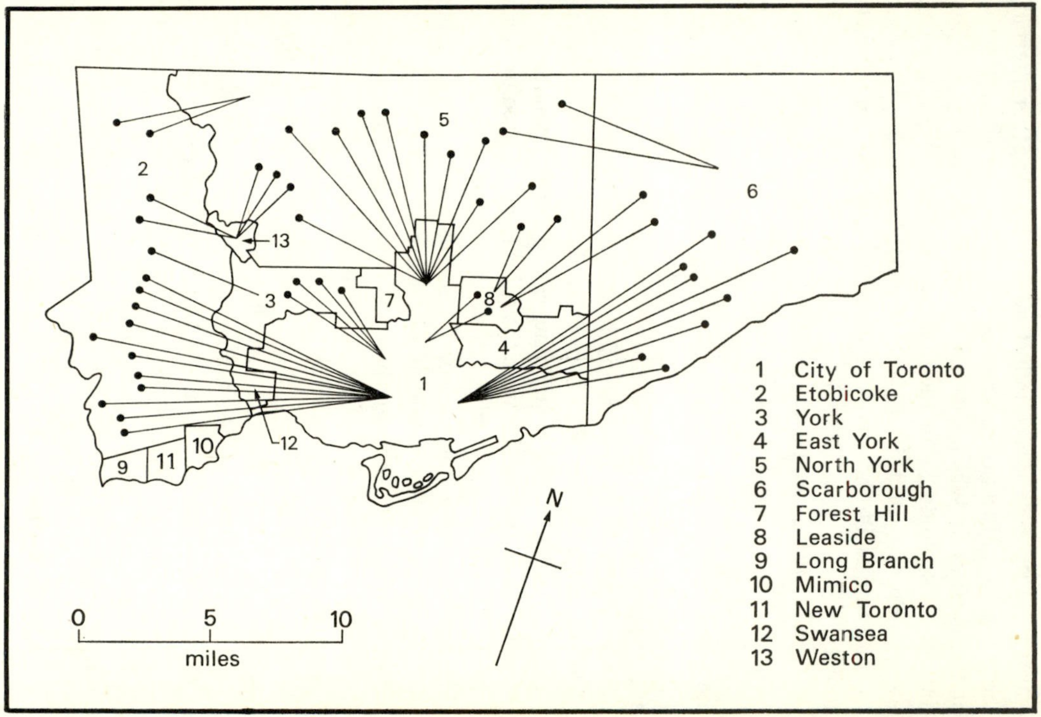

1 City of Toronto
2 Etobicoke
3 York
4 East York
5 North York
6 Scarborough
7 Forest Hill
8 Leaside
9 Long Branch
10 Mimico
11 New Toronto
12 Swansea
13 Weston

0 5 10
miles

N

MAP 2 Destinations of fifty-one establishments relocating from Metropolitan Toronto 1961–65

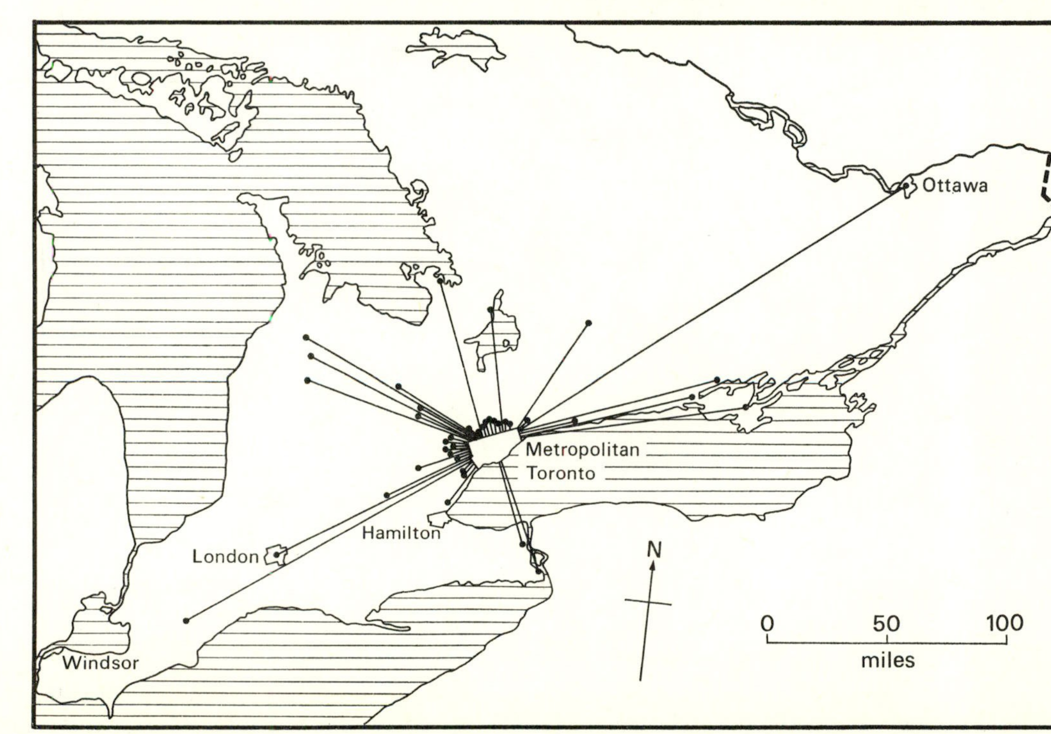

MAP 3 Origins of thirty-three establishments relocating to Metropolitan Toronto from Ontario 1961–65

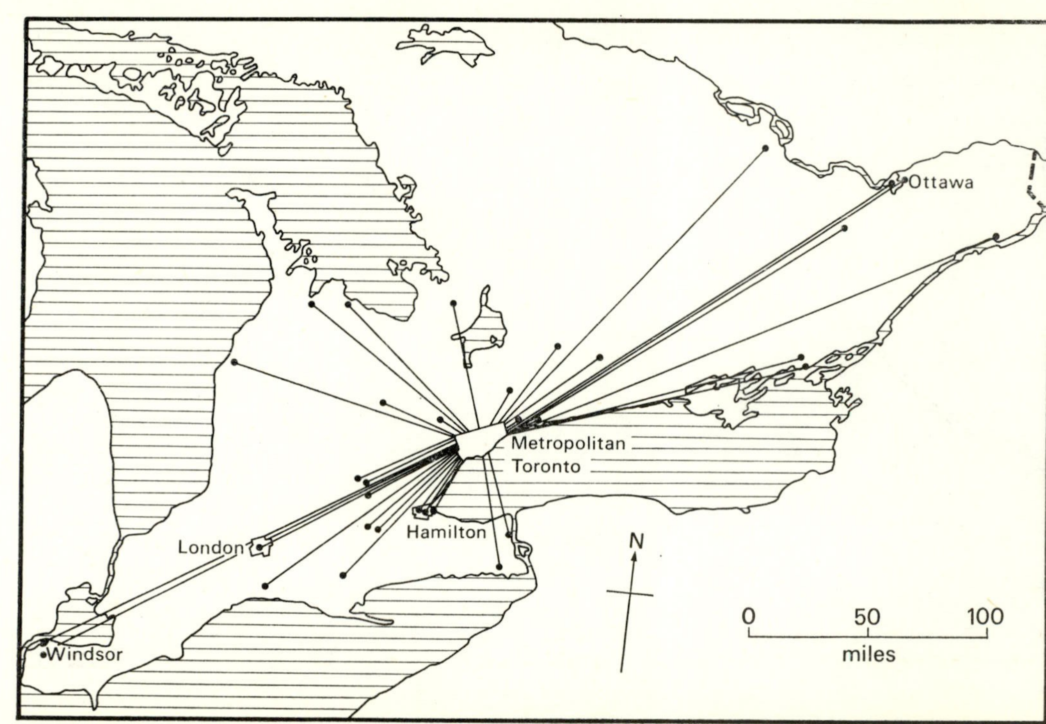

MAP 4 Origins and destinations of forty-six establishments relocating in Southern Ontario 1961–65

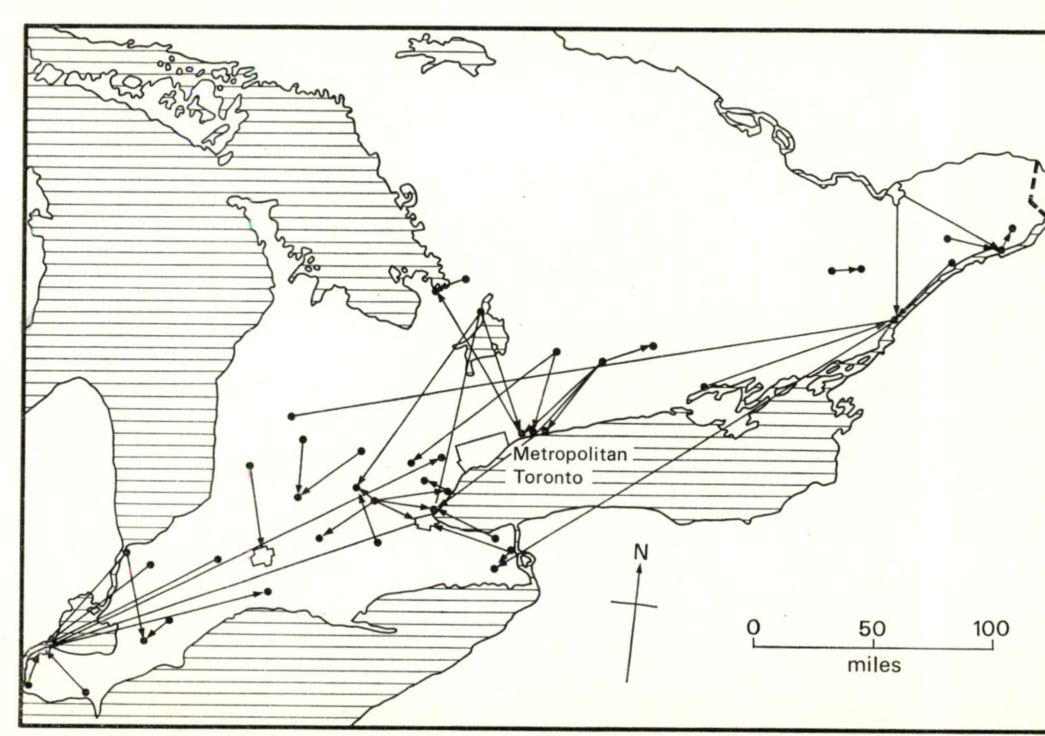

Toronto gave birth to 801 new establishments and lost 823. Toronto's natural decrease, therefore, was only 22 or 7·5 per cent of its total loss; hence 92·5 per cent of Toronto's loss for this period can be attributed to the migration process. On the other hand, Toronto's suburbs gained 276 plants during the same period – an increase of 6 per cent. Most of this increase was concentrated in the three suburbs of Etobicoke, Scarborough, and North York, where the respective natural increases accounted for 80, 64, and 43 per cent of the total gains. Further out in the Fringe townships natural increases accounted for between 80 and 100 per cent of the gains. Throughout the remaining towns and townships of Ontario birth and death rates varied little from the provincial averages of 7 per cent and 6·1 per cent respectively.

As already indicated, by far the largest component of change in Ontario with respect to 'migration' involved the relocation of 151 plants from the city of Toronto to its suburbs (*Map 1*). This suburbanization process was also presented, though to a lesser extent in the other four census metropolitan areas of Windsor, Hamilton, London, and Ottawa. At the same time, there was a significant movement of plants within Toronto's suburbs; a process which is here described as *suburban dispersion.* Plants also moved outwards from the Metropolitan areas as part of a *decentralization process* though 69 per cent of them moved to locations within a 50-mile radius of downtown Toronto (*Map 2*). Partly countering this centrifugal force, a smaller number of plants moved into the metropolitan area from towns and townships throughout Ontario and is viewed as a process of *centralization* (*Map 3*). Overlying these well marked patterns is one of *dispersion* throughout Ontario, that is to say, plants have moved from one town to another or from township to township without giving rise to any clearly recognizable pattern (*Map 4*).

Given this exceedingly complex picture of birth–death differentials and different spatial patterns of migration processes it remains to select that system of Markov states which will exhibit the greatest degree of mobility. Therefore, at this stage it is explicitly recognized that there is no locational theory to guide the selection of spatial states in the same way that Gibrat's concepts were used as a framework for selecting the states contained in the structural matrices.

Recalling the alternative systems of spatial states outlined earlier, the analyses tend to support the notion of increasing concentration in and around Metropolitan Toronto rather than that of widespread decentralization in southern Ontario. Perhaps then, a system of states based solely on the concept of 'distance bands' radiating outwards from Toronto may not be the most appropriate. Likewise, the analyses indicate no well-defined interregional character in the migration process. However, clearly discernible has been the tendency for plants to relocate from the city of Toronto to its suburbs and other centres; from the larger cities to their respective suburbs; and from smaller to larger urban centres. Such observations encourage the adoption of a system of states that gives emphasis to the varying degrees of industrial attractiveness, exhibited by urban areas rather than to that associated with distance bands or economic regions. The particular system adopted together with the associated transition probabilities for one year (1961–62) is shown in *Table 8*.

TABLE 8 Directional probabilities or relocations

		Toronto	*Tor. subs.*	*Large urban*	*L.U. subs.*	*Small urban*	*Rest of Ontario*
		1	*2*	*3*	*4*	*5*	*6*
Toronto	1	0·9567	0·0385			0·0017	0·0029
Tor. Subs	2	0·0115	0·9805	0·0008		0·0026	0·0044
Large Urban	3			0·9830	0·0072	0·0048	0·0003
L.U. Subs.	4			0·1063	0·8865		0·007·0
Small Urban	5	0·0004	0·0019			0·9866	0·0108
Rest Ont.	6		0·0022		0·0007	0·0477	0·9492

(Large Urban (L.U.) refers to the four cities of Hamilton, Windsor, London, and Ottawa. Small Urban refers to all towns over 10,000 in 1961.)

THE MARKOV MODEL: DESIGN AND APPLICATION

A null hypothesis is tested to establish whether or not the four independent annual structural matrices possess the Markov property. Formally, it is postulated that the movement of plants from one size category to another is statistically independent against the alternative that the observations are Markovian. The likelihood criteria provides the $-2 \log \lambda$ values shown in *Table 9* and the null hypothesis is rejected. Hence we can consider the structural matrices as realizations of a Markov chain. Similar tests show also that we can accept the spatial matrices as possesing the Markov property.

TABLE 9 Test of markovity for structural matrices

Realization	$-2 \log\lambda$	D.F. $(n-1)^2$
1961–62	20,444	169
1962–63	21,803	169
1963–64	22,959	169
1964–65	22,520	169

However, Markovity alone provides no indication of the specific order of the chain. Such additional information is obtainable only from cubic or three-way tally matrices which are necessary for testing the null hypothesis that the chain is first-order against the alternative that it is second-order. For the structural data four cubic matrices are developed:

(1) 1961 – 1962 – 1963
(2) 1962 – 1963 – 1964
(3) 1963 – 1964 – 1965
(4) 1961 – 1963 – 1965

For all realizations the computed values of $-2 \log \lambda$ are less than the appropriate degrees of freedom.

TABLE 10 Test of first-order property for structural matrices

Realization	$-2 \log$	D.F. $n(n-1)^2$
1961–63	697·62	2,366
1962–64	631·21	2,366
1963–65	607·78	2,366
1961–65	610·16	2,366

The null hypothesis is not rejected and the change in a plant's employment structure is considered to typify a first-order Markov process. However, for the spatial matrices the study's relatively short time period precludes the possibility of developing cubic matrices and the first-order property must be assumed.

Since the model is required as a predictive mechanism as well as for descriptive purposes it is necessary to determine that the serially independent Markov realizations are homogeneous or that the transition probabilities are 'stationary'. Two series are obtainable for both structural and spatial matrices:

(1) 1961 – 62, 1962 – 63, 1963 – 64, 1964 – 65
(2) 1961 – 63, 1963 – 65.

When tested with the minimum discrimination information statistic both series for the structural and spatial matrices indicated that the differences within each set are small enough to be attributed to random or chance fluctuation. The information components for the four annual structural matrices are listed in *Table 11*.

TABLE 11 Test of homogeneity for four annual structural matrices

Component due to	*Information*	*D.F.*
(i) homogeneity	31·36	39
(j/i) conditional homogeneity	284·43	546
(i,j) homogeneity	415·79	585

FIGURE 5 Observed distributions for permanent establishments, 1961 and 1965

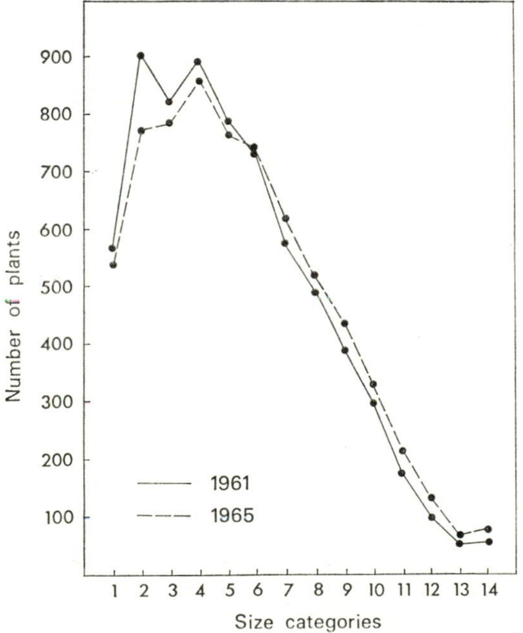

TABLE 12 Estimated distribution vectors 1962–65 from 1961–62 structural probability matrix for permanent establishments

	1	*2*	*3*	*4*	*5*	*6*	*7*	*8*	*9*	*10*	*11*	*12*	*13*	*14*
1962														
Ob.	568·0	873·0	770·0	927·0	763·0	702·0	615·0	503·0	404·0	294·0	194·0	97·0	67·0	58·0
Ex.	568·0	873·0	770·0	927·0	763·0	702·0	615·0	503·0	404·0	294·0	194·0	97·0	67·0	58·0
	Chi-square — 0·00													
1963														
Ob.	554·0	846·0	771·0	908·0	748·0	734·0	609·0	501·0	415·0	321·0	187·0	113·0	63·0	65·0
Ex.	555·2	843·5	739·0	933·0	748·8	680·8	640·5	523·1	421·9	300·2	212·4	99·6	78·8	58·1
	Chi-square — 19·09													
1964														
Ob.	525·0	819·0	771·0	838·0	777·0	718·0	606·0	528·0	416·0	327·0	202·0	120·0	67·0	71·0
Ex.	541·2	816·2	716·1	927·2	738·1	666·1	656·7	543·4	439·5	309·5	228·0	104·6	89·4	59·2
	Chi-square — 32·27													
1965														
Ob.	542·0	773·0	779·0	858·0	767·0	738·0	612·0	517·0	433·0	327·0	213·0	130·0	68·0	78·0
Ex.	526·6	791·2	696·9	915·7	728·2	655·5	667·5	562·2	457·0	320·6	242·2	110·9	99·5	61·0
	Chi-square — 57·79													

On this basis it is assumed that it is 'statistically safe' to apply the first-order Markov procedure for estimating changes in the value of the spatial and structural states. However, it must be recognized that in the test for the first-order property stationarity is assumed and in the test for stationarity the first-order property is assumed.

The actual change in the shape of the size distribution for the constant sample that occurred between 1961 and 1965 is shown in *Figure 5*. Multiplication of the initial distribution vector (1961) with successive powers of the 1961–62 matrix yields the estimated distribution vectors shown in *Table 12*, where they are compared with observed frequencies; the respective configurations of the estimated and observed distributions are shown in *Figure 6*.

FIGURE 6 Estimated distribution from 1961–62 structural matrix and observed distribution (1965) for permanent establishments

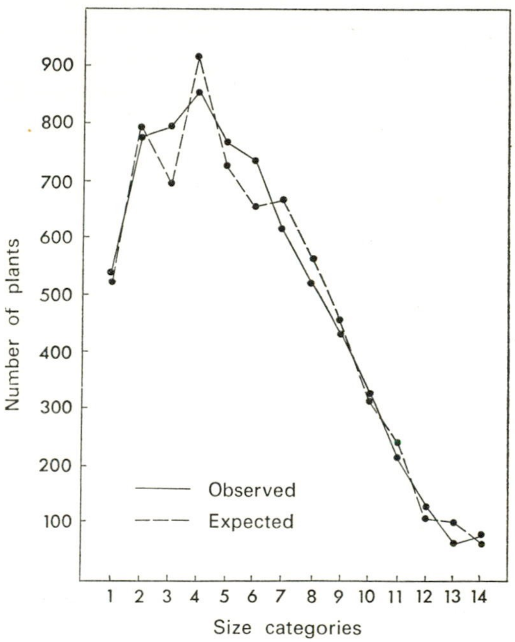

The initial results indicate the limited ability of transition probabilities estimated from a one-year interval to describe future annual changes. Even for this short time period the computed Chi-square

statistic used as a measure of the accuracy of the model indicates that the 'goodness of fit' is poor. Still more disturbing for predictive purposes is the tendency of the goodness of fit to deteriorate significantly with increasing time. In these circumstances it becomes necessary to modify and improve the model before it is extended to incorporate birth and death processes for predicting changes in the total population of establishments.

SMOOTHING SURFACES OF PROBABILITY MATRICES

One possible weakness in the annual transition matrices is the number of discontinuities which represent an incomplete estimation of the underlying fixed probabilities (*Tables 3–6*). Given a system of size categories and given that some plants will move one, two, or four size categories in any one time period, it is reasonable to assume that there is an underlying probability of a plant's moving three categories. Using the movement of plants from category two in the 1961–62 matrix (*Table 3*) as an example, there are probabilities of 0·0055 for a plant's moving to state five, 0·0011 for transition to state seven, and 0·0011 for transition to state eight; but there exists an estimated probability of 0·0 for movement to state six. Such discontinuities in the initial transition probabilities bounded by empirically derived upper and lower limits are not consistent with the theoretical expectations of the structural mobility of manufacturing establishments.

The provision of a continuous probability distribution around the main diagonal suggests a 'smoothing' process which can be accommodated with a matrix surface. Although any polynomial surface can be fitted in theory the specific form of the surface will depend on the underlying processes. It should be noted, however, that the concept is only appropriate under conditions of theoretically continuous distributions – as exist for the structural transition matrices. The fitting of a surface for example will smooth out irregularities and will 'fill' gaps in the distribution. Graphic analyses of the existing matrices indicate that the transition probabilities across the rows assume an almost normal distribution, the variance of which decreases systematically with increasing size. In this case a normal surface, but one that is modified to accommodate the 'taper' effect along the diagonal, seems appropriate; to incorporate this 'shifting mean' a three parameter model is minimal. The normal probability density function using only the mean and variance is given by

$$f(x) = \frac{1}{\sigma\sqrt{2\pi}} \cdot \exp\left[-\tfrac{1}{2}\,(x-m)^2/^2\sigma\right] - \infty < X < \infty$$

where m is the mean of the distribution and the variance is σ^2. Modifying this the required probabilities are

$$p_{ij} = C_i \exp\left[(j-i-T_1)^2/(T_2-iT_3)\right]$$

where C_i are normalizing constants, T_1, T_2, and T_3 are fitted parameters. The search procedure for fitting the surface, analogous to that used for deriving least squares estimates of the transition probabilities (Ashar and Wallace 1963:747–58), is applied iteratively using several starting points and the solution terminates with the 'best fit' measured in terms of the Minimum Average Absolute Deviation (MAAD). The average absolute error is used to give greater weights to the off-diagonal probabilities; the alternative of a 'weighted average' in which the squares of the errors are summed, would lessen the importance of the smaller probabilities in influencing the slope of the surface which would tend to 'fall off' more readily from the crest along the main diagonal. A normal surface fitted to the 1961–62

FIGURE 7 Estimated distribution from 1961–62 structural surface matrix and observed distribution (1965) for permanent establishments

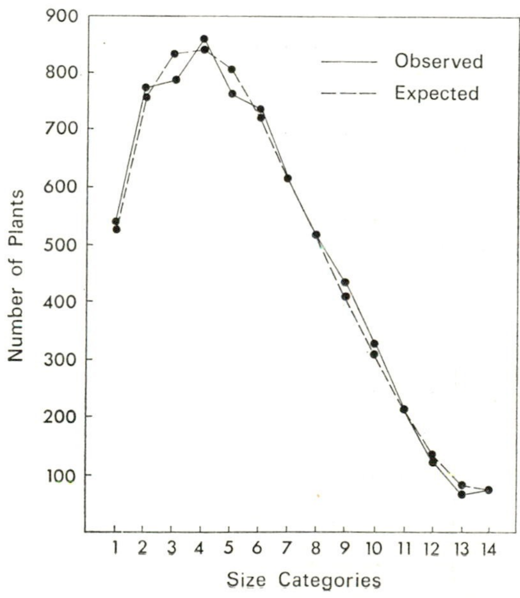

TABLE 13 Matrix surface of 1961–62 transition probabilities

1	·7765	·2200	·0035											
2	·1323	·6773	·1876	·0028										
3	·0013	·1294	·6821	·1847	·0026									
4		·0011	·1266	·6881	·1819	·0023								
5			·0010	·1237	·6942	·1790	·0021							
6				·0009	·1208	·7005	·1760	·0019						
7					·0008	·1178	·7069	·1729	·0017					
8						·0007	·1147	·7134	·1696	·0015				
9							·0006	·1116	·7201	·1663	·0014			
10								·0005	·1084	·7270	·1629	·0012		
11									·0005	·1051	·7340	·1594	·0011	
12										·0004	·1018	·7412	·1557	·0009
13											·0003	·0985	·7491	·1521
14												·0003	·1115	·8881

TABLE 14 Estimated distribution vectors 1962–65 from 1961–62 structural surface matrix for permanent establishments

	1	*2*	*3*	*4*	*5*	*6*	*7*	*8*	*9*	*10*	*11*	*12*	*13*	*14*
1962														
Ob.	568·0	873·0	770·0	927·0	763·0	702·0	615·0	503·0	404·0	294·0	194·0	97·0	67·0	58·0
Ex.	569·9	845·5	845·2	866·9	801·1	723·9	591·7	491·6	392·1	295·5	183·1	106·1	61·9	60·6
	Chi-square — 17·73													
1963														
Ob.	554·0	846·0	771·0	908·0	748·0	734·0	609·0	501·0	415·0	321·0	187·0	113·0	63·0	65·0
Ex.	555·4	808·3	847·7	854·7	803·9	722·5	604·0	498·3	398·9	300·1	193·9	114·3	69·8	63·3
	Chi-square — 19·23													
1964														
Ob.	525·0	819·0	771·0	888·0	777·0	718·1	606·0	528·0	416·0	327·0	202·0	120·0	67·0	71·0
Ex.	539·2	780·2	840·9	847·0	803·4	723·4	613·1	505·9	405·4	305·7	203·4	122·9	77·4	66·9
	Chi-square — 15·52													
1965														
Ob.	542·0	773·0	779·0	858·0	767·0	738·0	612·0	517·0	433·0	327·0	213·0	130·0	68·0	78·0
Ex.	522·9	756·8	830·0	840·4	801·8	725·1	620·7	513·7	412·1	311·9	212·2	131·5	84·8	71·3
	Chi-square — 12·18													

matrix with a MAAD of 0·0062 is shown in *Table 13.* It should be noted that this procedure involves the fitting of a surface to the whole matrix and is not merely a process of fitting a series of normal distribution curves across individual rows. This is apparent from the 'smoothness' of the main diagonal as opposed to the irregular diagonals of the annual matrices. The four estimated distribution vectors derived from the 1961–62 matrix are shown in *Table 14* and the 1965 estimated distribution is compared graphically with the observed 1965 distribution in *Figure 7* and is clearly superior to that derived from the observed 1961–62 probabilities.

Perhaps a more obvious alternative for improving the fit of the model and one which is possible where several realizations of a Markov chain are available, is the calculation of an average matrix. When computed and multiplied with the initial vector of state probabilities the matrix (*Table 15*) provides the estimated distribution vectors shown in *Table 16.* Although the fit of the model is better than the surface matrix it is to be noted that the estimations in this case are not 'true' predictions since they are derived from all the available data.

Moreover, examination of the average matrix shows that there is still evidence of 'noise' elements, or incomplete estimation of the underlying probabilities, in the off-diagonals. By combining the notions of matrix surfaces and average matrices it was hoped that the predictive accuracy of the model could be improved further. A surface fitted to the average matrix with a MAAD of 0·002 gave a total Chi-square value of 16·3 for the four years as opposed to the 15·7 for the average matrix. On this basis, the average matrix is used for further experiments designed to provide short and medium term forecasts for a fluctuating population of establishments. Such a model must allow for entry and exit from the system. This may be achieved by using two diagonal matrices: an attrition matrix which removes plants from the system and a birth matrix which adds plants to the system (Gale 1969). Adelman (1958) suggests a simpler approach and is the one adopted here: the addition of an extra state S_0, so that the row S_0 represents births, and the column S_0 represents deaths. An empirically derived reservoir of 900,000 to give the best results for the test year 1966 is employed.

The same procedure is applied to the spatial matrices from which are derived an average matrix (*Table 17*). The estimated distribution vectors and the observed vectors for the test period are shown in

TABLE 15 Average structural matrix for permanent establishments 1961–65

	1	*2*	*3*	*4*	*5*	*6*	*7*	*8*	*9*	*10*	*11*	*12*	*13*	*14*
1	·7871	·1887	·0189	·0049	·0005									
2	·1189	·7000	·1602	·0172	·0026	·0006	·0003	·0003						
3	·0080	·1411	·6645	·1714	·0118	·0025	·0006							
4	·0008	·0097	·1095	·7041	·1623	·0094	·0027	·0011	·0003					
5		·0009	·0049	·1287	·6874	·1641	·0120	·0019						
6		·0010	·0007	·0090	·0974	·7252	·1577	·0083	·0007					
7			·0008	·0017	·0087	·0936	·7187	·1672	·0079	·0008			·0004	
8			·0005	·0005	·0020	·0109	·0995	·7327	·1441	·0074	·0020			·0005
9				·0006		·0012	·0037	·0772	·7659	·1452	·0062			
10							·0008	·0032	·0907	·7733	·1296	·0024		
11						·0013	·0013	·0027	·0040	·0810	·7703	·1355	·0040	
12							·0023			·0023	·0979	·7716	·1166	·0093
13								·0040				·0840	·8080	·1040
14												·0119	·0356	·9526

TABLE 16 Estimated distribution vectors 1962–65 from average structural probability matrix for permanent establishments

	1	*2*	*3*	*4*	*5*	*6*	*7*	*8*	*9*	*10*	*11*	*12*	*13*	*14*
1962														
Ob.	568·0	873·0	770·0	927·0	763·0	702·0	615·0	503·0	404·0	294·0	194·0	97·0	67·0	58·0
Ex.	570·2	866·6	803·8	897·4	776·9	731·0	590·6	493·5	396·9	300·4	181·9	105·3	57·4	62·9
Chi-square = 8·75														
1963														
Ob.	554·0	846·0	771·0	908·0	748·0	734·0	609·0	501·0	415·0	321·0	187·0	113·0	63·0	65·0
Ex.	559·0	837·9	787·1	895·3	769·0	730·1	603·6	501·6	408·5	309·1	192·8	112·2	61·8	67·1
Chi-square = 2·10														
1964														
Ob.	525·0	819·0	771·0	888·0	777·0	718·0	606·0	528·0	416·0	327·0	202·0	120·0	67·0	71·0
Ex.	546·6	813·2	770·8	889·5	763·0	729·3	613·6	510·6	419·5	318·4	202·0	119·4	66·4	71·6
Chi-square = 2·29														
1965														
Ob.	542·0	773·0	779·0	858·0	767·0	738·0	612·0	517·0	433·0	327·0	213·0	130·0	68·0	78·0
Ex.	533·8	791·2	755·2	881·3	757·7	728·8	621·5	519·7	430·1	328·1	212·9	126·8	71·2	76·5
Chi-square = 2·58														

TABLE 17 Average spatial matrix with birth and death vectors for all establishments with two or more employees

	Deaths	*Tor-onto*	*Tor. subs.*	*Large urban*	*L.U. subs.*	*Small urban*	*Rest of Ont.*
Births	·99920	·00016	·00022	·00007	·00002	·00019	·00015
Toronto	·06076	·91306	·02259	·00012		·00108	·00239
Tor. Subs.	·06424	·00343	·92602	·00026		·00103	·00502
L. urban	·05176	·00046	·00074	·93822	·00603	·00186	·00093
L.u. Subs.	·08086			·05728	·81604	·01348	·03235
S. urban	·05670	·00030	·00150	·00300		·93578	·00543
Rest of Ont.	·05265	·00021	·00169	·00034	·00034	·01232	·93246

TABLE 18 Estimated vectors from average spatial matrix for all establishments and observed distributions 1961–66

	Toronto	*Toronto subs.*	*Large urban*	*L.u. subs.*	*Small urban*	*Rest of Ontario*
1962						
Ob.	2450·0	1648·0	1124·0	184·0	2730·0	2295·0
Ex.	2401·5	1603·3	1111·7	190·3	2757·3	2313·3
	Chi-square = 2·93					
1963						
Ob.	2398·0	1798·0	1135·0	180·0	2764·0	2354·0
Ex.	2344·0	1745·8	1119·2	180·8	2788·6	2328·0
	Chi-square = 3·55					
1964						
Ob.	2316·0	1944·0	1152·0	166·0	2799·0	2392·0
Ex.	2292·0	1876·5	1125·8	173·0	2818·0	2342·1
	Chi-square = 5·49					
1965						
Ob.	2234·0	2075·0	1174·0	153·0	2838·0	2409·0
Ex.	2245·0	1996·4	1131·5	166·8	2845·6	2355·7
	Chi-square = 6·87					
1966						
Ob.	2171·0	2130·0	1186·0	146·0	2880·0	2423·0
Ex.	2202·4	2106·4	1136·6	161·7	2871·7	2368·8
	Chi-square = 5·65					

FIGURE 8 Estimated trend lines 1962–75 for structural and spatial matrices

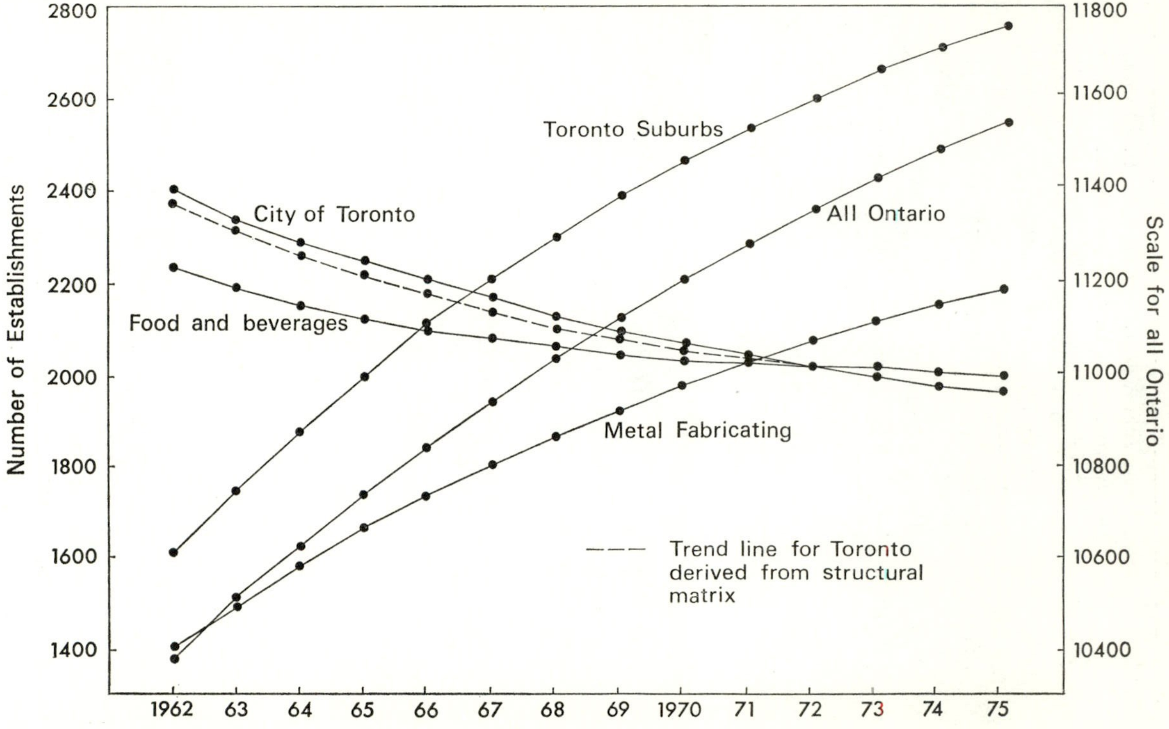

Table 18. Successive powering of the spatial matrix provides the 1962–75 estimated trend line shown in *Figure 8*, and the successive outcomes of each iteration for 1967–75 with the provincial totals are shown in *Table 19*. Application of the Markov procedure to the total

TABLE 19 Expected distribution vectors 1967–75 for the spatial matrix

Year	*Tor-onto*	*Tor. subs.*	*Large urban*	*Urb. subs*	*Small urban*	*Rest Ont.*	*Total*
1967	2164	2207	1141	157	2896	2381	10946
1968	2122	2300	1145	154	2919	2393	11040
1969	2097	2385	1148	152	2941	2405	11127
1970	2069	2463	1152	149	2961	2416	11209
1971	2043	2534	1155	147	2980	2427	11285
1972	2020	2600	1157	146	2999	2438	11360
1973	1999	2661	1160	145	3016	2448	11428
1974	1980	2716	1162	144	3032	2458	11492
1975	1963	2767	1164	143	3048	2467	11552

structural matrix provides estimated size distribution vectors for each point on the curvilinear trend line in *Figure 8*.

By 1970, for example, the structural matrix projects a total of 11,308 plants and for 1975, 11,716. The respective estimated size distributions of these establishments are shown in *Table 20*.

TABLE 20 Expected size distribution vectors 1970 and 1975

Year	*1*	*2*	*3*	*4*	*5*	*6*	*7*	*8*	*9*	*10*	*11*	*12*	*13*	*14*
A	1185	1583	1391	1494	1227	1094	909	738	598	430	281	172	98	112
B	1182	1584	1402	1521	1260	1135	953	781	644	474	320	203	118	141

(A = 1970, B = 1975)

The elements of these vectors show clearly that although the total number of establishments will continue to increase at a significant pace – a predicted increase of almost 1,000 from 1961 to 1975 – the actual size distribution will change very slightly. Most of the change will occur in the higher size categories but even by 1975 there will still be a greater proportion of small establishments than is predicted by the lognormal distribution.

Projected trend lines for individual industries will, of course, assume different configurations depending on the initial stochastic matrices. For example, the two largest industries with contrasting birth- and death-rates resulting in differential expansions, are metal-fabricating, and foods and beverages. Successive powering of the respective average transition matrices yields the trend lines shown in *Figure 8*. It is expected that the sharply increasing trend line for the metal-fabricating establishments will continue to climb at least to 1975, but the slightly decreasing trend line for foods and beverages is expected to level off after 1971 and to maintain approximately 2,000 establishments. If total population continues to increase at its existing rate, then we may expect a greater concentration of foods and beverage output among a slightly greater proportion of medium-sized and large-scale production units. Such a trend probably results from recent technological innovations in the manufacture of less perishable pre-packed food products which are not so market oriented as they have been in the past. Moreover, continuing improvements in transportation facilities have also encouraged food and beverage plants to take advantage of scale-economies in large, well-integrated establishments.

The long-term spatial trends of Ontario's manufacturing activity are observable from the equilibrium vector of the average spatial matrix. When normalized this vector takes the form:

= (0·153, 0·275, 0·094, 0·013, 0·256, 0·209)

and is very similar to the initial distribution of

1961 = (0·240, 0·141, 0·107, 0·020, 0·266, 0·224)

except that in 1961, 24 per cent of Ontario's manufacturing was located in Toronto and 14·1 per cent in the suburbs; in the limiting equilibrium state we would expect to find 15·3 per cent in Toronto and 27·5 per cent in the suburbs. Separate trend lines for these two areas up to 1975 are shown in *Figure 8*. For Toronto, two trend lines are presented: one is derived from powering the spatial matrix for all establishments in Ontario and the other is given by the structural matrix for Toronto. In the latter matrix, relocations out of the city are added to the death vector. Theoretically, successive powering of the spatial and structural matrices should provide identical totals, but in practice, differences of the estimated parameters resulting from approximated Markov processes contingent upon the classification of states creates inequalities. However, the maximum deviation in this case is only 1·5 per cent for 1965 and is not considered significant enough to detract from the value of the trend lines.

Changes in the internal structure of Ontario's manufacturing activity are provided in *Table 21*; by 1970 it is expected that Toronto will have far more small and medium-sized establishments than is predicted by the lognormal distribution. As already indicated, this trend is a result of the increasing tendency of large establishments to relocate to the suburbs rather than as a result of an increasingly high birth-rate among the smaller establishments. The total effect is to emphasize the growing phenomena of an industrial doughnut centred around the city of Toronto.

TABLE 21. Expected size distribution vectors for foods and beverages 1962–75.

Year	*1*	*2*	*3*	*4*	*5*	*6*	*7*	*8*	*9*	*10*	*11*	*12*	*13*	*14*
1962	428	421	350	284	207	162	123	90	71	48	31	12	6	8
1967	342	339	299	270	218	171	132	102	87	54	33	17	8	8
1970	319	319	284	261	216	173	136	107	94	58	35	19	9	8
1975	302	304	272	253	211	174	140	112	102	65	40	22	10	9

CONCLUSION

This paper, in a geographical context, has elaborated the use of a specific conceptual framework. Little attention has been given to the underlying philosophy for adopting such a model and no attempt has been made to show that a Markov chain is the best model or that the statistical tests are the most suitable for the particular problem involved. Rather, the focus has been on emphasizing the spatial problems which geographers encounter in using a model that has had widespread application in other social sciences.

The analyses have shown that whereas, in this case, geographers have recourse to economic theory to devise a system of aspatial states there is no corresponding geographical theory for calibrating a system of spatial states. The importance of this problem is not unique to Markov chain analysis since spatial classification or 'regionalization' is *the* major problem of many forms of geographical analysis. In this study, information on the spatial distribution of manufacturing activity has been available on a small-areal unit basis so that the problem has been one of grouping the units into a suitable number of meaningful classes. However, in most geographic studies, especially those reliant on published census data, the information is in aggregate form and all too often the aggregate classes are not the most appropriate for geographical analysis. In some studies therefore, the data have to be organized to fit the model whereas in others the model has to be refined to fit the data. Clearly, these are general problems and are of concern to other social sciences.

Despite such problems, it is to be hoped that further use of models in geography will continue to add descriptive and predictive powers to the respective analyses. However, it must be recognized that the interpretation of these analyses can be relevant only in the context of the assumptions embodied in each model framework.

NOTE

* The author wishes to acknowledge Statistics Canada for sponsoring the research on which this paper is based.

REFERENCES

ADELMAN, IRMA G. 1958. A Stochastic Analysis of the Size Distribution of Firms. *Journal, American Statistical Association* **53**: 893–904.

ARCHER, S. H., and MCGUIRE, J. 1965. Firm Size and Probabilities of Growth. *The Western Economic Journal* **3**: 233–46.

ASHAR, V., and WALLACE, T. D. 1963. A Sampling Study of Minimum Absolute Deviations Estimates. *Operations Research* **11**: 747–58.

BROWN, L. A. 1963. The Diffusion of Innovation: A Markov chain-type approach. Discussion Paper No. 3. Evanston, Ill.: Northwestern University.

CHAMPERNOWNE, D. G. 1953. A Model of Income Distribution. *Economic Journal* **63**: 318–51.

GALE, S. 1969. Probability and Interaction: A stochastic approach to intra-regional mobility. University of Michigan. Unpublished PhD thesis.

GIBRAT, R. 1931. *Les inegalités économiques.* Paris: Sirey.

——1957, On Economic Inequalities. *International Economic Papers,* No. 7: 53–70. Translated from the French by Elizabeth Henderson.

HART, P. E., and PRAIS, S. J. 1956. The Analysis of Business Concentration: A statistical approach. *Journal Royal Statistical Society* **119,** Series A,: 150–81.

KAPTEYN, J. C. 1903. *Skew Frequency Curves in Biology and Statistics.* Greningen: E. P. Noordhoff.

ROGERS, A. 1968. *Matrix Analysis of Interregional Population Growth and Distribution.* Berkeley: University of California Press.

SIMON, H. A. 1954. *Models of Man.* New York: John Wiley and Sons.

SIMON, H. A. and BONINI, C. P. 1958. The size distribution of business firms. *American Economic Review* **48**: 607–17.

STEINDL, J. 1965. *Random Processes and the Growth of Firms.* London: Charles Griffin & Co. Ltd.

Name Index

Subject Index